A History of Wales
1660–1815

WELSH HISTORY TEXT BOOKS

WELSH HISTORY TEXT BOOKS—VOLUME 2

A History of Wales
1660—1815

E. D. EVANS

UNIVERSITY OF WALES PRESS
CARDIFF
1976

ISBN   0   7083   0624   1

Printed by the
John Penry Press, Swansea

Preface

THIS book is the second of the trilogy on the history of modern Wales and, like its predecessor by Mr. Hugh Thomas, is designed to meet the needs of pupils in sixth-forms and students in various colleges. It is greatly hoped that it will be of some help to teachers of history in Wales to enable them to give to the teaching of Welsh history more prominence than it has received in the past.

Professor R. T. Jenkins's little classic *Hanes Cymru yn y Ddeunawfed Ganrif* has served the needs of Welsh readers from its appearance in 1928 but since then a great deal of research has been done which now needs to be synthesised. Professor David Williams's *A History of Modern Wales* has been the only standard work available to English readers and is a model of conciseness in distilling over four centuries of history into about 300 pages. The debt which this present work owes to these pioneer studies is only too apparent and is gratefully acknowledged. Whilst it will in no way replace them it is hoped that it will supplement them in some directions. I have to thank two other distinguished Welsh historians to whom I am under a deep obligation. I have leaned heavily on Professor A. H. Dodd, who has illuminated so many aspects of the period ; likewise on the work of Professor William Rees on the economic history of the period and his expertise in cartography.

My chapters on political history have incorporated a great deal of the work of Dr. P. D. G. Thomas and Dr. R. D. Rees and to both of these scholars I tender thanks. It will be equally apparent to the knowledgeable reader how much I have relied on the work of a host of scholars, too numerous to mention, in other fields. I trust that they will accept this as an acknowledgement of my indebtedness.

To Professor Glanmor Williams I owe a particular debt of gratitude ; first, for providing the initial stimulus and for his continuing interest thereafter. He was also good enough to read the typescript of the work at a time when he was burdened with much weightier responsibilities. Many of his suggestions have been acted upon but whatever defects remain are my sole responsibility.

I am grateful to Mrs. Phyllis Jones for typing the whole work, and to Mr. W. J. Jones for kindly reading the proofs.

Over the years that the book has been in progress, Dr. R. Brinley Jones has been a model of patience and for his courtesy and understanding I am sincerely grateful.

Calan Mai, 1975.   E. D. EVANS.

Contents

Maps

Abbreviations

Arch. Camb.	Archaeologia Cambrensis
B.B.C.S.	Bulletin of the Board of Celtic Studies
Carms. Ant.	Carmarthenshire Antiquary
Ch. Q. Rev.	Church Quarterly Review
E.H.R.	English Historical Review
Flints. H.S.Pub.	Flintshire Historical Society Publications
Glam. Hist.	Glamorgan Historian, ed. S. Williams
J.H.S.Ch. in W.	Journal of the Historical Society of the Church in Wales
J. Mer. H. & R.S.	Journal of the Merioneth Historical and Record Society
J. Welsh Bibl. Soc.	Journal of the Welsh Bibliographical Society
Mont. Coll.	Montgomeryshire Collections
N.L.W. Jnl.	National Library of Wales Journal
Traf. Cymd. Han. y Bed.	Trafodion Cymdeithas Hanes y Bedyddwyr
Trans. Angl. Ant. Soc.	Transactions of the Anglesey Antiquarian Society
Trans. Caerns. H.S.	Transactions of the Caernarvonshire Historical Society
Trans. Car. Nat. Soc.	Transactions of the Cardiff Naturalists Society
Trans. Cymmr.	Transactions of the Honourable Society of Cymmrodorion
Trans. Denbs. H.S.	Transactions of the Denbighshire Historical Society
W.H.R.	Welsh History Review

I GOFIO NHAD A MAM

JOHN AC ELIZABETH M. EVANS

1. The Representative System

The Constituencies

THE system under which Wales was represented at Westminster was that laid down by the Acts of Union of 1536 and 1542 whereby 27 constituencies returned members to Parliament.[1] It was fallaciously believed in the sixteenth century that thereby the Acts of Union conferred equal rights, liberties and privileges with the King's English subjects,[2] but in reality Wales only got half the representation given to England, probably as a concession to a poor country when M.P.s could claim fees. English counties were represented by two knights of the shire, Welsh counties by one, except for Monmouthshire. English boroughs were represented by two burgesses, Welsh boroughs by one and, with few exceptions, the burgess was elected not by one borough but by a group of boroughs consisting of the county borough and a number of ' out-boroughs '. Merioneth had no borough representation at all whilst Haverfordwest was granted county status and its own member of Parliament. When we bear in mind that the total population of Wales till about 1700 was still only about 400,000, the representation was not ungenerous and there were few complaints except from the burgesses of Merionethshire. The size of electorates was not determined by numbers of population but by the ability of rival groups in manipulating the franchise to their own advantage. The most striking feature of the system was its complete lack of uniformity.

The Counties

The proportion of voters to population in the counties varied from 1·8 to 4%. The smallest electorate was that of Caernarfonshire with about 500 voters and the largest were those of Denbighshire and Pembrokeshire with around 2,000. There

[1] See above, Vol. 1, pp. 73-9
[2] ibid, pp. 49-51

were six counties with between 1,000 and 1,500 voters and four
with under 1,000. Although the population grew within our
period, the electorate did not grow correspondingly ; indeed,
in some instances it declined. Still, the county electorates were
too large for direct bribery and it was generally assumed both
inside and outside Wales that the Welsh counties were free of
corruption. The qualification for the vote was the forty-
shilling freehold and the size of the Welsh county electorate
reflects the restricted number of freeholders because of the
smallness of the farming units. The term ' freeholder ' was
elastically interpreted in a way which often admitted people
with long leases and copyholds to the vote. When it suited
their electoral purposes landowners often created sham leases
in order to increase potential voters for their side at an impending election. The High Sheriff could at his discretion
investigate whether a voter's qualification was sufficient and
since he himself was usually partisan he might admit votes for
one side that he would disqualify for the other. The partiality
of the sheriff was as often as not what was complained of in
petitions relating to controverted elections.

Boroughs

There were several types of boroughs and their franchise
qualification was also diverse. By 1750 there were five single
borough constituencies, some having been so from the start like
Haverfordwest and Brecon, others having acquired the sole
right of electing a burgess because their out-boroughs had been
disfranchised, Montgomery being the latest instance of this in
1727. A borough's right to participate in election depended
on whether it had at any time contributed towards the fees of
the member but since payment of fees had so long lapsed it
was often difficult to secure proof. The practice of contributing
to the member's fee had brought the contributory boroughs
into existence which did not exist in England. In the case of the
Glamorgan boroughs seven out-boroughs shared with Cardiff,
the county-borough, the right of election; there were other
instances where three, four and five boroughs made up the
electorate. In practically every instance boroughs came under
the control of a patron but rarely was a patron able to control
all the out-boroughs. In Caernarfonshire, for instance, the

Wynns of Glynllifon who held the borough seat for a long period controlled only the borough of Nefyn and had some influence in Caernarfon because they held the county lieutenancy ; but it was the electoral pact which they made with the Vaughans of Corsygedol (Mer.) who controlled Pwllheli that ensured their return. In the case of the Cardiff group a pact between four borough patrons was necessary to secure control. The easiest to control were the single borough constituencies. In the case of Beaumaris the right of election was vested in the corporation which was a closed body to which nominations were made by the borough lord, Lord Bulkeley ; so Beaumaris became a Bulkeley pocket-borough. Brecon was comparable though not as closed a corporation as Beaumaris since the burgesses had a say in the election. But since the burgesses were chosen by the corporation which, in its turn, was dominated for long by the Morgans of Tredegar, the number of electors was purposely reduced until by 1805 there were only four. This made it more amenable to control and Brecon became a Morgan pocket-borough. This situation was averted in Carmarthen because there were two active political factions in the town and it was not until after 1765 that the ' Blue ' party established control. Most of the other Welsh boroughs were medium-sized with from 500 to 1,000 voters, the largest being the Cardigan group with about 4,000. In these, the right of election was usually vested in the freemen but this again gave rise to a variety of practices. In some boroughs, like Brecon, only resident freemen could vote, in others, like Cardigan, non-resident freemen were allowed. It was a common practice for the side which controlled the borough machinery to use its power to admit freemen to the roll merely to support its candidate at an election. Other boroughs purposely restricted the number of freemen especially if the borough owned property. To safeguard their selfish interests existing freemen denied entry to others in order to monopolise the benefits. Swansea was a case in point where the corporation acting in collusion with the borough lord, the Duke of Beaufort, put up the fees for entry into the freedom of the borough so high that few could afford it. Boroughs that had no property but had privileges such as exemption from tolls, which Cardigan and Monmouth enjoyed, naturally wished to extend the advantage to as many freemen as possible. The percentage of voters to population in the boroughs was much higher than in the counties and it is a significant fact that after the First Reform Act (1832) came into operation many Welsh boroughs actually had fewer voters than they had before.

Elections

The election of a member of Parliament usually took place at the first County Meeting of gentry and freeholders held after the writ had been served. The County Meeting retained its political importance to the end of our period and showed even greater political activity at the end of the eighteenth century than at its beginning. It was dominated by the gentry of the county whose lead the freeholders were content to follow. Deference was particularly paid to the premier landowners but no one could afford to be presumptuous. Noblemen, who were mostly non-resident in Wales, were expected to concur in the decisions of the County Meeting and attempts at domination by the aristocracy were resented and could lead to a revolt of the gentry in the name of independence as happened in Glamorgan in 1789 and in Carmarthenshire in 1796. Outside interference in the right of free election was resisted whether it stemmed from the Crown, as in the time of Charles II, or a great magnate like the Duke of Beaufort in the time of James II. The decision of the County Meeting was regarded as binding and any person who had the temerity to ignore it courted disaster if he entered a poll.

The number of elections which were actually carried to a poll within our period were few because contests were studiously avoided. Elections tended to germinate heat and acrimony and it was considered undesirable to disturb the peace of the county especially when violence was never very far below the surface. Elections could also encourage social insubordination when one side disparaged the other and this had to be avoided to preserve the social fabric. A more compelling reason for eschewing contests was the continually rising costs of elections throughout the period, since even if there was no poll, people expected to be entertained for their vociferous support and failing in the duties of hospitality was regarded as unbecoming of a gentleman. Contested elections could be outrageously expensive. The 1734 election in Flint boroughs contested between Sir George Wynne of Leeswood and Sir John Glynne of Hawarden, cost £70,000 between them. The ' lecsiwn fawr ' (big election) of 1802 in Carmarthenshire cost the unsuccessful candidate, Sir William Paxton, £15,700 and his opponent, James Hamlyn Williams, scarcely less and most of it went on wining and dining their supporters while the election dragged its course for three weeks. A normal expense for a contested election would be in the region of the £4,800 to £5,300 which the Wynns of Wynnstay and the Herberts of Powis Castle spent respectively in the 1774 Montgomeryshire election. There were more county than borough contests because the county seat was the premier honour and county electorates were not so easily manipulated as those of boroughs. Between 1754 and 1790 there were 17 county contests, 4 of them in Anglesey ; over the same period there were only 8 borough contests and 4 of those in New Radnor. By 1815, competition for seats was increasing and the solidarity which had been characteristic of the gentry in the eighteenth century was beginning to break up especially under the onset of money-ed wealth.

The owners of large landed estates in the county were recognised as having the foremost claim to a parliamentary seat and even if their political views were not always acceptable, their claim was respected. Some families were sufficiently dominant in their counties to be able to monopolise the representation for long periods. Such were the Vaughans of Corsygedol who represented Merionethshire for most of the eighteenth century and the Morgans of Tredegar who invariably held one of the Monmouthshire seats. Electoral contests only happened when there were several families aspiring to the honour and not enough seats to go round. Rising costs of election obliged many old territorial families which had been prominent in the representation to give up the struggle, the Philipps of Cwmgwili (Carms.) and the Owens of Orielton (Pembs.) being two casualties before 1815. Sometimes they were obliged to retire because of lack of heirs, and families which usually supplied members often had to yield the representation during the minority of an heir. To satisfy family honour and to avoid conflict, electoral pacts between families were often found to be necessary. In this way the Mostyns and the Glynnes had shared the Flintshire seats for a long period. Sometimes these pacts were marriages of convenience between families of different political complexions such as those between the Wynns and the Myddletons in Denbighshire and the Morgans and the Dukes of Beaufort in Monmouthshire. A *quid pro quo* was agreed upon in 1784 between the Bulkeleys and the Pagets in Anglesey whereby the Bulkeleys left Anglesey at the Pagets' disposal in return for electoral support in Caernarfonshire. In Carmarthenshire and Pembrokeshire electoral alliances had a more local flavour, the former having its Blue and Red parties, the latter its Blue and Orange parties and their political activities over-ran County boundaries. In general, local considerations predominated over national and family interests over political principles. Some families had traditional Whig or Tory affiliations which formed the basis of some political alliances but, in the main, party counted for little in the eighteenth century.

The duration of parliaments was fixed in 1694 at three years, extended to seven in 1716 by the Septennial Act, and eighteenth century parliaments usually ran their course which made election years predictable. Longer parliaments made a seat in them more sought after and added keenness to elections, and if money had to be laid out the prospect of a better return on it was enhanced ; so more effort went into the preparatory work for elections to ensure success. The choice of sheriff for election year was very material since he was responsible for the conduct of elections. The Government naturally had the advantage here and sheriffs who were partial to the Administration and who would exert influence on its behalf were naturally chosen. Although sheriffs were supposed to be impartial, everyone, including the Government, expected them to take sides. A sheriff could be prosecuted for misconduct if found out and that happened in Denbighshire in 1741. The Government could even nominate a person as sheriff to prevent him from standing as a candidate if it wanted to eliminate an opponent. Among misdemeanours cited in petitions following disputed elections, allegations of the partiality of the sheriff are the commonest. Usually the returning officer in a borough was the bailiff and he was usually the tool of a borough lord. In the Glamorgan boroughs it was the bailiff of Cardiff who acted in this capacity and it is not surprising to find a succession of nominees of Windsors and Butes, the lords of the town, holding the seat.

Before proceeding to a poll candidates usually made a preliminary canvass and these lists tell us a great deal about local politics. If the canvass was unpromising a candidate withdrew, there being sixteen occasions between 1790 and 1815 when this happened in the South Wales counties. Some candidates driven to desperation might even take the rash course of seizing the writ on its way to the sheriff in order to keep their opponents guessing and then spring a surprise election. Valentine Morris did this in Monmouthshire in 1771 for which he had to face a House of Commons inquiry and make condign apology. Elections were usually held at the county towns but in some counties the venue might alternate between two towns. In 1790, a partial Pembrokeshire sheriff held the election at Pembroke in the stronghold of the Owens of Orielton rather than at Haverfordwest which was secure in the control of their Picton Castle rivals. Government interference in free elections was most apparent when petitions following disputed elections were heard by the House of Commons. The Government always sought verdicts favourable to its supporters but the House, jealous of its own privileges, did not always oblige. Sir Watkin Williams Wynn petitioned alleging misdemeanours in the Denbighshire election of 1741 and this was the first of a number of such votes on which the Government was defeated and which led to Walpole's downfall.[1] Petitions, however, added to the expense of the election, and were often not heard or not proceeded with by the House of Commons. After losing the 1802 election in Carmarthenshire, Sir William Paxton petitioned but the expense of transporting a thousand witnesses to London and maintaining them there caused even this nabob to desist.

The direct interference of the Crown or the Government in Welsh elections was minimal. Neither had constituencies under its control as they had in England and any Court or Government servant who sought seats in Wales had to rely on his own and allied interests. The Court could not get anywhere without local co-operation, as the Duke of Beaufort and Lord Jeffreys

[1] See p. 65.

B

found out when they tried to ensure the return of candidates favourable to James II. It is alleged that George III intervened personally to obtain the return of Sir John Philipps for Pembrokeshire in 1761 ; it is more certain that he did so in the Glamorgan by-election of 1763 when Sir Edmund Thomas, a placeman, sought re-election. The King despatched Lord Talbot to still ' the frenzy of the times ' which had seized the electorate there and threatened to turn out Sir Edmund. In only one instance has it been proved that Secret Service money was used to support a Government candidate and that was at the Radnorshire election of 1755 when £173 was spent from that source. The patronage system worked more subtly and the Duke of Newcastle, ' the prince of patronage ', had a network of political agents throughout the country which kept him apprised of political intelligence at the local level. George Rice acted in this capacity in South Wales and the Earl of Powis in mid-Wales and Shropshire.

Powis's services were called for to settle disputes especially among aspiring Whig families as occurred in Caernarfonshire in 1754 and in Cardiganshire in 1761. Stewards of Crown lands also acted as political agents for the Government and the holder of this office in Radnorshire could command at least the borough seat if not the county seat as well if he had a substantial interest of his own. This combination had secured two families in the Radnorshire representation for a long time, the Howarths of Maes-llwch and the Lewises of Harpton.

The notion that every man had his price was widely held in the eighteenth century but instances of intimidation are more difficult to find. Complaints were laid in Cardiganshire in 1660 against lessees of Crown lands for using their position there for the purpose of ' extorting your Petitioners Voices at Publick Elections '. The Land Commission Report of 1896 did not discover any instances of intimidation and eviction before 1840. The situation in the eighteenth century was very different from what it was in the nineteenth. Landowners were still in contact with their community whether the latter were their economic dependants or not. Local solidarity demanded that people should support their natural leaders and the Welsh community operated on a basis of social obligations which outside commentators have wrongly described as the survival of feudalism. Landlords were able to commit their tenants' votes *en bloc* to the candidate they supported and it was rare for a tenant to refuse to comply. Even political opponents respected a landlord's right to dispose of his tenants' votes since this amounted to his political 'interest' in the county and county politics was always a matter of balance of interests. It is idle to look for political content or issues in elections until late eighteenth century, since politics meant no more than a trial of strength between families for primacy within their own county community.

The Representative Class

The Revolution of 1688 enhanced the importance of Parliament by making its meetings more regular whereas previously when it was summoned at will by the King there were often long lapses when it never met. With Parliament becoming a more integral part of government, its membership came to be more coveted as it conferred social status. The property qualification confined the representation to owners of land thus creating an oligarchy. In England it could be breached by the middle class converting their wealth to property and entering Parliament but in Wales they were not sufficiently numerous or wealthy to affect the monopoly of the established landed class. There were differing levels, however, inside the landed class and within our period we see the representation moving between them. Until the Civil War the representation had been shared by a number of landed families, some of them with only modest estates inasmuch as it was then considered a duty more than an honour to represent your community in Parliament. Social and economic changes in the seventeenth century depressed the portion of the lesser gentry very significantly and after 1660 they were largely eliminated from the representation. Their decline enabled the greater gentry to enter into their own and the eighteenth century became the golden age of the country squire. The gentry had been firmly established in most of the borough seats in the sixteenth century and this position had been greatly strengthened by the Corporation Act (1661). Welsh counties, with the exception of Monmouthshire, having only one county seat, the borough seat became a useful reserve in the game of political chess when so many claims had to be met. Thus there was no social difference between county and borough members although the former enjoyed precedence, and the same names keep recurring in the lists of representatives. Welsh boroughs had no independent corporate life and borough politics was intermixed with that of counties.

Rivalry between aristocracy and gentry, so marked a feature in England, is not much in evidence in Wales till the end of the eighteenth century. A connexion can be traced between members of Parliament from North Wales and the Nottingham-Finch aristocratic group at the end of the seventeenth century but it was mainly a matter of family relationships ; although this probably influenced the parliamentary conduct of the members concerned it had little bearing on the local situation since they came into Parliament on their own interests. In Glamorgan and Radnorshire aristocratic control was more in evidence, being a regular feature in the former and a somewhat more sporadic one in the latter. After 1790, we see aristocratic influence extending into counties like Carmarthenshire and Pembrokeshire where it was little in evidence before.

Between 1790 and 1830, it has been calculated that of 54 members of Parliament sitting for South Wales counties and boroughs, 45 owed their election to 9 families, 10 of them being accounted for by the Orielton and Tredegar families ; 15 members of Parliament were nominees of 4 English peers, Beaufort, Bute, Cawdor and Dynevor, whilst 6 were nominees of 3 Irish peers, Kensington, Lisburne and Milford. Many of these members of Parliament were sons, brothers or close relations to noblemen. This tendency in South Wales was also characteristic of North Wales, possibly to a somewhat lesser extent. The augmentation of estates by marriage increased the range of political interests whilst the loss of an estate meant that a family lost what interest it had. The growth of aristocratic power was in part due to marriages contracted by Welsh heiresses with scions of the English peerage but it was also partly due to the increasing interest shown by Welsh families in titles. Families like the Wynns of Wynnstay, Morgans of Tredegar and Owens of Orielton, might have been raised to the peerage at any time in the eighteenth century but had prided themselves on remaining commoners and for this reason there were hardly any indigenous families in the peerage. After 1770, parliamentary support came to be traded for such rewards and political attitudes were determined by hopeful expectation or disappointment of social advancement. Thus in 1776, three Welsh families obtained Irish peerages, that of Glynllifon becoming Lords Newborough, that of Picton Castle Lords Milford and that of Edwardes of Haverfordwest Lords Kensington. By the end of the eighteenth century a seat in Parliament was becoming the normal expectation of a peer's son when he came of age and it is significant that most of the younger members of Parliament were scions of aristocratic families whilst the older ones belonged to lower social groups who had often given a lifetime of service to their community.

The Member

Why did Welsh M.P.s go to Parliament? Being drawn from a class which was regarded as the natural leaders of the community many regarded a seat in Parliament as an obligation attached to high birth; as it acquired status and prestige there was also the family tradition and its standing in the county to be considered. The venality of the House of Commons during our period has often been alleged and no doubt Welsh members like English had some thoughts of gain. This is very evident in the Cavalier Parliament, the first after the Restoration, when many of the Welsh members were pensioners of the Crown and sold their parliamentary support in return for perquisites. They felt justified in doing so if only to recoup their losses during the Civil War period. Moreover, even to climb to such offices of local eminence as the Lieutenancy of their county they needed royal favour and faithful service to the Crown in Parliament and holding sundry offices at Court and in Administration was a means of securing attention.

In the Hanoverian period the interest of the country gentry was focused more upon their own localities than upon national politics but the workings of the patronage system still made an appearance at Westminster necessary. The anti-Hanoverian attitude of many Welsh M.P.s deprived them of public office but their economic and social standing ensured their local pre-eminence. Thus Sir Watkin Williams Wynn I steadfastly opposed Administration and never held government office but no one could deny his standing as one of the premier land-owners in North Wales.   M.P.s not only expected to be the recipients of patronage themselves, they also expected that their position would enable them to dispense patronage to their clients.   William Owen, who represented Pembrokeshire from 1722 to 1774, never held office nor took an active part in Parliament but his letters to Newcastle and Hardwicke are full of requests for favours for his supporters. As Peter Williams, the Methodist divine, so aptly put it in a request letter to a M.P., ' I apprehend that it is those who have none to solicit in their behalf are forgotten.'

Few Welsh M.P.s were career politicians, most of those who were came into prominence in the post-Restoration period. They had little advantage of birth but they had talent and it was their success in the Law which brought them to Court notice. Such were Sir John Trevor of Brynkynallt who became Master of the Rolls and Sir William Williams of Llanforda who became Solicitor-General and Speaker of the House of Commons.   The number of Welsh M.P.s who held offices other than purely local ones in the eighteenth century was small and what eminence most of them acquired in politics was won in the role of opposition. Most of them conformed to the type of country gentleman in the political sense of the term who was usually a silent member who watched the proceedings and made up his mind about issues on their merit. The hall-mark of the country gentleman was independence, especially inde-pendence of the ministers and being able to stand for election on his own interest. Many of them were Tories, others were either Government or Opposition Whigs but these were only traditional labels as far as they were concerned and in the main they eschewed political connexions.   Their parliamentary conduct was dictated by their independence and even their attendance at the House came second to county business ; those of the Opposition usually defied any attempt to organise them and acknowledged no leader which largely accounts for their political impotence.   They took a disinterested view of politics in the main and the fewness of Welsh professional men like lawyers and servicemen in Parliament suggests that they expected less from politics than English and Scottish members. It is significant that it was with the growing aristocratic domination of the electorate at the end of the eighteenth century that politics again became the high-road to a career for many Welsh M.P.s.

Some Welsh country gentry felt they had a responsibility to support the King's government in the interest of sound administration, but even they maintained a just sense of independence and to appear in the role of a placeman was one path to losing a county seat. John Campbell, who represented Pembrokeshire from 1727 to 1747 and gave his support to Administration, sums up this attitude thus : ' tho' an honest man may often comply with things not quite agreeable to him, rather than give any advantage against an Administration which he approves, yet there are some things in which he must follow his own judgment such as he has without regard to persons '. Other gentlemen took quite the opposite view of their role in politics. Parliament in the seventeenth century had been concerned with the threat of the growth of the executive power and many country gentry in politics in the eighteenth century still considered their parliamentary role as one of opposition to the Administration. Sir Thomas Hanmer from Flintshire, Speaker in Queen Anne's last parliament stated that ' Distrust of the executive is the principle on which the whole of our constitution is founded '. Many Welsh M.P.s belonged to this ' old constitutional school ' but their numbers thinned out by the end of the century and when Evan Lloyd Vaughan, the last of the Corsygedol family to represent Merionethshire, died in 1791 a commentator remarked that ' one of the last independent Members of the old constitutional school ' had passed. By the end of the century considerations for economic development even concerned M.P.s and constituents came to expect that their representative in Parliament should use his services to promote their well-being. Some of the landed gentry who had estates to develop responded to these demands, notably the Morgans and their successors, the Goulds, of Tredegar, whereby Newport acquired a great advantage over its rivals by being exempted from coal duties in the eastern part of the Bristol Channel. No wonder that Cardiff and the other Glamorgan ports saw fit to complain about the inactivity of their moribund members, Thomas Wyndham and Lord William Stuart. The winds of change had begun to blow and the advent of Benjamin

Hall, an industrialist, in 1814 as member for Glamorgan presaged the dawn of a new era.

What was it that commended members to their constituents? Very important in Wales was lineage and the possession of an ancient pedigree wedded to an estate. Against this combination outsiders had little chance and attempts by English moneyed men to gain a seat were almost certain to earn a rebuff as happened in Carmarthenshire in 1794 to the banker Dorien Magens. Although much was made of a candidate's native origin little was said about his proficiency in the Welsh language. Residence in the county was considered essential ; this was a drawback which the non-resident Benjamin Hall was quick to appreciate and made amends by buying the Hensol estate in Glamorgan. Service to the community in the role of magistrate at Quarter Sessions was considered a good proving ground which told to the advantage of age rather than youth and which excused many an errant member his absences from the House. Local patronage and hospitality were noticed and John Adams's gift of £4,000 to rebuild Carmarthen Guildhall was not untypical. The development of local newspapers and journals, such as *The Cambrian* launched in 1804, did a great deal to publicise a member's conduct and made him more responsive.

The Welsh members increasingly lost a sense of identity with the people they were supposed to represent. There were few issues which caused them to act together as they had sometimes done in the 17th century. Their upbringing made them similar to English M.P.s in most things. More and more of the sons of Welsh gentry went to English public schools, Westminster being the most popular and Eton next. It was the younger sons and the sons of the lesser gentry that continued to go to grammar schools like Ruthin. Between 1754 and 1790 about half the Welsh M.P.s had been to University, mostly Oxford, whilst the Inns of Court, once so fashionable, attracted fewer and fewer. With this growing estrangement it is little wonder that the Welsh people began to look around for alternative leadership.

SUGGESTED READING

General:

Y Bywgraffiadur Cymreig, Llundain, 1953, *Dictionary of Welsh Biography*, London, 1959.

R. T. Jenkins, *Hanes Cymru yn y Ddeunawfed Ganrif*, Caerdydd, 1945.

———, *Hanes Cymru yn y Bedwaredd ganrif ar bymtheg*, Caerdydd, 1933.

W. Rees, *An Historical Atlas of Wales*, Cardiff, 1951, 1959, 1966.

A. J. Roderick, *Wales through the Ages*, Vol. II, Llandybie, 1960.

D. Williams, *Modern Wales*, London, 1962.

G. Williams (ed.), *The History of Glamorgan*, Vol. IV, Cardiff, 1974.

Chapter I:

L. B. Namier, *The Structure of Politics at the accession of George III*, London, 1957.

L. B. Namier and John Brooke, *History of Parliament, The House of Commons*, 1754-90, 3 vols., H.M.S.O., 1964.

T. H. B. Oldfield, *The Representative History of Great Britain and Ireland*, 6 vols., London, 1816. (Vol. VI refers to Wales).

E. and A. G. Porritt, *The Unreformed House of Commons*, 2 vols., Cambridge, 1909. (Vol. 1, chap. 6 refers to Wales).

R. Sedgwick, *The History of Parliament, The House of Commons*, 1715-54, 2 vols., H.M.S.O., 1970.

W. R. Williams, *Parliamentary History of Wales*, Brecknock, 1895.

2. Restoration Politics
1660—1714

The Cavalier Parliament and the Exclusion Crisis

The loyalty of Welshmen to the Stuarts was scarcely less than it had been to the Tudors and during the Interregnum many families opted out of public life rather than serve the Protectorate. Some had participated in loyalist plots which had anticipated the Restoration and several North Wales squires were involved in the Booth Rebellion of 1658. The lesser gentry who had been prominent in county government especially after 1658 gave way once more in 1660 to the traditional families. Many of them had been impoverished by fines and sequestrations but their hopes of compensation were soon dashed. The greater families recovered quickly especially if they had not been too committed in the Civil War and emerged unscathed or had changed sides in good time like the Myddeltons of Chirk. Some pinned their faith on young sprigs of the family who were too young to be involved in the Civil War and far from taking a despondent view of the future many regarded the time as congenial for making careers, especially in Law. Marriages were contracted to enhance family fortunes and many turned to politics to further their plans. Perquisites like the stewardships of royal manors, receiverships and constableships fell into the laps of politicians as the reward of political support. Families, like the Carters of Kinmel, created by the marriage of Parliamentary officers into old landed families were left unmolested and even those who had come into possession of sequestered estates, like Col. Philip Jones of Fonmon, kept them. The Regicides alone suffered for their part in the Civil War ; Thomas Wogan fled abroad, and Colonel John Jones, Maesygarnedd, was executed in London. His son was allowed to keep his pre-1646 estates and remained in the circle of the lesser gentry of North Wales. Puritans remained under surveillance especially after the discovery of a plot of Commonwealth men in 1661 when many of the associates of Vavasor Powell were imprisoned at Caernarfon.

When the Convention Parliament was summoned in 1660 about one-third of the Welsh members were Cavaliers despite attempts at excluding them; but the Roundheads, including some Presbyterians who were in the majority, were ready to come to terms. Moderation was more in evidence than royalist enthusiasm and apart from the effusions of poets like Huw Morus, royalist propaganda was not pronounced nor was the anti-Presbyterianism so common elsewhere evident here. Few of the elections were contested, about half of the members elected having previous parliamentary experience and despite the preponderance of youth in England it was about equally balanced with age in Wales. In the election of 1661 to the Cavalier Parliament, as it came to be known, moderation was again the note with only about six contested elections, mainly in the boroughs ; about half the members had sat in previous Parliaments and about half could be designated Cavaliers. When this Parliament wound up eighteen years later, the number of loyalists had risen to about two-thirds as younger members were returned at twentyfour by-elections. The royalist tide ran strongly till 1667 when Clarendon fell from power.[1] It was he who began building a ' Court ' party in the Commons and many Welsh members, especially those elected pre-1667, were drawn into it. The ' Country ' members resented this attempt to dominate Parliament and among those who encompassed Clarendon's fall some Welshmen were prominent, notably Sir John Vaughan of Trawsgoed. Danby continued and extended Clarendon's clientage system and after 1673 it was reckoned that 22 of the Welsh members were pensioners of the Crown, county as well as borough members being included. Reaction was already setting in before the Parliament ended in 1678 and the new men elected in its last years mostly joined the ' Country ' opposition. The only defence for this unprecedented degree of venality is the poverty of the members because of sequestration suffered by many in the Civil War and their need for financial support to be able to come into Parliament. Opportunities for preferment were sought as much as financial

[1] For the Penal or ' Clarendon ' Code see p. 32

reward, some becoming court officials and placemen but there were also career politicians like Sir John Trevor of Trefalun who became Secretary of State and Lord John Vaughan (Carmarthen) who became Governor of Jamaica.

Early in the seventies news began to filter through to the House of Commons of disaffection in Monmouthshire, allegations being made that Catholic J.P.s sheltering under the protection of the Raglan family were discriminating in favour of their co-religionists. Mixed with it was a good deal of resentment against the Marquis of Worcester on account of family aggrandisement and of personal arrogance, especially when he began to use his power and influence as newly-created Lord President of the Council in the Marches (1672) to intervene in elections to secure the return of Court candidates. His chief enemies in Monmouthshire, Sir Trevor Williams and John Arnold, were no doubt inspired by personal animosity as well as concern for the Protestant religion. It was against this background that the hysteria of the Popish Plot spread in 1678 which had great repercussions in Monmouthshire. William Bedloe, a Monmouthshire man, was one of Titus Oates's accomplices and he alleged the existence of a plot whereby Lord Powis was to seize Chepstow Castle and then join with prominent Catholics to restore Popery. There was extreme Protestant reaction in the county led by John Arnold, and a witch-hunt of Catholic priests mainly based on the seminary at Cwm ended in the execution of four of them.[1] The Catholic threat assumed more substance when a murderous attempt was made on Arnold's life.

The Popish Plot was the prelude to the Exclusion Crisis when Parliament attempted to exclude the Catholic James, Duke of York, from the succession. From 1678, the Marquis of Worcester was active in purging the Commissions of the Peace of opponents in anticipation of an election for a new parliament. The First Exclusion Parliament elected early in 1679 nevertheless had a number of critics of the Court returned from Wales including some old Parliament men of pre-Restoration days like Bussy Mansel. Worcester received a personal rebuff in his own territory of Monmouthshire and Brecknockshire when he tried to rig the election to bring in loyalists. Among

[1] See p. 34

those who drew up the First Exclusion Bill were two Welsh lawyers of the Country party, Edward Vaughan (Cardiganshire) and William Williams of Llanforda, and although slightly more Welsh members voted for than against it no clear pattern emerges. The election to the Second Exclusion Parliament in September 1679 again showed no swing either way from the previous parliament. When it met after a year's delay, William Williams, one of the foremost critics of the Court, was elected Speaker. The Second Exclusion Bill which it introduced was more extreme than the first and feeling was running high when the King prorogued Parliament, but not before it had voted the imprisonment of five Catholic peers, including Lord Powis, in the Tower. In the interval before the Third Exclusion Parliament was elected the Court made a determined bid to re-fashion local government in a way advantageous to itself ; 27 J.P.s were removed from the Commissions of the Peace mainly in the south-east and Montgomeryshire, many of them aggressive Protestants and a few supporters of the Duke of Monmouth, the proposed Protestant successor ; the charters of the corporations of Brecon, Carmarthen and Cardiff were re-modelled to permit greater royal control. No doubt the exercise paid off but more important was the rising tide of royalist reaction which set in when cooler heads began to draw parallels with the situation of the 1640s. The election was a stormy one in North Wales accompanied by riots at Wrexham but courtiers were returned in some constituencies where they had no look-in before, although Tory gains were on the whole modest. After the Rye House Plot had discredited the Whigs, Worcester seized his advantage to avenge himself on his personal enemies. Sir Trevor Williams and John Arnold were proceeded against in King's Bench and were heavily fined to the extent that they had to seek clemency. Worcester, created Duke of Beaufort in 1682, set out on a vice-regal progress through Wales which took some weeks and was courteously received; by the time Charles II died in 1685, the heat had been taken out of the situation.

The reign of Charles II serves to indicate fairly clearly the extent to which Welsh M.P.s had become involved in English politics. Both in the attack on Clarendon and in the impeachment of Danby Welsh M.P.s had been prominent. At no time

in the history of Parliament were Welshmen more conspicuous
in high office ; Court adherents like the two Sir John Trevors,
Sir Leoline Jenkins and Judge Jeffreys served as Ministers of
the Crown, whilst Sir John Vaughan of Trawsgoed and his son
Edward, and William Williams were prominent in the rise of
the Country party. When Welsh members were so drawn into
the vortex of high politics it is no wonder that Welsh issues were
inconspicuous.   Concern was shown by most Welsh M.P.s
about the importation of Irish cattle to the detriment of Welsh
breeders and concern for the woollen industry, so important
to the Welsh economy, led to a measure which compelled the
burial of people in woollen cloth.   More controversial was the
issue of the Council in the Marches which had been revived
in 1660 and which in the hands of the Marquis of Worcester
had stirred up much disaffection, being presented by the Grand
Jury of Monmouthshire as a grievance.   The Second Exclusion
Parliament tried to abolish it hoping thereby to strike at the
Crown's prerogative and at Worcester's power at the same
time, but it survived for a few more years.   The Court of Great
Sessions, which also stemmed from the Acts of Union, was
viewed in a different light when it came under attack early in
the Cavalier Parliament; Welsh M.P.s rallied in its support
assisted by the great learning of Sir John Vaughan of Trawsgoed who published a pamphlet entitled *Process into Wales*
which clarified the legal position and left the Court unmolested
till 1830.

James II and the Revolution of 1688
    The succession of James II passed without incident in Wales
and there is no evidence that Welshmen were involved in the
Monmouth Rebellion saving Lord Jeffreys' part in the ' Bloody
Assize ' which was a prelude to his becoming Lord Chancellor.
James's only parliament was presided over by Sir John Trevor
of Brynkynallt who later became Master of the Rolls. William
Williams who had been so prominent a member of the Country
party in Exclusion days was won over probably because of his
standing with Dissenters and became Solicitor-General. During
this brief reign seven of the principal law officers of the Crown
hailed from Wales and the borderland and that at a time when
the judiciary was looked upon as a branch of royal adminis-

tration which was concerned with furthering royal policy. The Parliament of 1685 was as amenable as James could wish, but despite this, he soon fell foul of it when his intention of putting Catholics into positions even in the Army became known. The significance of James's pilgrimage to Holywell in 1686 was not lost on the people of Wales. In April 1687, he proclaimed his first Declaration of Indulgence which granted toleration to Dissenters as well as Catholics for which he received three votes of thanks from Wales. It is unlikely that this represented the attitude of the majority of Welsh Dissenters to this un-constitutional Act and James was disappointed with the re-ception it had. Judges on circuit were instructed to prompt Grand Juries in the counties to return thanks for the Indulgence but only the Grand Jury of Merioneth responded. Attempts were made to sound out opinion about the religious tests. Beaufort summoned the Deputy Lieutenants and the justices of the peace to meet him at Ludlow but less than one half of the 320 expected turned up. Three questions were put to them; the first, whether they would support the repeal of the Penal Laws if they were elected members of Parliament ; the second, if they would vote for such M.P.s as favoured repeal ; the third, whether they would live peaceably with people of a different religion. The replies were generally evasive and only the last question drew any positive response.

Nevertheless, James continued his wooing of Dissenters and five of them were put into the Commission of the Peace in North Wales and five in the South ; what is even more signifi-cant is the fact that they were drawn from among the lower gentry. The son of John Jones, Maesygarnedd, even, was nominated as High Sheriff of Merionethshire but for some reason was vetoed. The process of re-modelling corporations went on and Swansea's charter was changed so that the Crown could remove any officials by Order in Council. On May 22, 1688, the second Declaration of Indulgence was announced which the clergy were required to read from their pulpits. The Archbishop of Canterbury and seven bishops, including William Lloyd of St. Asaph, petitioned the King to withdraw it for which they were put on trial, the case for the Crown being led by William Williams as Solicitor-General. One of the judges at their trial was Sir John Powell, a Carmarthenshire

man, who declared that to concede the King's right to suspend
the laws ' amounts to an utter repeal of all the laws '. The
bishops's acquittal was tremendously popular and Lloyd was
hailed by the poets Huw Morus and Edward Morris, and his
progress home was a triumphal affair.

The trial of the seven bishops was the curtain-raiser for the
Revolution of 1688 which came before the excitement had died
down in north-east Wales. James's fate was sealed when a son
was born to his queen and Lady Powis, an avowed Catholic,
was appointed as his governess. Tories joined Whigs in inviting William of Orange over but even at this late hour the
King could still draw a response from Wales. Beaufort anticipated no difficulty in raising 10,000 men here and Edward
Carne of Ewenni, of an old Catholic family, set about recruiting
a special regiment in Glamorgan. North Wales squires expressed a willingness to raise forces locally and Sir Robert
Owen of Clenennau declared his intention of supplying 500
men. James realised the futility of it in time inasmuch as the
Army could not be relied on nor was the allegiance of the
squirearchy assured, it being known, for instance, that there
was a party favourable to the Prince of Orange in Glamorgan.
The threat of an Irish army landing in Wales could always be
relied on to create anti-Catholic feeling and rumour was rife.
When news of the Revolution reached Dolgellau the gaol was
opened and the High Sheriff's authority denied. Excise commissioners making for the town were taken for Irishmen and
set upon. At Welshpool, where the Marquis of Powis had his
seat, there were fights between Catholics and Protestants in the
streets and Powis Castle was attacked. The panic did not last
long but it took rather longer to adjust to the new regime. Few
Welshmen followed James into exile, the Marquis, created
Duke, of Powis being the only person of note, but many
remained at home resolved not to be reconciled to the Revolution Settlement. Beaufort came to terms and saw many of his
enemies returned to the Convention Parliament which abolished
the Council in the Marches over which he had presided. The
abolition of the Council meant that Wales was no longer
considered as a separate unit of government and henceforth
came to be treated as an extension of England. The somewhat
mystical attachment which Welshmen had had for the Crown

did not survive the Revolution either. Although the Revolution had little impact on Wales it was the end of an era.

Non-juring clergy were not alone in refusing to change their allegiance, many gentry and corporations showing much tardiness in taking the oath to William and Mary, and many gentry refusing to become J.P.s. Abergavenny was deprived of its charter because its burgesses refused to take the oath and news of disaffection spread as far as Pembrokeshire and as late as 1693. William aggravated the situation in Wales by granting the confiscated Powis estates and the lordships of Bromfield and Yale, worth some £100,000 to the Crown, to his Dutch favourite Bentinck, created Duke of Portland. The gentry of north-east Wales and the lordships' tenants expressed great resentment and the matter was raised in the House of Commons. The occasion evoked a famous speech by Robert Price of Giler (Denbs.), member for Weobley, which contained a great deal of national sentiment and some veiled threats. The House carried a unanimous resolution asking the King to revoke the grants, which he did with ill-grace. William's stock only rose in Wales when news of an attempted assassination in 1696 made people realise what the consequences might have been. James Owen, a prominent Welsh Dissenter, published a sermon of thanksgiving for his deliverance. A Welsh member, Rowland Gwynne (Radnorshire) proposed an Oath of Association in defence of the King which all were invited to take and copies were circulated throughout the country. The Glamorgan signatories numbered 760 but many did not sign, including nine M.P.s, which can be taken as an indication of Jacobite sympathy. With the emergence of parties political allegiance came to be influenced less by attitude to the Crown than to the Revolution after 1688. Welsh M.P.s became increasingly drawn to the English political connexions, the Nottingham-Finch group, for instance, drawing many adherents from North Wales and the northern border. Robert Harley (Radnor boroughs) led the Harley-Foley group with which several members from South Wales and the southern border were identified. William's main claim to Welsh support was his conquest of Ireland which Harley described as ' a very great mercy '.

The Crown retrieved its popularity in Wales in the reign of

C

Anne but the battle between Whigs and Tories became the focus of attention at elections. The High Church party, dominant in the Church and favoured by the Queen, renewed its attack on toleration and picked on the practice of occasional conformity which had fallen into bad odour when in 1697, the Lord Mayor of London, Sir Humphrey Edwin, a Welsh landowner, repaired to a Dissenting meeting-house after taking the Sacrament in Church. The tactics which the High Church Tories adopted discredited the attempt since they brought in a measure which was 'tacked' to a money bill hoping that thereby it would pass unnoticed. Jacobitism could be openly expressed in the reign of Anne and many sought to identify the Queen with their views, two judges on circuit in North Wales asserting that the Queen had intimated that she regarded the Non-jurors as her father's best friends. This led some misguided Merionethshire J.P.s to refuse levies for the army and to disband soldiers already enlisted. The Whig government misjudged the situation badly in 1709 when it sought to impeach Dr. Sacheverell, a spokesman of the more arrogant section of the High Church party, for preaching a sermon before the Lord Mayor at St. Paul's in which he attacked the Revolution. The Doctor was impeached and found guilty but his sentence was so mild that it was interpreted as an acquittal. Seventeen Welsh votes which can be identified as Tory were cast for the Doctor and seven which were Whig were cast against him. No less triumphant was his journey towards north-east Wales to his new living at Selattyn, in the diocese of St. Asaph, being greeted by vast concourses at Shrewsbury and Wrexham and entertained by the gentry in a manner reminiscent of Bishop Lloyd's return in 1688. It was a sufficient demonstration at least of the Tory sympathies of the majority of the Welsh squirearchy and an ironical sequel to the events which had produced the Revolution of 1688.

SUGGESTED READING

A. H. Dodd, *Studies in Stuart Wales*, Cardiff, 1971.
T. Richards, *Wales under the Penal Code*, 1662-87, London, 1925.
——, *Wales under the Indulgence*, 1672–75, London, 1928.
——, *Piwritaniaeth a Pholitics*, 1689–1719, Wrecsam, 1927.

Articles:
A. H. Dodd, 'Caernarvonshire and the Restoration', *Trans. Caerns. H.S.*, XI, 1950.
——, 'Tuning the Welsh Bench', *N.L.W.Jnl.*, VI, 1950.
——, 'Flintshire Politics in the Seventeenth Century', *Flints. H.S. Pub.*, XIV, 1952–3.
J. R. Evans, 'The Popish Plot', *N.L.W.Jnl.*, VI, 1949.
F. Jones, 'Disaffection and dissent in Pembrokeshire', *Trans. Cymmr.*, 1946–7.
G. W. Keeton, 'Judge Jeffreys: Towards a reappraisal', *W.H.R.*, I, 3, 1962.
D. Matthew, 'The Welsh influence among the legal advisers of James II', *Trans. Cymmr.*, 1938.
T. Richards, 'Declarasiwn 1687', *Traf. Cymd. Han. y Bed.*, 1924.
——, 'The Glamorganshire Loyalists, 1696, *B.B.C.S.*, III, 1926.
C. J. Skeel, 'The Council in the Marches in the Seventeenth Century', *E.H.R.*, 1915.
J. G. Williams, 'Sir John Vaughan of Trawscoed', *N.L.W.Jnl.*, VIII, 1953–4.

3. Religion under the Penal Code

The Restoration Church

The Restoration of 1660 was not merely the restoration of a king to his throne but also of the pillars of the Old Order, the Church and the landed class. But it was impossible to turn the clock back to 1649 because the intervening years had witnessed changes in the Church as well as in government, and diocesan and parochial organisation had been seriously disrupted. Out of Cromwell's religious toleration sectarianism had grown up, and when it was abolished at the Restoration, Nonconformity became as much of an established fact as Roman Catholic recusancy. Despite the King's partiality for toleration Parliament was hostile to it and as the power of the Presbyterians declined in Parliament the hope of finding an acceptable settlement receded especially after the failure of Anglicans and Presbyterians to reach agreement at the Savoy Conference (1661). Parliament's attitude hardened to the point of resorting to penal laws against all who dissented from the Church but it relaxed the moral sanctions which had characterised the period of Puritan austerity.

The opportunity of reforming some of the more obvious abuses in Church organisation was lost in reverting to the old system. The size of dioceses was unchanged, which left St. David's embracing the greater part of South Wales as the second largest diocese in England and Wales. This explains why Nonconformity reared its head in some of the remoter corners of the diocese far from the administrative centre at Abergwili. The inherent weaknesses of the Church for which geography was responsible were aggravated by organisational weaknesses. The administrative machinery at the level of the archdeaconry and rural deanery was weak and often non-existent. Thus there was no effective link between bishop and clergy and if diocesan organisation was weak there was no reinforcement from below. Parishes were also overlarge with churches badly sited. Churchwardens had to discharge civil as well as ecclesiastical duties and parish funds had to meet all contingencies such as the relief of the poor. Non-churchmen were admitted to the parish vestry and so had a say in Church as well as in parish affairs. Parochial revenues were always inadequate and the impropriations of a previous age which produced this state of affairs remained to become one of the major grievances of the eighteenth century Church. Patronage of livings was mainly in lay hands ; the Bishop of Llandaff, for example, did not have a single living in his gift in the Glamorgan half of his diocese. The power of the bishops to reform the system was thus limited even assuming that there was a disposition towards it.

The calibre of the episcopal bench of the Restoration Church was generally superior to that of the succeeding Hanoverian period. Most of the bishops appointed were Welsh-speaking at least down to the 1690s and this was equally true of Llandaff as of Bangor. Whatever the limitations of the Restoration episcopal bench many of them had solid pretensions to scholarship. William Lloyd of St. Asaph was an able controversialist and Humphrey Lloyd was well-versed in ecclesiastical law. Bishop Bull of St. David's had written weighty volumes against the growth of Arian doctrine in theology. Bishop Humphrey Humphreys was an acknowledged Welsh scholar and a patron of literary men whose elevation to Bangor in 1689 caused M.P.s as well as the bards to rejoice. Both Humphreys and William Lloyd of St. Asaph encouraged the use of the Welsh language for official purposes and addressed their episcopal queries to the clergy in it. The Welsh bench suffered through frequent translations of bishops to English sees since Welsh sees were regarded merely as stepping stones to preferment. This accounts for the inordinate number of Welshmen holding English sees at this period. Unfortunately, few were in their Welsh dioceses long enough to carry out any programme of reform although some notable exceptions like Humphreys of Bangor and Beveridge of St. Asaph did make some effort. Bishops, as yet, spent a substantial part of the year in their diocese as far as attendance on the House of Lords and Convocation permitted but there was a tendency for these demands to increase from the time of William III on. More reprehensible was the practice of holding a Welsh bishopric along with an English office like a deanery and residing outside Wales, all too common in the case of Llandaff. During Tyler's incumbency Llandaff ordinands had to seek him out at Hereford, where he was Dean, in order to be ordained. Canonical duties were on the whole regularly performed between 1660 and 1714. In the case of St. David's there was some evidence even of a spiritual revival after Bishop Bull's succession in 1705.

The religious bitterness and tension of the early part of the century were still active in the post-Restoration period and were exacerbated by the efforts of Church and State to stamp out Nonconformity. The Welsh bishops showed as uncompromising an attitude as any towards Dissent and were impatient with the half-hearted attempts made by J.P.s and Justices of Great Sessions to extirpate it. Bishop Lucy of St. David's thought the Brecon magistrates very remiss in not silencing some preachers who came near that town. Some bishops made a genuine effort to hold a dialogue with the Dissenters but not with a view to making concessions but to persuading them to re-enter the Church. Argument was preferable to coercion but equally ineffective. Both Bishops Hugh Lloyd and Francis Davies tried to win back Samuel Jones, Brynllywarch, but failed and Bishop Davies resorted to persecution and had him imprisoned. William Lloyd of St. Asaph had meetings with leading Quakers like Richard Davies and the brothers Charles and Thomas Lloyd of Dolobran and even held a public disputation at Llanfyllin. He also met Presbyterian divines like Philip Henry and James Owen and the leaders of the Wrexham Dissenters. They were all abortive and, writing to Archbishop Sheldon, he expressed the view that the Dissenters' obstinacy was the dragon's teeth which had sprung from the seed sown by the firebrand preacher Vavasor Powell who languished in prison till his death in 1670. The Rye House Plot (1683) caused more suspicion to fall on Dissenters and even Bishop Lloyd took to sterner measures to discipline them. One can only conclude that a reverend gentleman who refers to them in such terms as ' bloody wretches ' must have had his patience sorely tried.

The Welsh Trust also got less encouragement from the Welsh prelates than from the lesser clergy or indeed from some English bishops.[1] The Trust had offended by opening unlicensed schools and by publishing new editions of the Bible without episcopal authority. The similarity between the work of the Welsh Trust and that of the Propagation Commission must have been unpalatable to them and an unpleasant reminder of times past. The Toleration Act of 1689 brought to an end the persecution of Dissenters but not their proscription and it certainly did not change the attitude of the Church towards them, nor were the Dissenters likely to be more amenable now that their religion had the protection of law.

Contemporary opinions differ about the state of the Church in the half-century following the Restoration. It was from the ranks of the clergy that most of the correspondents of the S.P.C.K. were drawn and their letters throw much light upon this subject. Some who were puritanically inclined like Griffith Jones took a very gloomy view and attributed the general ignorance of parishioners to the negligence and bad example of the clergy. The Rev. William Wynne refused to believe that Wales was worse than it had been or that it owed its salvation to Gouge and the Puritans. Erasmus Saunders, describing the Church in the first two decades of the eighteenth century, confirms Griffith Jones's view but attributes it to the root cause of poverty. He found people generally well-disposed towards religion and prepared to make a great effort to attend services from which it appears that ignorance rather than indifference was the besetting sin. Though Griffith Jones and Saunders were speaking of what they saw in the diocese of St. David's, Browne-Willis, who had a much wider experience, maintained that the situation was no worse there than elsewhere.

The ministry was inadequate because of a shortage of clergy which encouraged pluralism despite genuine efforts by the Church to curb it. Plurality returns indicate that there were 28 pluralists in St. Asaph, 51 in St. David's and the situation was no better in Llandaff. Much of the responsibility rested with lay impropriators by reason of whose meanness Griffith Jones alleged many clergy ' were pinched with poverty and

[1] See Chapter 4, p. 43

forced to officiate in three or four parishes '. The King had
expressed a wish in 1660 that the incomes of vicars and curates
in poor parishes be augmented out of the revenues appropri-
ated to the higher cathedral clergy. In the decade after 1660
St. David's had set aside only £400, St. Asaph £660 and Llandaff £1,200 for this purpose which was quite an inadequate
response to the problem. Sir John Philipps, writing to the
S.P.C.K., stated that the Duke of Somerset drew £900 a year
from some Carmarthenshire parishes and spent but £70 on
the stipends of six curates to look after them. He proposed
that money be raised to buy up these impropriations thus
reviving an idea first put forward by the Welsh Trust.

The effects of this poverty were bound to be reflected in the
calibre of the clergy whose ignorance stemmed from their lack
of education since the Church made no provision for clerical
education in Wales. The number of graduates in the Welsh
ministry was relatively low since many Welshmen who had
been to University sought more remunerative livings in
England as the number of Welshmen who served as prison
chaplains in London indicates. It has been alleged that the
clergy ejected for their Puritanism between 1660 and 1662
were replaced by graduates but of those ordained in St. David's
between 1664 and 1670 less than a quarter had been to University. Of 23 clergymen who were correspondents of the
S.P.C.K., nine only had been to University. A university
education came to be looked upon as an ideal rather than a
necessity and Bishop Henry Lloyd asserted that it was not
practicable to fill the Welsh ministry with graduates. Of the
two, he considered it more important that they should be
Welsh-speaking than graduates which he enlarged upon by
saying, ' of those I have ordained the graduates have not been
always the best scholars '. As Bishop Humphreys wisely commented, more could not be expected because of the straitened
means of the clergy and ' their learning will be proportionable
to their means of attaining it '. The majority had to be content
with the smattering of a classical education which they could
pick up at local grammar schools like Carmarthen or even at
Dissenting academies, since Dissenters took much more trouble
over ministerial education than the Anglicans did. Despite
their handicaps there were many conscientious and dutiful

clergy who were active in many parts of the country in promoting pious works such as founding charity schools, an activity which reached its climax under the S.P.C.K. in 1715. As early as 1701, Sir John Philipps had found a group of 31 clergy who had come together to promote this work and to seek the sponsorship of the Archbishop of Canterbury. Clergymen were equally prominent in the publishing work of the S.P.C.K. in order to provide a supply of pious literature in Welsh.

The Stuart period ended somewhat better than it started since there are unmistakable signs of a revival of Church life in the reign of Queen Anne who was very popular for her munificence towards the Church and she is the idol of Ellis Wynne's *Gweledigaetheu y Bardd Cwsc.*[1] ' Queen Anne's Bounty ', if it did not solve the financial problems of the Church, went some way towards relieving them. Its impact on Wales was considerable where the Governors of the Fund found an inordinate number of livings worth less than £50 per annum. Royal briefs came to be resorted to more frequently to raise money for repairing or rebuilding churches.

About 1709, an improvement came about in Church services. Archbishop Tillotson's sermon on ' Frequent Communion ' was circulated and given some heed, and the churchwardens' presentments indicate a reform of the public services and more frequent communion in many churches. Vigorous efforts were made to restore public catechising and Bishop Beveridge of St. Asaph urged its more regular observance on his clergy. The sermon became more popular and there appears to have been some evangelical zeal in the diocese of St. David's inspired by the saintly Bishop Bull. Bishop William Lloyd went as far as to urge his clergy to emulate the Dissenters' way of preaching. Nor were the needs of Welshmen in exile in the American colonies and West Indies overlooked. The S.P.G.,[2] the missionary arm of the S.P.C.K., was urged to provide preachers and teachers who could minister in Welsh and they scored some notable success in winning converts in America even from the Quakers.[3] Evangelical laymen were also active in philanthropic work, Sir John Philipps and John Vaughan showing much concern for prison reform. Thomas Pryce of Merthyr wanted

[1] Visions of the Sleeping Bard, published in 1704
[2] Society for the Propagation of the Gospel
[3] See Chapter 14, p. 255

to place a library in prisons and Robert Powell wanted religious services to be held there regularly. Branches of the Society for the Reformation of Manners were formed in Caernarfonshire, Carmarthenshire, Pembrokeshire and Monmouthshire after 1692 and were directed at enforcing the anti-vice laws.

Such then was the Church which presumed by means of parliamentary legislation to enforce every person to belong to it and to no other. That many should consider it unworthy to submit to its authority is not strange and the story of the conflict between the Church and the Dissenters is the least complimentary aspect of its history during this period.

The Penal Code

The Penal or Clarendon Code was the work of the predominantly Anglican Cavalier Parliament and destroyed all attempts at comprehension of Presbyterians and sectaries within the Church. The Corporation Act (1661) was directed mainly against the political power of Dissenters in corporate towns and required the swearing of an oath of passive obedience which in effect threatened the existence of Dissent. It also required people who held public office to receive communion in Church and to obtain a certificate of their having done so. The Act of Uniformity which followed in 1662 ejected clergy and teachers who did not subscribe to the Book of Common Prayer and the liturgy of the Church. Although its impact on Wales was considerably less than on England only 25 being turned out, this was only so because 93 Puritan clergy had already been ejected here to make room for those Anglicans they had replaced during the Interregnum. The Corporation Act forbade Dissenting ministers from keeping schools, the Act of Uniformity subjected schoolmasters to ecclesiastical control. The Conventicle Act (1664) made it illegal for more than five persons to meet anywhere for worship other than in a church unless a family keeping family devotions, and was directed against religious gatherings in private houses. It was ineffective, but when Archbishop Sheldon inquired into its operation the Welsh bishops were very secretive. The Bishop of Bangor denied the existence of any conventicles in his diocese although it is known that Dissenters met in three counties within it and the same was true elsewhere. When the Act was renewed in

1670 the penalties became severe to the point that it defeated its own ends. Sir John Vaughan of Trawsgoed struck a truly Elizabethan note when he declared that ' as long as persons conform outwardly to the law, we have no inquisition into opinion '. He only feared that making an exception of Dissenters by the grant of toleration would undermine the law. The Five Mile Act (1665) which forbade ejected clergy from living within five miles of a town was intended to suppress Dissenting schools in order to wean the younger generation from Dissent. Despite the Act, Bishop Lucy testifies to the continued existence of schools in towns like Brecon, Carmarthen, Haverfordwest, Swansea and Cardigan in 1672.

How effective the Penal Laws were in their application is inconclusive. Bishops often complained of the tardiness of sheriffs in executing writs and even of Great Sessions judges for obstructiveness which was not surprising when the Lord Chief Justice, Sir John Vaughan, was against their indiscriminate use. Some J.P.s were notorious baiters and their names were noted in Puritan records. Many were indifferent and some who had social or family relations with Puritans acted in collusion to mitigate the severity of the law. In the words of Dr. John Owen, many wise and judicious magistrates had ' openly declined all engagements in these persecutions '. Persecution was at worst sporadic and the years 1660-2, 1664-7, 1670-2 and 1681-4 stand out. J.P.s tended to take their cue from Westminster and it was not till 1681 when political necessity caused Charles II to fall in with the High Church Tories that persecution entered upon its worst aspect in that and the years which followed. The brunt always fell on the Quakers against whom even their fellow-sectaries showed animosity. The eighties witnessed emigration on a scale which alarmed Sir Leoline Jenkins, the Welsh Secretary of State, and Quakers were very prominent amongst the emigrants.

Roman Catholics were fellow-sufferers with the sectaries despite the efforts of the Court to protect them. Parliament was nevertheless intent on harassing them especially after the signing of the Treaty of Dover in 1670 when its suspicions of royal intentions were aroused. Demands to enforce the anti-Catholic laws were made to safeguard the Protestant Establishment. In 1672, the King decided to chance his arm and proclaimed the Declaration of Indulgence which suspended the Penal Laws. This raised the constitutional question of the King's right to suspend Parliamentary legislation in which he was opposed by the judges. Dissenters were placed in a cleft stick since, much as they desired toleration, they did not seek it by illegal means. Nevertheless, the King received three addresses of thanks from Wales ; more indicative, perhaps, was the number of licences which were taken out by Dissenting congregations and preachers—185 in all throughout Wales, 136 of them being in South Wales. This figure does not account for all the congregations known to have existed but belies the efforts of the bishops to play down the strength of Nonconformity. The Indulgence was short-lived since the House of Commons insisted on its revocation, but after 1672 the situation was never quite the same Dissent having been recognised by royal proclamation and this was the beginning of royal dalliance with them in an effort to find allies to counterbalance the High Church Anglicans.

The Test Act of 1673 with which Parliament retaliated was directed at Roman Catholics since it required all office holders to take the Oath of Supremacy as well as the Oath of Allegiance which led to the increased harassment of Catholics, nowhere more so than in Wales. Returns made to Archbishop Sheldon in 1676 put their number at 1,085, about one quarter that of the Dissenters, and concentrated mainly in three counties. In Monmouthshire they enjoyed the powerful protection of the Beaufort family, but their arch-enemy, Sir Trevor Williams, the county member, succeeded in having an investigation opened into their activities which disclosed that Mass was being publicly celebrated and Catholics assembling in defiance of the law. Some J.P.s were even alleged to be Catholics and using their position to protect their co-religionists while harassing Protestant Dissenters. The scare associated with the Popish Plot after 1678 created an atmosphere in which persecution thrived and Catholic priests were hounded to death, David Lewis 'the father of the poor' at Usk, Philip Evans and John Lloyd at Cardiff ; the Catholic seminary over the border at Cwm was ransacked and closed.[1] The Catholic cause in Wales did not recover from the blow it received in 1679 and

[1] See p. 18

the following years. Now that Catholics were the focus of attention Parliament's attitude towards Dissenters mellowed somewhat in an attempt to dissociate them from each other and during the reign of James II both King and Parliament were wooing the Dissenters. In 1687, the King put them to the test by enquiring what their attitude towards Catholics would be in the event of the Penal Laws being removed. The most the Dissenters would concede was that they would live peaceably with them but were resolved not to support the repeal of the Penal Laws except by Parliamentary consent which was a remarkable change from 1672.[1] Dissenters were only too well aware that the King was merely trying to use them as a pawn in the game and their resistance to his overtures made the acceptance of the Toleration Act easier in 1689.

James II's determination to set aside the Penal Laws led to his undoing when both bishops and clergy resisted his second Indulgence in 1688. The Archbishop of Canterbury and seven bishops petitioned the King remonstrating against the Declaration knowing that the Church was solidly behind them. One of the seven bishops clapped in the Tower was William Lloyd of St. Asaph who had handed the petition to the King. The acquittal of the bishops on a charge of seditious libel was followed by Bishop Lloyd's triumphal return to St. Asaph and the occasion for a demonstration of support throughout north-east Wales, in which spirit the Revolution of 1688 which soon followed was greeted too. When the Revolution necessitated breaking their oath to James II and taking another to William III some clergy demurred and amongst their leaders was William Lloyd, the Welsh Bishop of Norwich. The number of Non-jurors in Wales was only eighteen and at least some of them were ejected from their livings. It caused very little disturbance in the Welsh Church and before the end of Anne's reign most of the Non-jurors were dead. In her reign the reinvigorated Church attempted to renew the harassing of Dissenters by the Occasional Conformity Act to stop the practice of taking communion in Church merely to qualify for office. The attempt failed but the renewed attempt in 1711 succeeded as the result of some political horse-trading. The Schism Act of 1714 would have destroyed Nonconformist

[1] See p. 21

schools but both measures remained inoperative and were repealed in 1719 since the spirit of persecution had gone out by then and Dissent had survived, strengthened and purified in adversity and shorn of its fellow travellers who had succumbed to the heat of the day.

Old Dissent

It was the Act of Uniformity of 1662 which brought Nonconformity into existence although the sects and creeds which formed it go back in some cases beyond the Interregnum. The number of ejections in 1660-2 indicates that it was strongest in South Wales probably because it was more susceptible to English influences. The Nonconformity which emerged in the half century after the Restoration acquired very distinct Welsh characteristics and had a particular regard for the language. The process of identification was a gradual one because there was always a quality of élitism attached to Puritanism.

Socially, the Dissenters were drawn from the ranks of the minor gentry like the Owens of Bronyclydwr (Mer.) and the Prices of Ty'n Ton (Glam.), and also from among more substantial freeholders, tenants and townsmen. It was reported from Denbigh in 1715 that there was one member of the congregation worth £4,000 to £5,000 a year, and three worth £500 each. There was a member worth £1,400 at Trelawnyd in Flintshire and the congregation at Llanfyllin (Monts.) counted five gentlemen amongst them. Several gentry houses were licensed for worship under the Indulgence of 1672. Most of the Dissenters were men of substance rather than affluence and the social status of a few like the Bradfords of Tir Iarll (Glam.) allowed them to sport armorial bearings. Many of them were owners of modest libraries displaying a fairly catholic choice of books other than on religion. Traders were also in evidence and one needs remember that Puritanism flourished more in the small towns than in the countryside. Stephen Hughes was the son of a silk-merchant and when he lost his living he settled in Swansea in fairly comfortable circumstances. Artisans and yeomen were prominent as the figures of Dissenters who emigrated to America show clearly. It was not an exclusive caste, nevertheless, and humble labourers were to be found in some numbers in the congregation. An analysis of the ten Dissenting congregations in Monmouthshire gives a fair cross-section of the social complement of Puritanism : number of members, 1,300 ; this included 1 squire, 37 gentlemen, 115 yeomen, 137 merchants, 85 farmers and 167 labourers.

'Gathered' churches had existed in Wales before the Puritan Revolution, Llanfaches being the first and Cardiff next. The churches which emerged after the Restoration were also of this nature but they were organised on a county basis or even a wider area. Churches tended to form where some eminent preacher had been labouring as in Montgomeryshire which had been part of the mission field of Vavasor Powell who for a time lived at Kerry. Henry Maurice, writing after 1672, states that there were twelve Independent churches in Wales ; one in every county except Anglesey, Merioneth and Flint, but with Glamorgan and Monmouth having two each. The Church met at several places within the county which might be described as branches of the one county church. Thus the church of Cardiganshire associated with Cilgwyn had congregations at at least eight other places attached to it but it constituted one church. An itinerant minister served all the congregations and sometimes churches in neighbouring counties since circuits were carefully organised. The church also gathered together periodically for the celebration of communion and all the branches were subject to a common discipline. Churches often grew up near county boundaries before 1670, as in the case of the Olchon Valley on the Hereford-Brecknockshire boundary, so that members could make their escape if a conventicle was disturbed.

In the early years Presbyterians, Baptists and Independents were found in the 'gathered' church. Baptists and Independents were often yoked together and Vavasor Powell even after he had become a Baptist used all his endeavour to keep the two sects together. The two sects had adopted a congregationalist system wherein each church was independent and had no central authority imposed on it. The Presbyterians had a more closely-knit organisation with a centralised authority. By 1678, differences were beginning to divide the Presbyterians from the Baptists and Independents mainly about the form of organisation but before the end of the century doctrinal differences also widened the gap between them.

Exclusiveness was the characteristic of the ' gathered ' church since membership was only offered when a person gave convincing proof of conviction and that after a long period of preparation. Hence the Dissenting churches were small in the size of their membership. It was probably fortunate that Dissent was not more closely organised than it was since, if it had evolved into churches of a conventional kind with a settled ministry, its chances of surviving the persecution of the seventies and eighties would have been much less. Movements under persecution tend to split up into small cells which are better able to avoid detection and Dissent survived in its conventicles which often met in secret and out-of-the-way places. It was the elasticity of its organisation which proved such an asset in the days of tribulation since the preachers, or ' teachers ' as they were frequently called, moved about serving several communities in much the same way as the Catholic missionaries had done. Unlike Catholicism, however, Dissent was never wholly dependent on the patronage of great people and so did not fall a casualty as often when a family deserted a cause.

The Indulgence of 1672 enabled congregations to come out into the open and congregations and ministers to take out licences so that a more formal kind of Dissent emerged and many causes date their inception from 1672. Despite the revocation of the Indulgence and the renewal of persecution it never lost its identity, it had been given a start which even the persecution of 1682 could not efface. Nevertheless, the granting of toleration in 1689 was timely since the evidence of church-wardens' accounts is that between 1672 and 1682 there had been a considerable falling-off in the numbers of Dissenters. The Independents and Presbyterians responded to the Toleration Act by setting up a Common Fund in London in 1691 to support their churches and particularly to make provision for ministerial education which increased the number of ministers to expand their work. Resentment against the interference of ' *gwŷr y* Fund ' (the Fund men) was often expressed and some churches refused Fund support rather than sacrifice their independence. The Common Fund also brought together religious leaders whose doctrinal views were at variance who had hitherto been content to work together in relative harmony, but now that they were yoked together differences became more accentuated than common interests. So in 1694, the Congregational Board set up its own separate fund from which grants of from £30 to £50 were regularly made to churches in South Wales.

By the end of the seventeenth century we see a growing tendency for churches to sort themselves out on the basis of doctrinal belief and the days of the ' gathered ' churches from then on were numbered. Dissenters still made common cause against the harassment of the Anglican authorities and the justices of the peace, since churches were denied licences, Dissenters were denied burial in parish cemeteries, individuals were pressed into public offices which would cause them to fall foul of the law by holding, and other malicious practices. In their own defence the Dissenters of the London area formed in 1732 the Committee of Dissenting Deputies which took up cases and even resorted to the law-courts to seek redress. Although it was representative only of the Dissenters in and around London, it came to be looked upon by Dissenters throughout the country as the protector of their rights and the champion of their liberties.

Having rejected the ' religion of the magistrate ', as they termed the Anglican faith, the Dissenters just as readily opposed any authoritarianism in matters of belief. Holding that religion was a matter of inner conviction they brooked no interference between a man and his conscience. Their approach was intellectual rather than emotional and the Presbyterians among them came increasingly under the influence of the rationalist trend which became evident towards the end of the seventeenth century. There was a gradual moving away from High Calvinism even among sections of the Baptists and Independents because it emphasized the depravity of Man and reduced him completely to an instrument of the Divine Will which did not go down well in an Age of Reason. Since so much rested on understanding it is not surprising that so much emphasis should be laid upon an educated ministry.

Even Puritan laymen must have received a higher than average education since otherwise the kind of sermon which was directed at them could hardly have been appreciated. The derisive term '*Sentars sych*' (' dry Dissenters') suggests very strongly the length and weightiness of their sermons which

D

were directed towards a select hearing rather than a mass audience. The church was as much a school to instruct as a society of worshippers. In their public worship the emphasis was on hearing the Word proclaimed rather than on ritual upon which they frowned. For this reason a pretentious building or even any building at all was unnecessary and the term ' *tŷ cwrdd* ' (meeting house) indicates the purpose of their coming together. When they did start erecting chapels in the early eighteenth century they were usually no more than rectangular boxes with the pulpit in a place of prominence but with no decoration or any trace of symbolism.

Although Sunday observance was emphasized this did not of necessity mean regular or several Sunday services. One sermon per Sunday was normal and where a minister served more than one congregation a service every other or even every third Sunday was not unusual. Communion was not frequently celebrated, again indicating that they laid no stress on ritual. Hymn-singing became an early feature of their worship as a means whereby the congregation could participate actively in the service. The Puritan ethic, however, dominated more than their formal meetings, it also coloured their lives. Austerity was practised and the eschewing of any form of extravagance was undoubtedly one of the reasons for their worldly success. Their social influence was very decidedly in the direction of raising moral standards as well as banishing ignorance. This moral attitude they applied also towards politics and contributed to the growth of a social conscience in the eighteenth century.

The Calvin-Armin controversy tore many congregations apart in the eighteenth century, the Independents being mainly affected but the Baptists did not go unscathed. The first great upheaval, known as the ' first schism ' of 1707 began at Wrexham and spread to Henllan (Cards.) when the High Calvinists were forced out of the church. Thereafter, there followed a great winnowing of congregations which gradually became more homogeneous according to which religious doctrine they subscribed to. The Baptists, being the only sect that insisted on adult baptism, drew apart from the others, whilst the Presbyterians drew nearer towards Unitarianism to the sorrow of Old Dissenters. Even so, the newly-emerging denominational churches were far from monolithic and throughout the eighteenth century the situation remained fluid. Congregations still disputed points of theology and schisms were almost endemic. It was not until the end of the eighteenth century that modern day sects began to assume their definite form and characteristics.

SUGGESTED READING

E. T. Davies, *The story of the Church in Glamorgan*, London, 1962.

R. T. Jones, *Hanes Annibynwyr Cymru*, Abertawe, 1966.

M. O'Keeffe, *Four Martyrs of South Wales and the Marches*, Cardiff, 1970.

T. M. Rees, *A history of the Quakers in Wales*, Carmarthen, 1925.

T. Richards, *Wales under the Penal Code*, *1662–87*, London, 1925.

——, *Wales under the Indulgence*, *1672–5*, London, 1928.

——, *Piwritaniaeth a Pholitics*, *1689–1719*, Wrecsam, 1927.

E. Saunders, *A view of the state of religion in the Diocese of St. David's*, 1721, repr. Cardiff, 1949.

Articles:

A. H. Dodd, 'The background of the Welsh Quaker migration to Pennsylvania', *J. Mer. H. and R.S.*, III, 2, 1958.

G. J. Williams, 'Stephen Hughes, a'i gyfnod,' *Y Cofiadur*, 1926.

E. G. Wright, 'Humphrey Humphreys', *J.H.S. Ch. in W.*, II, 1950.

4. Charity Education

Introduction

THE educational movements of the end of the seventeenth and the early part of the eighteenth century were the product of piety or ' Puritanism in action '. The Act for the Better Propagation of the Gospel in Wales (1650) had established the tradition of making education the hand-maid for spiritual and moral improvement. The translation of the Bible into the vernacular had the effect of enhancing literacy and the Puritan resort to the written and spoken word in pamphlet and sermon along with the emphasis upon an educated ministry added to the importance of education and literacy. Puritans feared diminishing the ' power of the Spirit ' by Man's ' natural parts ' but a concession was made to learning as a weapon capable of banishing ignorance and increasing godliness. They appointed lecturers and Puritan ministers were commonly known as ' teachers '. Puritan leaders showed concern for a ' complete and generous education ' and had revived the idea of a University in Wales. The desire ' to remove ignorance and profaneness ' which had motivated the Propagation Act[1] continued to inspire Puritan educational endeavour for one and a half centuries.

Puritans, especially from the distance of London, were concerned at the alleged decline of Wales into ignorance and barbarism and so it early became the object of Puritan piety. Inasmuch as many of the Puritan benefactors were Englishmen or English-speaking Welshmen, the language problem was a complication from the start. Puritans had recognised the need to address Welsh people in their own language during the Interregnum in political pamphlets and broadsheets written in or rendered into Welsh in order to win their ear. This did not, however, modify their aim of making proficiency in English the goal and allowed very little place for Welsh in their educational schemes.

[1] See Volume 1, 218

Austerity and moral rectitude were the hall-marks of the Puritan, expected in their schoolmasters as much as in their ministers. There are also indications that they used their schools to uphold the social order as well as to promote spiritual welfare. Under the Propagation Act, Church revenue had borne the expense of educational provisions, but the Restoration period was hostile to such ideas and education once again had to fall back on charity. The excess of zeal and intolerance of the Propagation Commissioners was the cause of much hostility from the clergy and lay impropriators to the efforts of later Puritan educational pioneers in the post-Restoration period.

The Propagation experiment had awakened interest in education and some of the persons who had been involved in it continued their interest, forming links with the new pioneering efforts. The first decade of the Restoration period was hardly a conducive period for reviving Puritan schemes and a more tolerant climate had to be awaited. The Declaration of Indulgence of 1672 briefly provided such a respite. Continuity of interest in education tended to run in families and is best illustrated by the Philipps family of Picton Castle. Erasmus Philipps was a Propagation Commissioner and later showed an interest in the Welsh Trust whilst his son, Sir John Philipps, became one of the pillars of the S.P.C.K. and patron of Griffith Jones. The tradition continued into the third generation and so this family represents over a century of philanthropic endeavour whilst other families, like the Vaughans of Derllys, exhibit a similar interest over a briefer period. It was the gentry, especially the minor gentry, who were the chief patrons especially in the borderland and the more Anglicized areas. Their patronage was necessary to the success of any local effort and the distribution of the charity schools is closely related to patronage. A continuity of tradition existed in some market towns where the climate was more amenable to Puritan activity. Local interest in education was thus maintained despite the apathy of the Anglican Church between 1660 and 1700 and this could be fanned into a flame when opportunity arose.

The Welsh Trust
Although the Puritans had looked to the State during the

Interregnum to supply the needs of education they were not short of initiative when thrown upon their own resources in the post-Restoration era. The Act of Uniformity of 1662 was in a way a fortunate accident since many of the ministers ejected from their livings turned to keep school, albeit unlicensed, for their living. So numerous did they become that the Cavalier Parliament directed its Five Mile Act (1665) against them, forbidding Puritan ministers to hold schools within five miles of a corporate town, hoping thereby to arrest the spread of Dissent into the younger generation. This measure exhibits the negative attitude of the official Anglican Church newly restored to its position and privileges which it was intent on holding even by persecution. Persecuting schoolmasters was a poor substitute for providing schools and such a sterile policy was bound to founder ; it even aroused sympathy for its victims. Nowhere were the Penal laws more ' laid asleep ' than in London where sympathy for the Puritan cause was still active. The seventies heralded a more tolerant age and the Indulgence (1672) gave Dissent, at least by implication, an official recognition which would make its suppression more difficult.

It was during this period of greater tolerance and accommodation that the first voluntary educational movement to do with Wales was born, the Welsh Trust. Apart from its educational work, it was an interesting experiment in co-operation between ' men of latitude ' inside the Anglican Church and among the Dissenters. It exhibits that spirit of accommodation which surmounted sectarian differences in the common endeavour to raise spiritual and moral standards through education. It attracted some of the most outstanding Anglican divines of the time in Tillotson, Stillingfleet and Whichcote, matched on the Dissenters' side by such men as Richard Baxter, William Bates and Thomas Firmin. The keystone which bound them together was Thomas Gouge, the ejected minister of St. Sepulchre, Southwark. The Lord Mayor and Court of Aldermen of the City of London added lustre and patronage to the movement which was London-based and even in 1699 the Welsh Trust was still spoken of as ' this favour of the Londoners toward poor children begun divers years ago in North and South Wales '.

The initiative was taken not by an organised movement in London but by two individuals working independently of each other, Thomas Gouge in London and Stephen Hughes in Carmarthenshire. It may be argued that some educational effort would have matured in Wales anyway, but without London backing it is doubtful whether it would have attained such proportions as it did. Stephen Hughes, like Gouge, was an ejected minister who had served the parish of Meidrim, Carmarthenshire. Although he would not compromise with his faith in 1662 he did not suffer ostracism in the circles in which he turned and he succeeded in keeping the friendship of people of widely different views. Calamy has described him as ' a plain, methodical, affectionate preacher who insisted much upon the substantial things of religion '. His tolerance and moderation allowed him to preach in parish churches after his ejection as well as elsewhere, since he remained acceptable not only to the clergy but also to the gentry of the neighbourhood. Successful as a preacher, he is nevertheless remembered principally for his educational work. He was excommunicated for keeping school without a licence which could only be obtained from the bishop, whereby he controlled education in the diocese.

Hughes also appreciated the power of the printed word as well as the spoken which impelled him to take steps towards spreading literacy and providing reading material for those who could read. It was he who undertook the publication of Vicar Prichard's ever-popular verse which appeared as *Canwyll y Cymry* ('Welshmen's Candle') in 1672, thereby ensuring its permanence and a wider circulation. He also published a translation of the Catechism, the Psalms, New Testament and Bunyan's *Pilgrim's Progress* in Welsh, being assisted therein by a circle of scholarly friends, Anglican and Dissenting, like Charles Edwards, Richard Jones, Dr. William Thomas and Samuel Jones, Brynllywarch. It was probably this intense literary activity which took him to London since there were no printing presses in Wales as yet, making it necessary for an author or editor to spend weeks in the metropolis seeing his work through the press. It is believed that it was this which brought him into touch with like-minded people in London such as Thomas Gouge.

Gouge, who was an evangelical, was probably aware of the missionary enterprise conducted by the Propagation Commission. He shared with Joseph Alleine of Taunton, whose *Life* he read in 1671, a passionate desire to evangelise Wales. He also had the means and the time to devote to the enterprise. He made his first visit to ' the skirts of Wales ' in 1671-2 to undertake some itinerant preaching. He saw the need for providing Bibles in Welsh and on his return to London set about the task of raising funds. The publication and distribution of literature in Welsh on the scale that he contemplated made necessary the establishment of the Welsh Trust, which dates from 1674. Bishops and clergy and ' the quality around London ' responded to its appeal for help. Welsh gentry also became patrons and members of local organisations ; names like Edward Harley, Edward Mansel, Thomas Mostyn, Trevor Williams, John Trevor, Erasmus Philipps and John Awbrey indicate the interest of some of the leading families in Wales and the Puritan connections of some may be noted.

The work of the Trust falls into two parts ; firstly, the supplying of Welsh devotional literature, and secondly, the opening of schools for children. Much co-operation was received from Stephen Hughes and his collaborators in the first of these tasks as the writing and translating of suitable literature into Welsh made necessary. Existing supplies of the Welsh Bible met only a small part of the need and so Stephen Hughes undertook a new edition of 8,000 copies in 1678. The Church Catechism and the Common Prayer Book were published alongside religious classics like *The Whole Duty of Man* and *The Practice of Piety*, which shows an absence of prejudice against Anglican manuals in the two Dissenters, Hughes and Gouge. Over a hundred towns and villages were appointed as distributing centres which, together with the number of works published, indicate a substantial reading public despite the lack of schools since the expiry of the Propagation experiment. The English patrons agreed with Hughes that it was useless directing literature at an adult audience in any language other than Welsh and so co-operation in this field of activity continued till the Trust's work came to an end in 1681.

Whereas the English sponsors were prepared to make a concession to adult readers rather than jeopardise their chances of salvation, in the schools of the Trust they set their faces against the use of Welsh as a medium of instruction. It was deemed that the best interests of the children would be served by their acquiring fluency in English and abandoning their native tongue. The belief that Welsh was an encumbrance whilst English was the high-road to success which dominated education for so long has unmistakable Puritan origins.

The Trust's approach to schooling was severely practical with the goal of producing honest, hard-working citizens as well as good Christians. The Puritans were only somewhat less eager to acquire the possessions of this world than the heavenly reward and this is summed up in the aim of the Trust which was, to teach children to read ' our English Bible and be more serviceable to their country and to live more comfortably in the world '. So, simple arithmetic took its place alongside English reading. Stephen Hughes was averse to the emphasis on English from the start and voiced his protest as early as 1672. Whilst the dearth of material in Welsh made the use of English imperative at first, the force of this argument diminished as the Welsh publishing activities of the Trust increased. The determination of the Trust sponsors to press the use of English increasingly by 1675 led to some estrangement between them and Hughes who was receiving encouragement from the gentry of his neighbourhood in establishing Welsh schools. In view of the experience of later voluntary movements, the policy of the Trust in regard to language was unfortunate and it seems a tremendous pity that so much endeavour was productive of so little achievement.

This was not due to lack of enthusiasm on the part of the Welsh people. The Trust's Reports show that by 1675 some 87 schools were in being, the number in attendance at each varying from 10 to 60. Archbishop Tillotson testified to 1,600 to 2,000 children being put to school annually under Gouge's provision. The expense was borne partly by the Trust, partly by Gouge himself and partly by towns which were ' excited to bring up at their own charge the like number of children in the like manner '. How many children passed through the schools cannot be assessed because the pupils' length of stay is not known. By 1678, when the Reports mention 71 schools, it is apparent that decline was setting in.

The activities of the Trust were wound up in 1681, the year which saw the death of Thomas Gouge and the imprisonment of Richard Baxter. By this time, the religious and political climate had changed for the worse as Charles II abandoned his wooing of Dissenters and men of toleration and made an alliance with the High Church Tories. Persecution was renewed and Anglican clergy turned ' the force of their zeal almost wholly against Dissenters '. Erstwhile supporters like Stillingfleet turned their backs fearing that co-operation would lead to the spread of Dissent. The Welsh bishops became more openly hostile and in Archbishop Sheldon found a sympathetic ear when they accused the Trust of ' drawing the credulous common people into a disaffection for the government and liturgy of the Church '. No doubt, the bishops had been annoyed by the Trust's publication of the Bible in 1678, a task which had always been regarded as the prerogative of the bishops. Their control over school appointments also diminished after the verdict in Bates's Case in 1670 allowed patrons to appoint masters to schools which they had endowed. No wonder the Bishop of St. David's complained of patrons and ' great purses ' supporting unlicensed schoolmasters and mistresses. This hardening of official attitude made Anglican co-operation in the movement increasingly difficult and although Tillotson in his funeral sermon on Gouge talked about finding a successor to him, none was found.

The Trust schools lapsed but there is no reason to suppose that schools founded by private patrons and town corporations did. It is significant that the S.P.C.K. later reported schools at 30 centres where there had been Trust schools which may well indicate a continuity of existence. The real importance of the Welsh Trust is that it formed a link between the State experiment of the 1650's and the voluntary efforts of the eighteenth century, providing a continuity not only of idea but, to a remarkable degree, of personnel. The Welsh Trust has, therefore, been rightly regarded as the parent of the educational movements of the eighteenth century but this does not detract from its interest as an experiment in co-operation between seventeenth century ' men of latitude ' before toleration had come to be accepted as a principle.

The S.P.C.K. and the Charity School Movement

The Society for Promoting Christian Knowledge was founded in London in 1699. Of its five founder members the only cleric was Dr. Thomas Bray of Oswestry, a town with very close Welsh connections ; Sir Humphrey Mackworth, the Neath industrialist whose mining activities extended into Cardiganshire, was also in at the start. Though not a founder member, Sir John Philipps of Picton Castle, very early became involved in its activities which he generously patronised and, more than anyone, encouraged the Society's interest in Wales.

The aims of the Society were two-fold, to carry the Gospel into foreign parts and to establish catechetical schools at home. The missionary zeal which inspired the former was also applied to the latter in Wales in a manner reminiscent of the Welsh Trust. The Society organised its work on a territorial basis, appointing local correspondents, in which capacity gentry and clergy served the movement well ; prominent amongst them were country squires like Sir John Philipps who applied his private fortune to the task. He was better educated than most of his own class and his discernment and sensibility mark him out as a paragon of his time. A relation by marriage and a neighbouring squire, John Vaughan of Derllys, shared similar interests and encouraged the participation of his brother gentry in them. He showed sound common sense and appreciated the practical difficulties which beset the movement, advising that poor children be clothed to ensure their attendance. Philipps and Vaughan showed a generous tolerance towards Dissenters and a disposition to co-operate towards the common good. The movement interested female patrons also, Mrs. Vaughan of Llwydiarth (Monts.), the wife of the knight of the shire, being a conspicuous example. The ladies of Brecon raised funds to maintain a girls' school and several ladies made bequests to endow schools to educate poor children. Financial help came both from within and from outside Wales and, considering the number of English patrons there was no undue interference with the work which the Society endeavoured to carry out.

Unlike the Welsh Trust, the S.P.C.K. was a society composed solely of Anglicans. For a short time at its inception the four Welsh bishops supported the movement to educate the Welsh people, and this was an incentive for the clergy to do likewise. Despite the accusation of apathy which is levelled at the clergy of this period it is safe to say that without their support the movement would not have flourished as it did. It was they who encouraged parents to send their children to school and their letters to the Society bear evidence of great interest and concern. Some clergy and more curates taught in the schools and the masters were often ' exhorted to proficiency ' by a diligent cleric.

The efforts of Welsh reformers to combat religious ignorance and spiritual apathy were second to none, but the emphasis in the Society's schools in Wales was different from that of other countries in the British Isles. There was less emphasis here on conditioning poor children to work than in England, but social deference was nevertheless instilled. Nor were the blessings which an alien culture bestowed upon them emphasized as in Scotland, and the need to rescue children from the toils of Rome did not arise in Wales as in Ireland. The Welsh reformers had a simple singularity of purpose which was the saving of souls to which all other things were incidental. The need to teach children how to work was less necessary among children who were long inured to it from an early age.

Between 1699 and 1737, when Sir John Philipps died, 96 schools were established under S.P.C.K. auspices throughout Wales with the exception of the county of Flint. There was a heavy concentration in the southern counties amounting to 76 schools almost half of which were in the counties of Carmarthen and Pembroke. This can be explained by the presence there of such men as Sir John Philipps and John Vaughan who had a great influence upon the clergy so that the parishes adjacent to the Taf Valley were well supplied with schools and it was here that Griffith Jones, Llanddowror, a protégé of Sir John Philipps, came into contact with the movement. Cardiganshire, noted by Erasmus Saunders, is a case in point where there was no patron ready to further the work of the Society and hence hardly any schools. The role of the patron was very important when we remember how the schools were organised.

Although the S.P.C.K. sponsored schools it did not finance them unless there were exceptional circumstances. Money had to be raised locally, the collection taken at the celebration of the sacraments often going to the purpose. Sometimes a school was founded by local endowment as in the case of Llangynog (Carms.) which was endowed by John Vaughan and the freeholders of his manor. Thus the task really owed more to local effort than to the Society whose contribution lay mainly in the provision of books and materials necessary for teaching and whose London headquarters became a distributing centre. The financial outlay of the S.P.C.K. schools was much greater than that of the Welsh Trust which preceded it or that of Griffith Jones's Circulating Schools which succeeded it. School buildings had to be provided where none existed and the Society had to meet the cost of salaries of its regular teaching staff. As an inducement to get children to attend, clothing allowances were often made and at Pembrey (Carms.) and Llanfyllin (Monts.) free meals were given. The expenses attendant on such ancillary services slowed down the work of the movement but they were very necessary because the poverty of families made parents reluctant to send their children to school. The situation was clearly put before the Society by Dean John Jones of Bangor in describing the plight of the poor of Anglesey and Caernarfonshire where no provision for parish relief existed and children had to go begging from door to door.

We have no means of knowing for how long children stayed on at school but probably for much less than the four-year curriculum which was operative in England. The proverbial 'quarter of schooling' ('*cwarter o ysgol*') was probably considered adequate for tuition in the Catechism and principles of the Church of England which formed the core of the course of instruction. Reading and writing were taught ; the boys were taught arithmetic and the girls to spin and ' sew plain work '. Such was the curriculum of the Llanfyllin school which was probably common to all with local variations. Though work training was not as prominent in Welsh schools as elsewhere, Sir John Philipps expressed disquiet about any instruction which disposed children too much towards the ' mechanics trades ' and tried to persuade the Society to print ' an agreeable treatise upon agriculture fitted to the capacity's of youth ', an understandable enough attitude for a country landlord. Opposition was voiced from other quarters against the teaching of reading and writing because it unsuited children for hus-

bandry. Some relief was provided in some Welsh schools by
the inclusion of music, an activity considered to be too dis-
ruptive a social and political influence in the schools of England.

The language problem confronted the S.P.C.K. like the
Welsh Trust but unlike the latter the former did not adopt a
language policy. Whereas English was the usual language of
instruction the Society did not exhibit any prejudice against
the use of Welsh. It sometimes even erred by sending Welsh
publications into areas which were English-speaking. Object-
ion to teaching English was raised in some quarters, by Lewis
Morris among others, because it encouraged people to migrate
to England ' to the utter ruin of the place of their nativity '.
The Rev. John Morgan, Matchin (Essex), a Welsh exile of
long standing, urged his friend Moses Williams, when setting
out on a journey through Wales to collect for a new edition of
the Bible, to agitate against English teaching wherever he could.
Pleas for Welsh language schools came from some areas. Dr.
Robert Wynne, writing from Gresford (Denbs.) in 1700, noted
the lack of schools in those parts, but emphasizing that any
that should be founded must be Welsh ones and the clergy
societies of Denbighshire, Flintshire and Montgomeryshire
supported this view. Dean John Jones of Bangor, one of the
foremost promoters of the Society's work in North Wales,
established some Welsh schools and in his will left endowments
for them on condition ' the children were to learn Welsh
perfectly '. Unfortunately, bishops like Humphrey Humphreys
and John Evans who had encouraged the early work of the
Society gave way to less sympathetic successors like Philip
Bisse of St. David's, who even opposed translating works into
Welsh. There is little doubt that the schools of North Wales
were carried on in Welsh whilst the signs are that English was
commonly used in the South. Sir Humphrey Mackworth
sought a schoolmaster from London for his works' school at
Neath but on the grounds of experience and qualifications
rather than on language. It would be interesting to know
what language was in use at his other works' school at Esgair-
hir in Cardiganshire. No doubt, it was the prevalence of
English which prompted Griffith Jones, Llanddowror, to
embark on his charity schools since Welsh schools were completely lacking in his neighbourhood. Erasmus Saunders,

writing in 1721, notes the complete absence of Welsh schools and the dearth of English ones ' except it be in market towns ' in the diocese of St. David's, especially in Cardiganshire which was then monoglot Welsh. This might well account for the decline of the movement in its stronghold, Carmarthenshire and Pembrokeshire, areas which later on were to nurture the schools of Griffith Jones.

The S.P.C.K. employed a regular teaching staff but the work was retarded by an insufficient supply of suitable teachers. This led Sir John Philipps to suggest to the Society that it should embark upon the training of teachers, but lack of funds prevented it from pursuing the idea. It was Sir Humphrey Mackworth in 1719 who fathered the idea of itinerant teachers, a suggestion later taken up by Griffith Jones. The wages paid to the schoolmasters were low even by contemporary standards, usually about £4 to £5 a year, the equivalent of a curate's stipend. Indeed, many of the masters were curates who took on the work to augment their income. Although the Society set its face against fee-paying pupils at first, later on they were admitted and this supplemented the master's wages somewhat. Despite these handicaps the schools were served by some notable men, amongst them Griffith Jones, who had the reputation of being a very severe pedagogue.

The movement achieved its greatest success in Wales in its early period between 1699 and 1715 when 68 out of the total 96 S.P.C.K. schools were founded. This coincides with that burst of activity in Church life which was a feature of the reign of Queen Anne only to be followed by a period of wrangling between the High and Broad Church parties each trying to control the schools. Some historians attribute the post-1714 decline to the Hanoverian succession which alienated Jacobites from the Establishment and many of the Society's foremost patrons in Wales were Jacobites. Dr. Isaac Watts attributes their decline to the withdrawal of Dissenting support after the Schism Act of 1714 but that would be giving too much weight to the influence of Dissent in Wales at this period. All these may have been contributory reasons for the schools' decline but it rather overlooks the fact that the decline was apparent at least by 1713 even in Carmarthenshire and Pembrokeshire. Out of 31 schools founded in Pembrokeshire, 26 fall within the period 1704-13. In Carmarthenshire, only 9 S.P.C.K. schools were founded between 1714 and 1737. After 1727 the decline was general throughout Wales and it rather suggests a diminution of interest in the English-medium schools of the Society rather than a decline of interest in education. This is confirmed by the fact that although the Society's schools were dwindling in numbers, other provisions in the form of independent endowments and foundations were increasing. Between 1699 and 1715, 17 schools were established of this kind ; between 1716 and 1727, 14 ; between 1728 and 1740, 30. This makes a total of 61 which amounts to almost two-thirds of the number of schools established by the S.P.C.K. over the same period, the greatest increase being observable in the period when the Society's schools were declining in numbers. Competition from independent foundations thus contributed to the waning of the S.P.C.K. schools especially since these foundations had greater permanence and survival prospects as they were often supported by testamentary bequests or rent charges on property or other sources of secure income. Many of these schools survived the century and passed into the hands of the National Society after 1811.

It is difficult to assess the impact which the S.P.C.K. schools made upon their day and age. From the testimony of good churchmen like Erasmus Saunders and Griffith Jones it appears to have been very small. They talked about the ignorance and the illiteracy of the people in the diocese of St. David's where most of the S.P.C.K. schools were concentrated. On the other hand, reports to the Society in London from all parts of Wales were usually full of praise about the work of the schools. It is probably safe to say that the Society served Wales better in other ways than through its schools but it helped to maintain a continuity of educational effort keeping interest alive and often stimulating individuals to private efforts.

We have no means of knowing how many private, fee-paying schools existed over the same period. William Lewis of Margam writing to the S.P.C.K. in 1724, stated that there was hardly any parish thereabouts without a private school to teach children to read but very few charity schools. The Dissenters often made separate arrangements for educating their children and a number of their schools existed around Carmarthen.

The most organised Dissenting scheme was that established under the will of Dr. Daniel Williams for setting up eight schools in North Wales. Despite clerical opposition schools were opened at Wrexham, Denbigh, Newmarket, Montgomery, Llanuwchllyn, Caernarfon and Pwllheli. In the few places in Wales where workhouses existed pauper children received some measure of education there. The tradition of informal teaching which Griffith Jones was to exploit later was well-established in Wales and Erasmus Saunders attributes the standard of literacy which did exist to the ' peasant schools ' where a person with reading knowledge taught those with whom he came in contact. This makes it difficult to assess the extent of literacy and the means by which it was propagated but it was probably more general than the gloomy comments of religious reformers would lead us to believe.

The S.P.C.K. set up as a publishing house to which the debt of Welsh education for publishing Welsh literature is immense. As a well-organised charity it was able to raise sufficient funds and that over a long period to finance the printing of works composed in Welsh or which had been translated from English. Most of these works were pious and devotional in character and included some of the best-known English classics of this *genre*. In addition, Church catechisms, some of them specially written, psalmodies and several editions of the Welsh Bible which ran into thousands of copies were provided. There was no organisation in Wales, public or private, which could have done this volume of work so expeditiously for it was a triumph of organisation to get this work produced, printed and distribut-ed and to satisfy the persistent and extensive demands which were made. The Society was more than generous to all who sought its help and its resources were made available irrespect-ive of whether the schools were conducted under its auspices or not. Long after its schools were defunct this service con-tinued unabated at least till the end of the eighteenth century. Its example was an encouragement to others to sponsor publi-cations in Welsh. John Vaughan and Sir John Philipps were constantly making suggestions to the Society concerning suitable material and undertook the cost themselves on more occasions than we know. Mrs. Vaughan of Llwydiarth (Monts.) got Edward Morus, Perthillwydion, to translate *Y Rhybuddiwr*

E

Cristnogawl ('Christian Warning') at her own expense and this is no isolated example of the patronage of the gentry in this matter.

One of the most modern aspects of the Society's work was the foundation of libraries. John Vaughan of Derllys was one of the earliest sponsors of the idea which was also very close to the heart of Dr. Bray. Vaughan's idea stretched to a network of libraries extending from diocesan centres down to parish level. It is not strange that when the idea was implemented that the first library should have been established at Carmarthen and that its organisation was entrusted to Vaughan. By 1711, others had followed at Bangor, Cowbridge and St. Asaph. The idea of parochial libraries was not extended beyond the founding of eight of them for clerical use. Vaughan wanted to make them available to all with necessary safeguards but it was probably felt that the need of the clergy was greatest so that they could 'administer wholesome and sound doctrine'. Vaughan even suggested home libraries for children and the *Young Christian's Library* was translated into Welsh. In 1717 Moses Williams completed the task of compiling a catalogue of all books printed in Welsh. What debt the eighteenth century literary revival owed to the S.P.C.K. cannot be estimated but the work it performed in the publishing field was a very important contribution to literature, education and religion.

SUGGESTED READING

M. Clement, *The S.P.C.K. and Wales*, London, 1954.
M. G. Jones, *The Charity School Movement*, Cambridge, 1938.

Articles:
T. Shankland, 'Sir John Philipps and the Charity School Movement', *Trans. Cymmr.*, 1904–5.
E. G. Wright, 'Dean John Jones', *Trans. Angl. Ant. Soc.*, 1952.

5. The Hanoverian Succession 1714—70

The accession of George I in 1714 passed peacefully with only token demonstrations of protest from Jacobites in certain areas. Watkin Williams Wynn of Wynnstay incited his miners at Rhosllannerchrugog to march down to Wrexham to sack two Dissenting meeting houses and the bells of Wrexham church were silenced. Lord Bulkeley chose to retire from politics as a mark of disapproval but by 1722 realised his mistake since he had only eased the way for his political opponents and had lost several offices which were almost hereditary in his family. Lewis Pryse of Gogerddan was elected in Cardiganshire in 1715 but showed his contempt by absenting himself from the House from which he was expelled in 1716. Such die-hard attitudes were not typical and about half the Tories came to terms with the new dynasty, some, like the Joneses of Buckland (Brecs.), abandoning Jacobitism for Whiggism. In the last parliament of Queen Anne about three-quarters of the Welsh members had been Tories but the election of 1715 produced an equal balance between the parties by the Whigs capturing about six Tory seats but some of the remaining Tories were known Jacobites. In Radnorshire, the Whigs succeeded in breaking the long-standing hold of the Harley family. Toleration was an issue which had been handed down from the previous reign when the Act against Occasional Conformity and the Schism Act had been passed as the result of political horse-trading between the Whigs and some reactionary Tory lords to harass Harley. In view of such hostility it is no wonder that Dissenters had cause to rejoice at the Hanoverian succession and a deputation led by Dr. Daniel Williams, one of the foremost Presbyterians of his day, waited upon the King. The repeal of the two Acts stirred little enthusiasm in Welsh M.P.s most of whom, including some Whigs, voted against the measure. It indicates that the Dissenters were not as yet a political lobby of any consequence in Wales and the only county where they were taken note of was Monmouth whose Dissenters received a *douceur* of £100 annually from the Government through the hands of the Hanburys of Pontypool. Whig electioneering was for some time concerned with counteracting the political influence of the High Church and as late as 1734 Bussy Mansel had to deny allegations of hostility against Dissenters in Glamorgan. Sir Watkin Williams Wynn on the other hand could with impunity imprison Peter Williams, the Methodist preacher, in his dog kennels.

Jacobitism

Apart from the Marquis of Powis few of his Welsh adherents had followed James II into exile ; two David Lloyds, father and son from Cardiganshire and Henry Lloyd from Merioneth, drawn from the lesser gentry, were the only representatives of their class. Most Jacobites remained at home to guard their interests and to nurture their disaffection at no cost or discomfort to themselves and to indulge in braggart but clandestine activities. Jacobitism existed before the Hanoverian succession and enjoyed some popularity in Anne's reign ; in 1709-10 we hear of Jacobites assembling in the town house of the Pryses of Gogerddan at Aberystwyth to drink toasts to ' the King over the water '. The Cycle of the White Rose which was the premier Jacobite society was founded in 1710 though even in 1722 it had only fourteen members drawn from the gentry of North Wales, but many confirmed Jacobites were not members of it. There were two Jacobite clubs in Montgomeryshire and despite the fiasco of the Atterbury Plot in 1722 a resurgence of Jacobite activity took place about 1725. The Sea Serjeants, which was the Jacobite society of the southwest and whose origins are obscure, was revived in that year and the Cycle of the White Rose became more active under the energetic leadership of Watkin Williams Wynn. The Sea Serjeants were not as politically demonstrative as the White Rose Society and even denied political motives, their meetings being confined to an annual week of races, balls and conviviality. William Bulkeley's diary for 1738 mentions the existence of a Jacobite society in Anglesey for the past three years. Despite the proliferation of societies there is no evidence that any attempt was made to link them or to concert action between them.

The ' Fifteen ' caused hardly a ripple in Wales though rejoicing at its suppression was cut short in Pembrokeshire by a Jacobite mob armed with cudgels. Various persons were convicted of seditious talk and drinking toasts, most of them of humble origin. Rumour about such activities embarrassed loyalists and in 1715 some Whig gentry and clergy connected with Wales founded in London the Society of Ancient Britons in defence of the House of Hanover and to counter reports of disaffection by loyal addresses, one of which was signed in September by 200 Welsh gentlemen in London and Wales. Its social activities were held annually on St. David's day and it enjoyed the patronage of the Princess of Wales whose birthday fell on that day. In 1717, the Earl of Mar at Innsbruck was corresponding with Lewis Pryse, Gogerddan, about a proposed landing at Milford Haven which did not materialise. The year 1722 was an election year and though Walpole made political capital of the Atterbury Plot it made little difference in Wales. The Cycle was active in North Wales elections as far as Anglesey where Lord Bulkeley was attempting to reassert his authority. The attempt by the Whig gentry of Denbighshire to organise a loyal address to the King following the disclosure of the Plot had to be dropped to avoid contention.

The ' Forty-five ' was likewise a non-event in Wales. Henry Lloyd (Cwm Bychan) came in advance to make a survey but it is not known whom he saw. One thing is certain, there was no attempt at planning or concerting action and the outbreak of rebellion in Scotland was unexpected in Wales where it was considered badly timed following so close on the death of the Duke of Beaufort and when Sir Watkin Williams Wynn was reputedly short of cash. Sir Watkin's promised support was conditional on the Pretender landing in this country at the head of a French army whereas Charles Edward landed in Scotland with only seven men. His journey south via Preston was purported to link up with North Wales Jacobites. The authorities were certainly alerted, Lord Herbert of Chirbury as Lord Lieutenant of Shropshire being warned to be ready to deal with a Jacobite incursion, and bridges over the River

Mersey were demolished in expectation of an attack on Chester. But no army advanced from Wales, only a few zealous individuals like the two Vaughan brothers of Courtfield in Welsh Bicknor and David Morgan of Pencraig-taf near Merthyr. The latter, a London barrister, became the Pretender's ' counsellor ' and urged him to fall back on Wales rather than on Scotland. Morgan was taken and executed but the Vaughans made good their escape, William entering the service of the King of Spain and becoming a general. Henry Lloyd was captured but was released for lack of evidence and he lived out his life in exile, becoming a general in the Russian army and a European authority on the art of war.

In view of this complete lack of planning it would have been more remarkable had a rebellion broken out in Wales than that it did not. Although Sir Watkin Williams Wynn is regarded as the key man the designated leader was Lord Barrymore, a Cheshire peer. Sir Watkin's conduct is often considered enigmatic but although it is tinged with some duplicity it is not without explanation. It has been suggested that he did not get the Pretender's summons ; alternatively, that he sent Lord Barrymore's son as an envoy but the Pretender had already retreated. The Welsh Jacobites waited on the turn of events and avoided incriminating themselves in any way and though John Murray of Broughton, the Pretender's secretary, turned King's evidence, no proceedings were preferred against any of them. Sir Watkin was at the height of his political power by this time and the Government could not afford a failure in prosecution. He continued to correspond with the Pretender after 1745 and was somewhat embarrassed to explain his non-co-operation which he said ' was owing more to the want in them of concert and unanimity than that of real zeal and dutiful attachment '. His counsel was invariably given against rash attempts at further landings in 1747 when one was again mooted.

The nature of the Movement ; why it failed

Jacobitism was an affair of the country gentry, a few leading families in several counties being affected ; the Pryses in Cardiganshire ; the Kemeys, Lewises and Raglan associates in Glamorgan ; the Wynnstay, Brogyntyn and Baron Hill families in North Wales; the Picton Castle and Slebech families in Pembrokeshire; the Beaufort family in Monmouthshire. The great families drew many lesser families into their orbit as well as some clergy despite the Roman Catholic associations of the Pretender. These families met in social circles in London where it is known that Sir Watkin Williams Wynn and his political cronies assembled at the Somerset coffee-house. Their need for conviviality was scarcely less in the country and led to the founding of clubs, the social aspect of the Jacobite clubs being more prominent than any. The Cycle members met at country houses, their meetings being as well-regulated as any social club; their main centre was Daniel Porter's hostelry, afterwards the Wynnstay Arms, at Wrexham. The members attracted a certain amount of notoriety from drinking treasonable toasts in specially engraved glassware and the number of Jacobite relics which have survived is astonishing. Complaints from political opponents suggest that they dominated local government in many localities, John Meller, a Denbighshire Whig thus describing the power of Wynnstay in his county : ' Neither is it a small influence which they have over the middling gentry who, observing that at the Quarter Sessions the Bench of Justices is generally swayed by the Tory party and generally side with Sir William Williams's interest, they think it advisable to be of the strongest side '. Similar complaints came out of Pembrokeshire and Anglesey too. Some would attribute to the Movement a nationalist character interpreting it as a protest against English oppression ; this ignores the fact that at this period the Welsh gentry were more concerned with assimilation into the English social and political scene than otherwise. At his trial, David Morgan of Pencraig-taf protested against the anglicisation of the Church and some would interpret Jacobitism in that light but it is an ironical explanation of a movement whose aim was to restore a Roman Catholic dynasty. Yet there were some distinct nationalist sentiments voiced now and again in these circles. Robert Price's protest against William III's land grants had emphasized the separate identity of Wales and Sir Watkin often alleged that corruption in electioneering was an English characteristic not a Welsh one.

The Jacobite movement suffered from over-optimism and the dalliance of the Welsh gentry with the cause was interpret ed too seriously at the distance of St. Germains. A spontaneous rising was expected when the Pretender landed in Scotland but the Welsh leaders were too judicious in calculating the chances to be implicated in something which was in the nature of a gamble. The survey which the Jacobite agents made in 1721 was totally unrealistic, claiming, for instance, that all the Welsh counties except Brecknock, Radnor and Carmarthen were under Jacobite control ; even more optimistic was the French envoy's opinion in 1743 that all Wales was Jacobite. This betrays poor intelligence of the actual situation and an unrealistic assessment of persons, Sir Charles Kemeys, a modest Glamorgan squire being accorded the status of one of the four most important Jacobites in Britain and the influence of families like the Bulkeleys being grossly inflated. 'Jacobite' was so often a term of abuse indiscriminately used by Whigs against any Tory that their numbers can be over-estimated. Whatever hold Jacobitism had on Wales was slackening by the 1740s as even the most committed Jacobites were becoming tired of political sterility and being debarred from local offices such as J.P.s as well as parliamentary power. Sir Watkin was already a parliamentary figure of some stature and had evidently mellowed by the time he entered into his estate and baronetcy in 1740. He was one of Walpole's most feared opponents, enjoying a reputation as the champion of independence and the sternest critic of political corruption. The electors of Westminster had elected him steward of their annual celebrations and a more independent body of electors could not be found. In his own country he was regarded as *yr hen Gymro cyfiawn* (the just old Welshman), as Jac Glan y Gors called him. He was one of the engineers of Walpole's fall and he and Sir John Philipps were two of the three Tories chosen to concert with the opposition Whigs how best to harass the Government after this event. The Pelhams, who succeeded to the mantle of Walpole, were more amenable and Sir Watkin even found it possible to support their limited war policy to the extent of voting for the payment of Hanoverian troops, generally an unpopular measure. Unlike Sir John Philipps, he refrained from joining the 'Broad-Bottom' Administration in 1744 and his conduct was generally less rash than Sir John's. Sir Watkin even contributed to a fund for opposing the Pretender and when the ' Forty-five ' was being inquired into he remained aloof except for protesting against the arrest of Jacobite agents on the ground that it had no parliamentary sanction.

The old Tory party disintegrated after its leader, Gower, and twelve Tories joined the Broad-Bottom Administration in 1744 and in the vacuum which followed, the young Duke of Beaufort seized the leadership. It was he who negotiated on behalf of the Tories the agreement with Pelham whereby ' in all commissions of the peace hereafter to be issued, all proper regard shall be had to gentlemen of figure and fortune, well-affected to His Majesty's government without distinction of parties '. This opened the door to the re-admission of Tories into local government offices and already by 1748 Tories were being appointed J.P.s in Cardiganshire. The younger Tories rejected Jacobitism, recognising it as a romantic sentiment rather than a political creed for which their families had paid the price of being deprived of political influence for half a century. It had achieved such prominence because of a lack of political issues at a period in parliamentary history which Sir Keith Feiling has described as ' a flat plain '. No one aspired to the Jacobite leadership left vacant by the death of Sir Watkin and Lord Barrymore in 1749. The accession of George III in 1760 enabled Tories once more to associate themselves with the throne and Jacobites like Sir John Philipps made their way to Court and established contacts with active politicians.

The Development of Political Activity

The Welsh members had no separate identity in Parliament nor were they a political force as the Scottish members who arrived later on the scene could be. They had been completely assimilated by the eighteenth century, more rather than less so than the Scots as has been suggested.[1] In their desire to be accepted as part of the English social scene to which they were becoming increasingly attached by marriage, Welsh M.P.s seldom mentioned their separate identity. Few of them were tried in office and their talents were more in evidence in opposition. Most of them were independent country gentry for whom politics was a leisurely interest rather than a career. They paraded party labels which signified little difference

[1] John Brooke, *The House of Commons*, 1754-90, I, 175

since Whigs and Tories came from the same social background and had the same interests. The attachment to them was nevertheless real in Wales and lip service at least was paid to party principles. In 1721, Edward Bayly refused his vote to Lord Bulkeley because of the difference in their political principles and in a town like Carmarthen where political feeling ran high party strife was endemic. Attachments were traditional family ones, Dr. J. B. Owen describing the Tories as ' those whose ancestors were Tories and who continued to behave as members of a Country party opposed in general to the measures of the Court '.

One significant development in this period is the organisation of political activity in the constituencies. Watkin Williams Wynn was busy soon after 1720 building up a political following in North Wales but this was entirely on a territorial basis and when he was invited to intervene in a Glamorgan election in 1745 to ensure fair play, he declined on the grounds that it was outside his province. Sir John Philipps attempted something similar in the south-west and in 1761 a Tory bloc emerged in Radnorshire led by the Marquis of Carnarvon. In the main the element of political conflict was supplied by the Whigs in their endeavour to dislodge the Tories from long-entrenched positions. The election of 1727 was the first to return more Whig than Tory members from Wales. In hearing the petitions which followed the Commons disfranchised the out-boroughs of Montgomery and the non-resident freemen of Brecon which served to reduce the constituencies to Whig pocket-boroughs. However, the House did not deviate from the line of duty in rejecting the Whig candidate's claim to the rights of the burgesses of Newborough to participate in elections nor did the Walpolian candidate succeed in persuading it to restrict the vote to the ' scot and lot ' voters of Flint boroughs. In the determination of these petitions five Welsh Whigs who normally supported the Government asserted their independence and voted against it to uphold the integrity of the House. The Excise Bill of 1733 excited political passions in Wales because of the traditional prejudice against excisemen and their insidious political influence at elections. The vote in the House of Commons was more or less on a party basis although some Welsh Whigs voted with the opposition. Walpole wreaked his vengeance on deserters, the Duke of Bolton being deprived of his Lieutenancy of Carmarthenshire. The election of 1734 followed before the dust had settled and the Duke of Newcastle sent his election agent, Jessop, to prepare the way in the Welsh border counties. Riots broke out at Flint and a person was killed ; at Knighton where Walpole's effigy was burnt it was deemed necessary to quarter a troop of soldiers on the town for a time.

In preparation for the 1741 election the Whigs followed the Tory example and laid plans to counteract Sir Watkin's influence in North Wales. Walpole was intent on getting rid of his arch-enemy and was party to the plans to overthrow him. There were six contests in Wales which was quite abnormal. In preparation for the Denbighshire election a Whig sheriff had been chosen for election year and although Sir Watkin polled most votes it was his rival John Myddelton who was returned by the sheriff. Sir Watkin countered by causing his brother Robert to stand down in Montgomeryshire where he stood as a candidate and was returned. Back in the House of Commons he petitioned against the Denbighshire return and this was the first division of several to be carried against the Government on election petitions, many of Walpole's regular followers absenting themselves which led directly to his fall. The sheriff's conduct of the Denbighshire election was investigated and he was heavily fined. Sir Watkin resumed his seat for Denbighshire and relinquished his Montgomeryshire seat where his brother Robert was returned, his other brother, Richard, being seated on petition in Flint boroughs. Sir Watkin's only disappointment was his failure to carry the election in Denbigh boroughs where a Whig candidate was elected, the House upholding the return when a petition was presented against it. Even this minor triumph was a matter of exultation for the Whigs, Horace Walpole remarking in a letter, ' I am this moment come from the House where we have carried a great Welsh election against Sir Watkin Williams by 26 '. No mention was made of all the discomfitures they had received. When the nine petitions which went up from Wales were before the House the counties of Anglesey, Denbigh, Flint and Montgomery and the boroughs of Flint, Carmarthen and Monmouth sent ' instructions ' to their Members demanding a strict inquiry into past measures and the punishment of guilty men. They were obviously Tory inspired but they are significant as early instances of the assertion of the principle of the accountability of members to their constituents.

A matter which touched the Welsh members closely was the demand for an inquiry into the conduct of Admiral Thomas Mathews at the Battle of Toulon in 1745 when he failed to deploy his numerical superiority to destroy an inferior Franco-Spanish fleet. Blame was put on Mathews or on his deputy Vice-Admiral Lestock according to one's political leanings and in the divisions in the House of Commons the Tories carried a hostile motion against Mathews. Much of the opposition to Mathews arose, as Horace Walpole divined, from his election for Glamorgan in 1745 through the services of a partial sheriff against Sir Charles Kemeys Tynte and the Tory phalanx. In anticipation of the 1747 election the Tories joined hands with Frederick, Prince of Wales and his following, the proposals being submitted to a committee of fourteen leading Tories including the Duke of Beaufort, Lord Windsor and Sir Watkin Williams Wynn. Although the election confirmed the Pelhams in office this move signifies the political reorientation of the Tories now that they were exploiting the reversionary interest to bring them to power. Some even dallied with Administration, changing places from the ' opponents ' column to the 'doubtful' one in Newcastle's interminable lists.

Newcastle's hand is evident in the Welsh elections of 1754 and 1761, the Earl of Powis acting as his election agent. The occasions were contentions between Whig families for seats in Caernarfonshire and Cardiganshire. Even more embarrassing was the demand of the Marquis of Carnarvon for the Radnorshire seat on account of the size of his estate and interest in that county. Carnarvon was no friend of Administration and Radnorshire had been under Whig control for forty years. Newcastle felt that his whim had to be gratified and Howell Gwynne, the sitting member, had to be found a Treasury borough ; the stewardship of Crown lands in the county also passed from the Whiggish Lewises of Harpton to Lord Harley. Crown lands were mixed up with politics in Cardiganshire, too, especially with the discovery of mineral wealth on them. Esgair-mwyn was a particularly rich mine and there were many competitors for its lease. Pelham wanted it for his son, but the Duke of Cumberland, the King's son, also coveted it and as Commander-in-Chief refused troops for its protection when requested. Lord Powis, already involved in mineral development, also desired to acquire the lease and through the good offices of the Duke of Newcastle eventually succeeded. It was essential, therefore, to appease the neighbouring gentry, Thomas Johnes and Wilmot Vaughan, who were both Whigs but opponents and involved in mineral working, being often at odds with the Crown deputy-steward, Lewis Morris.

The fall of the Duke of Newcastle in 1761 was like the eclipse of a fixed star in the political firmament of the Welsh Whigs but it soon became apparent from desertions that their attachment was to his office rather than to himself. Some became attached to Bute whose star was in the ascendant, others to Grenville and when Fox was steering the preliminaries of the Treaty of Paris (1763) through the House he had cause to be grateful for the support of most of the Welsh members since the War, whose conduct they had approved of under Pitt, had become a serious cause of hardship. Equally unpopular was the post-war taxation which was needed to pay for it. Protests and disturbances occurred in some of the border counties following the Cider Tax and the disaffection spread to south-east Wales. As Lord Egmont noted, ' the Welsh counties adjacent, Monmouth and Hereford (*sic*.), are made of stuff to kindle with a very little fire, and Somerset, Devon, and Cornwall are divided from Glamorgan by the Severn only '. It was in this atmosphere that a by-election was held in Glamorgan in April 1763, when Sir Edmund Thomas had to seek re-election on appointment to a minor place. He was very apprehensive of the result on account of ' the frenzy of the times' and Lord Talbot had to be sent by George III to arrange matters at the County Meeting. The agitation continued into May when Sir John Philipps, passing through Monmouth, was ' grossly affronted and insulted ' by a riotous mob for his support of the Cider Tax. Before the trouble had died down the Wilkes affair broke upon the country which kept the pot boiling for the next two decades. Wilkes had a number of Welsh friends and so it was no wonder that his fame spread through the Welsh hills as was claimed and this was reflected in the hostility to government in the 1768 elections in Wales when the rights of the electors of Middlesex was a live issue. When Wilkes was released from prison in 1770 balls were held at Denbigh and Ruthin in his honour and a coffee-house at Denbigh was named after him. There is no evidence that a petition was sent from Wales during the great petitioning campaign of 1769 although one was mooted in Pembrokeshire and Glamorgan. Three addresses were sent from Cardiganshire, Carmarthenshire and Pembrokeshire to Lord Mayor Crosby and Aldermen Wilkes and Oliver when they were committed to the Tower in 1771 and were commemorated in a contemporary print. These were probably instigated by Sir Watkin Lewes, a Cardiganshire man, who was active in the Wilkes controversy and became Lord Mayor and M.P. for the City of London through his involvement. Out of the Wilkes agitation the Society of the Bill of Rights came forth and its first secretary was Robert Morris whose family was connected with copper works at Morriston. Dr. Richard Price was a member and a link with the American protest movement against the Stamp Act. Robert Jones of Fonmon, a Glamorgan J.P. was an active member and organised a meeting at Westminster Hall for drawing up a petition concerning the Middlesex election.

The political situation had dramatically changed by the 1770s and although geographically distant from the centre of affairs Wales's political involvement was becoming deeper than ever it was in the Jacobite cause.

SUGGESTED READING

The titles at the end of Chapter 1 are relevant.

G. N. Evans, *Religion and politics in mid-eighteenth century Anglesey*, Cardiff, 1953.

Articles:

G. M. Griffiths, 'Chirk Castle Election activities, 1600–1750', *N.L.W.Jnl.*, XI, 1957–8.

W. T. Morgan, 'County elections in Monmouthshire, 1705–1847', *N.L.W.Jnl.*, X, 1957–8.

G. Roberts, 'The county representation of Anglesey in the eighteenth century', *Trans. Angl. Ant. Soc.*, 1930.

——, 'Political affairs (in Carmarthenshire) from 1536 to 1900', in J. E. Lloyd, *History of Carmarthenshire*, Vol. II, 1939.

——, 'The Glynnes and Wynns of Glynllifon', *Trans. Caerns. H.S.*, IX, 1948.

D. Ll. Thomas, 'Lewis Morris in Cardiganshire', *Y Cymmrodor*, XV, 1902.

P. D. G. Thomas, 'Jacobitism in Wales', *W.H.R.*, I, 3, 1962.

——, Articles on the political history of several counties in the following journals :

Trans. Angl. Ant. Soc., 1962; *Brycheiniog*, VI, 1960;

Trans. Caerns. H.S., XIX, 1958, XX, 1959;

Carms. Ant., IV, 1963; *Ceredigion*, VI, 1967;

Flints. H.S. Pub., XX, 1962; *J. Mer. H. and R. Soc.*, III, 2, 1958;

Mont. Coll., LIX, 1966; *Morgannwg*, VI, 1962.

——, 'Wynnstay versus Chirk,' *N.L.W. Jnl.*, XI, 1959.

——, 'The Montgomery Borough Constituency,' *B.B.C.S.*, XX, 1963.

D. Williams, 'Cardiganshire politics in the mid-eighteenth century,' *Ceredigion*, III, 1959.

6. The Methodist Revival

The Anglican Church on the eve of Revival

> 'Pan oedd Cymru gynt yn gorwedd mewn rhyw dywyll farwol
>   hun,
>   Heb na Phresbyter na 'ffeirad, nac un Esgob ar ddihun;
>   Yn y cyfnod tywyll pygddu . . . '[1]

Thus wrote William Williams, Pantycelyn, in his elegy to
Howell Harris looking back over a period of almost forty years.
In so doing, he established what was a Methodist view of the
religious history of the period which was long to hold sway.
Evidently Williams implied this spiritual somnolence to be a
criticism of the Church to which he belonged and which he had
served as ordained clergyman but which resisted all attempts
to reform it by people like himself. No doubt, the Methodists
were genuine enough in their sense of urgency about the state
of religion as references in Harris's diary to ' poor dark North
Wales ' and of failing to find ' any religion in Anglesey or
Flintshire but Papists' indicate. Methodism was a spontaneous
movement—the only genuinely native product since the
Pelagian heresy. So it is not strange to find impatience with the
established order which had become ossified into an over-
formalised religion. Both Harris's and Williams's views were,
however, blinkered and they failed to acknowledge any merit
except among persons of their own outlook. They failed to
recognize themselves even as the spiritual heirs of the Puritans
of the previous century and a Puritan element had been active
in the Church from the time of Vicar Prichard. Nevertheless, it
is to the discredit of the Anglican Church in Wales that it failed
to come to terms with this spontaneous movement which had
grown up within it and the growing anglicisation of the

[1] (When Wales lay formerly in a dark, fatal sleep, without a presbyter or
clergyman or one bishop astir ; in that dark, stygian period . . .)

Establishment rendered it even more unassimilable as time went on. Even in Williams's lifetime the claim that Wales owed its salvation to the Methodists did not go unchallenged and critics even accused them of arrogance. Edmund Jones of Pontypool, the doyen of South Wales Dissenters, describes Williams's claim in the elegy to Harris as ' a shameless untruth printed ', and goes on to name many godly men in different parts of Wales, churchmen like Griffith Jones among them, who had laboured for reform and accuses Williams of failing to acknowledge the debt of the Methodists to their predecessors. The censure was not undeserved.

The revival in Church life which was noted in the time of Queen Anne was shortlived and the Hanoverian succession brought a crop of fresh problems as well as exacerbating old ones. The High Church party, dominant under Queen Anne, was opposed to both comprehension and toleration. The Latitudinarians who were in the ascendant under the Hanoverians were pledged to the Revolution Settlement and to toleration. This was reflected in the nominations to episcopal and other high offices in the Church when persons of ' broad views ' were preferred ; the lesser clergy whom they ruled remained predominantly High Church as in Anne's day, thus producing a cleavage which was much more serious than that occasioned by the Non-jurors. In addition, the Hanoverian bishops were English since, when John Evans was translated from Bangor to Meath in Ireland in 1716, Wales was deprived of its last Welsh-speaking bishop till 1870. Translations were frequent. During the reigns of the first two Georges, of nine bishops appointed to Bangor, eight were translated ; in Llandaff four out of six ; in St. Asaph five out of six ; in St. David's five out of six. Bishop Hoadly, the sycophantic Whig prelate who never once visited Bangor during his incumbency, was more excusable than many inasmuch as he was a cripple. During his tenure he preached his famous sermon before George I which started the celebrated ' Bangorian Controversy ' which created such a rift amongst Anglicans, especially between the Upper and Lower Houses of Convocation that they were suspended indefinitely.

The abuse of absenteeism common in the Restoration Church now became much more accentuated. Even more reprehensible was the old-established practice of holding

F

livings ' in commendam ' by the higher clergy in order to augment their stipends whilst a lowly-paid curate was entrusted with the pastoral duties. Nepotism occurred too frequently to be merely accidental and episcopal families like the Otleys enriched themselves from Church offices. Their estrangement from their dioceses meant that bishops failed to establish their needs at first hand and often led to unwise appointments.

The fulminations of the Morris Brothers and their circle against *yr Esgyb Eingl* (the English bishops) had even more point when scholarly Welsh clerics could not find livings in Wales whilst monoglot Englishmen were appointed to Welsh-speaking parishes. Some bishops were more careful than others on this point. Bishop Willis, writing to Bishop Otley, complained that Hoadly had appointed an English Chancellor of Bangor and added that ' Englishmen when they creep in care for nothing but the pence '. Shute Barrington, who was bishop of Llandaff from 1770 to 1782, an uncommonly long period, was very careful about appointing Welsh clergy to Welsh-speaking parishes. This was in marked contrast to the views of an earlier Bishop of St. Asaph, Drummond, who thought it desirable to eradicate the Welsh language as quickly as possible. Matters came to a head in 1766 when an Englishman, Dr. Bowles, was instituted to the parishes of Trefdraeth and Llangwyfan in Anglesey where but 5 of his 500 parishioners understood any English. This became a test-case in which the recently formed Cymmrodorion Society took a leading part. Money was raised and support was forthcoming from leading Welsh landowners who had themselves long forsaken the language they now championed. The case proceeded to the Court of Arches which declared that ignorance of Welsh was sufficient to bar a person from appointment to a Welsh-speaking parish but at the same time ruled that since Dr. Bowles had been properly instituted he should be allowed to enjoy the living. The ruling in the Trefdraeth case did not prevent its recurrence many times over. Even liberal-minded bishops like Shipley of St. Asaph and Watson of Llandaff failed to show due appreciation of the language problem and, needless to say, the Hanoverian prelates contributed singularly little to the culture and literature of their adopted land.

Important as the role of the bishops was to the success of the

Church even more so was that of the parish clergy who were in close and immediate contact with the people. Many strictures have been laid upon them to the effect that they were wholly unworthy pastors of the flock. All too often the standards which those of the meaner sort set have been taken as a reflection of the whole profession. It is strange, however, that most of the clergy we know anything about seem to have been worthy men in some field or other. Their contribution to educational movements has been noted elsewhere,[1] and they were largely responsible for the great increase in Welsh book publication between. 1660 and 1730. Many of them were knowledgeable in the history and antiquities of their parishes and were consulted by scholars like Edward Lhuyd who addressed his questionnaires to them. Though they formed the most numerous professional class in Wales their status was much lower than that of the English clergy and the close affinity which existed between squire and parson in England was less in evidence in Wales, and there is little indication of social intercourse between them. The houses which most of the clergy occupied scarcely gave much room for entertainment. Shortage of suitable accommodation frequently forced incumbents to live outside the parishes if they sought a house becoming their dignity. In the deanery of Ultra-Aeron nine parishes were without vicarages. This made it more difficult for the clergyman to minister to the needs of his flock and involved him in a great deal of travelling. The plea made by Bishop Watson to give each incumbent a stipend of £100 and a house in order to abolish pluralities and enforce residence fell on deaf ears.

Comments about the irregularity of services and infrequent ministration of the sacraments are frequent but it must be remembered that the Sabbatarian principles of the nineteenth century do not apply to the eighteenth. One service on Sunday was the norm and three was uncommon. Nor was the preaching of a sermon at each service considered necessary. In Ultra-Aeron only eleven churches had a sermon every Sunday and ten had one on alternate Sundays. In three churches of the Deanery the Lord's Supper had not been celebrated in living memory and seldom was it ministered oftener than once a

[1] Chapter 4

month anywhere. The number of communicants in proportion to the population was small and despite the religious ferment of the period there does not appear to have been a significant increase in their numbers. This suggests that the Dissenting sects were more the beneficiaries of the Methodist Revival than the Anglican Church. The physical evidence was to be seen in dilapidated church buildings when even the Cathedral church of Llandaff became a ruin and was replaced by an Italianate temple. Heath Malkin's comment made in 1803 appears to have been apt when he stated that ' the natives of the Welsh mountains worship their Maker where an Englishman would not litter the most ignoble quadruped . . . .'

On the credit side, evidence exists that societies of clergy were wont to come together in different parts of the country for devotions and fellowship along the lines of the London religious societies about which Dr. Josiah Woodward had written. As early as 1712, Sir John Philipps discovered such a society of nine persons meeting in Pembrokeshire and the S.P.C.K. correspondence has many references to religious societies in the bishopric of Bangor in the time of Bishops Humphreys and John Evans. This movement undoubtedly drew much stimulus from the S.P.C.K. which disseminated information and gave practical support through its publications and funds. Some modification in church services was also made such as the introduction of hymn singing as well as psalmody although it seems to have been officially frowned upon. The popularity of carols and *halsingod* and their value for moral and spiritual instruction was not ignored by clergy in many parts of the country.

The general picture which emerges is one of a Church with inadequate resources both human and material grappling with an unequal task. There were many abuses and shortcomings which cannot be glossed over but it was not as indifferent as the traditional view of the period would have us believe. The main criticism that can be levelled against it is that it was hide-bound by its institutionalism and the victory went to those enterprising spirits—most of them young Anglican clergymen—who formed the Methodist movement and had vision and boldness enough to innovate. Without the pioneering work done by Anglicans and Dissenters alike in which both cleric and lay played a part the success of the Methodist Revival would not have been assured. They prepared the ground from which the Methodists garnered an abundant harvest.

The early history of the Methodist Movement

The Methodist Revival came as a reaction to the climate of thought and feeling of the first half of the eighteenth century. It was a period which has been labelled the ' Age of Reason ' because of the hold which rationalism had established over the whole of the intellectual field. An age which had produced Newton in science and which had accepted the validity of scientific enquiry found it amenable to apply these methods to all fields of knowledge. The spirit of scepticism which pervaded the intellectual field could not be shut out from the field of religion. Some thinkers found religion a fair game for their criticism since it was fundamentally based on the premise of revealed truth and in the course of centuries had acquired a great accretion of practices and beliefs many of which savoured of superstition. Even those who defended the claims of religion found it necessary to make concessions to the rationalistic cult of the age and endeavoured to show that Christianity was credible on the score that it was reasonable. Many of the younger generation of clerics who came to be known as 'Methodists' in both England and Wales protested by word and implication against a scheme of things which tended to elevate Man and place him on a pedestal whilst at the same time relegating God to a passive role in the universe.

Methodism was part of a much wider movement of ' enthusiasm ' which was then afoot. The phenomenon was already apparent as early as 1678 in London when a number of pious men came together to found a religious society. This was the progenitor of others, and in 1697 Dr. Josiah Woodward published *An Account of the Rise and Progress of the Religious Societies of the City of London*. It is more than a possibility that Howell Harris might have known of this work through his contacts with Griffith Jones whose patron, Sir John Philipps, was in touch not only with the London societies but also with the Pietist Movement centred on Halle in Saxony. The Pietists were actively involved in the Danish Mission working in Coromandel (India) in which several Welshmen, including Bishop John

Evans, were interested. Another continental movement which was known in Wales and which later established a tenuous hold here was that of the Moravian Brethren in which Howell Harris was very interested and for the sake of which he almost abandoned Methodism. Harris's interests extended beyond Wales and he was the only Welsh Methodist leader who was actively concerned in the English Movement. His diary also reveals an interest in religious developments in Scotland and America and he actively supported George Whitefield's mission to Georgia and deputised for him at the London Tabernacle in his absence. Pietism widely penetrated evangelical circles in many countries and represented a missionary approach to religion.

The term ' Methodist Revival' is really a misnomer and apt to mislead. Although the year 1735 is an important milestone inasmuch as Howell Harris and Daniel Rowland experienced their conversion in that year it should not be thought that the Revival was a single occurrence or even a sustained one. Nor did it occur on any ' national' scale for revivals were generally local in character and usually occurred after the visit of some gifted evangelical preacher. Very often the fire was soon damped down only to be rekindled by another visiting preacher at some later time. There were many precedents, such as the revival in which Griffith Jones was involved in Carmarthenshire. The Old Dissenting sects after 1690 showed greater missionary zeal in which Presbyterians and even Quakers had some part. This activity was already afoot when the Methodist Revival broke out. It does appear, therefore, that set in this context it was nothing like ' a bolt from the blue '. It was more intense and longer lasting and wider in its ramifications than earlier occurrences but it was not fundamentally different. The Methodists brought to the situation a talent for organisation which ensured the permanent success of their efforts whilst those we have noted earlier tended to be evanescent.

The characteristic of Methodism which struck contemporaries most was their ' enthusiasm' and Methodists were frequently referred to as ' enthusiasts' which in an age of moderation and good taste savoured of disparagement. So it appeared to the Rev. Theophilus Evans whose book *A History of Modern Enthusiasm from the Reformation to the Present Times* (1752) has been described as the eighteenth century text-book on the subject. It asserted the traditional view that ' enthusiasts ' were rebels in Church and State and this was a reputation which had not been laid in Wales even at the time of the French Revolutionary Wars. The Methodists found the demonstrativeness of their followers an embarrassment because memories of religious excesses die hard and those of the seventeenth century had not been obliterated from people's memories. The leaders of the societies were also constantly on their guard to detect any dissimulation or self-deception and needed assurance of conviction when examining any candidate for admission. Every effort was made to prevent those who had been converted on an emotional wave from becoming back-sliders and this was always regarded as a danger.

The relationship between Griffith Jones and early Methodism is an ambiguous one. His life's work and especially his early interest in preaching marks him as being in the evangelical tradition of the Church. He could also claim to have had a spiritual conversion in his youth and this is the hall-mark of evangelical religion. His enemies often accused him of being ' the father of Methodism ' and at least three of the Methodist leaders acknowledged him as their spiritual father, Howell Harris being a frequent visitor to Llanddowror for spiritual counsel. Although Griffith Jones strongly disowned the Methodists he never denounced them, rather did he criticise them for their excesses and urged moderation upon them. His censure fell upon the practice of exhorting particularly, and exhorters in Carmarthenshire perforce had to walk more warily than elsewhere. His own emphasis had decidedly moved away from the emotional appeal to emphasis upon knowledge of the Word gained through catechising. He also forbade his Methodist curate, Howell Davies, from itinerant preaching and Howell Harris was much grieved that ' the old saint ' had so turned against them. No doubt, Griffith Jones was motivated by concern for his schools and the fact that many of his teachers were accused of exhorting. It has been shown, for instance, that about one-third of the farm-houses in Carmarthenshire where his schools were held between 1738 and 1777 also became meeting-places for societies. The success of Methodism owed much to Griffith Jones and to his schools and the Methodists acknowledged it and held him in the highest esteem.

Methodism not only benefited from the spade-work done by Anglicans but also from the work of the Old Dissenting sects, especially the Independents. Dissenting historians have rightly pointed out that it was in areas where Dissenting ministers had long been working that Methodism reaped its greatest success. Relations between the Methodists and Dissenting preachers were at first cordial and it was by invitation of and with the support of sympathetic Dissenting ministers such as Edmund Jones, Pontypool, that Methodist preachers first made their appearance in several areas. Moreover, the religious situation at the mid-century was a very fluid one when it was difficult to assign people to any definite religious sects. Methodists and Independents co-existed in many societies which created a situation reminiscent of the old ' gathered ' churches. Edmund Jones defines the situation very nearly when he describes certain people as being of ' the Methodist way ', whether they be Anglican, Baptist or Independent, which suggests an inclination more than a definite commitment. Gradually, many of the Independents either broke away from the societies and established their own or cast out the Methodists with whom they did not want to be associated because of their excesses, and thus the societies became more homogeneous towards the end of the century. The Methodists lost much ground in this way first to the Independents and then to the Baptists, a situation which was never retrieved in South Wales. Tension over the ministration of the sacraments early appeared since some Methodists of more Anglican inclinations like Howell Harris were reluctant to accept communion from the hands of Dissenting ministers whilst Dissenters often expressed a strong aversion to accepting it from unworthy clergymen. Doctrinal differences which did not bother Harris in the early stages became more accentuated and from about 1740 there was constant winnowing of the societies.

The cordial relations which had once existed between Methodists and Dissenters became strained to the point of recriminations. Harris was prone to accuse the Dissenters of aridness, lukewarmness and even sins of the flesh which he fancied he saw in the Watford congregation among others. He also accused their minister, David Williams of ' more oratory than demonstration of spirit and experience and heartsearching doctrine'. The victims retaliated in kind and Williams exposed Harris as an example of the bigotry which he had once so vigorously condemned. Co-operation became increasingly difficult after 1740 when attempts to form a joint Association between Methodists and Independents failed. By that time Methodism was firmly established, thanks being due in no small measure to the early encouragement it had received from sympathetic Dissenting ministers. It was only just that the Dissenters should in their turn share in the harvest which the Methodists were garnering by their efforts.

The Leaders

The Methodist leaders did not doubt that they were called to their work by divine election. Quite independently, Daniel Rowland and Howell Harris had experienced a religious conversion in 1735, the first at Llanddewibrefi through the ministry of Griffith Jones, Llanddowror, the latter through the ministry of his own vicar, the Rev. Price Davies, at Talgarth. It was not until 1737 that Rowland and Harris met and decided to combine their efforts but since 1735 each had been working in his own sphere. Until the time they separated in 1750, the movement was dominated by these two men. Usually coupled with their names and generally better known is William Williams, Pantycelyn, who was somewhat younger and started his career in the role of Daniel Rowland's assistant although after Harris's departure Williams became a leading figure. In a somewhat lesser role we find Howell Davies, known as ' the apostle of Pembrokeshire ' because his activities were mainly confined to that county. Peter Williams might also have come to the forefront had he not been cast out for heresy. These men constituted the first generation of Methodist leaders and with the exception of Harris they were all ordained clergy of the Church of England. This is a significant fact which accounts for the continuance of Methodism within the Established Church while they were alive. It also ensured the initial success of Methodism since it in no way constrained people to abandon old loyalties for new but merely breathed new life into existing institutions, or so the leaders hoped. The single

exception who was not in Holy Orders, Howell Harris, was in
many respects the central figure of the movement and the
greatest enigma.

Howell Harris (1714-73)

Despite the volume of correspondence which has survived
as well as his diary we know little about Harris the man apart
from his spiritual state ; likewise, about the places he visited
and the people he met he is uninformative apart from their
religious associations. Nevertheless, his journals are amongst
the most important sources for the history of Methodism as he
intended them to be since they were written with an eye on
history. An inveterate traveller, he carried out his journeys
for the purpose of field-preaching, an activity which had
started in Wales at least three years before the Methodists
embarked upon it in England and which had been initiated
by Howell Harris. His conversion in 1735 was central to his
whole career and he interpreted it as a divine summons to
carry out the work of God. It also placed him in a dilemma
because he was not prepared in any formal sense for the call.

Educated at Llwyn-llwyd Academy, a Dissenting institution,
Harris did not proceed to university though he went to
Oxford to matriculate. He once expressed an intention of
becoming a missionary but why he did not seek ordination
initially is not clear. Later he made at least four applications
for ordination but this was after he had started going round
preaching which proved an insurmountable obstacle to his
admission into Orders especially since Harris laid down his
own conditions which were unacceptable to any bishop.
Undoubtedly, Harris saw the advantages of ordination but
exulted in the fact that he was a man with God's mark upon
him and that the divine call was superior to any episcopal
laying on of hands. At the same time Harris had a profound
respect for the Church, its institutions and the status of the
clergy, and though he prided himself on the uniqueness of his
own situation he was also very sensitive about it. He fancied
that his lack of clerical status prejudiced people against him, as
it undoubtedly did, and prevented his acceptance as unquestioned head of the movement. The alternative to Church
ordination was to become a Dissenting minister which was

abhorrent to Harris with his strong ties of loyalty to the Church. He failed to appreciate that the objections raised were not directed against him personally as against the precedent it would create.

Although he did not admit to preaching, only 'exhorting', he drew large congregations and John Wesley testified that he was a great and moving orator ' both by nature and by Grace '. In a period which believed that art and education heightened natural parts he owed little to either. Harris was possessed of ' that impulse to win souls for Christ which asks few questions about Church and order and discipline ', about which Archbishop Ramsey speaks. ' Such love, such power, such simplicity was irresistible ', according to Wesley. His great natural gifts were heightened by inspiration but his lack of preparation of a more conventional kind was a handicap and raised many obstacles. Though an avid reader he had no theological training and his essays into this field, which were unavoidable for a preacher, were often uncertain and unsound. Daniel Rowland, commonly regarded as the greater theologian, found it necessary to warn him more than once to look to his doctrine which sometimes veered towards Antinomianism and Patripassianism which were considered heretical and which betray the influence of Moravianism upon him. Matters were moving to a critical stage in 1749 when Rowland published a pamphlet entitled *Ymddiddan rhwng Uniongred a Chamsyniol* ('Conversation between Orthodox and Mistaken') which has been described as ' the pamphlet of the disruption '. The unorthodoxy of his doctrine contributed to Harris's rejection by the clerical members as leader of the movement.

Harris's quarrel with the Church was not on account of its doctrine but because of the laziness and pride of the bishops whose shortcomings he, like others, hoped would be put to rights with the accession of Frederick, Prince of Wales. Though he did not give primacy to doctrine he recognised the need to initiate converts into it and produced a pamphlet *Sail, Dibenion a Rheolau'r Societies* ('The Foundation, Purposes and Rules of the Societies'). He even contemplated a form of Confession of Faith or handbook of instruction on doctrine but if such had been agreeable to his fellow-Methodists Harris would have been the last to whom they would have entrusted it. His emphasis was, however, squarely laid on ' evidence of the Spirit ' as the condition for entry into the private society which was the most select gathering of converts. Harris even demanded assurance of salvation as a condition of entry which his colleagues felt was setting too high a standard. In the dilemma which faced many society members about receiving communion from unworthy clergymen Harris preferred this to the alternative of receiving it from a Dissenting minister which appears illogical in a person who was so critical of the clergy's shortcomings. Harris dreaded the possible separation of the Methodists from the Church but this did not frighten him from contemplating the shape of things that might follow such an event.

Basically, Harris was conservative in his outlook towards the existing order. His action in joining the Brecknockshire Militia as an officer in 1759 has been interpreted as a gesture to demonstrate the loyalty of the Methodists to the Crown which it might have been in part, but one also suspects an inclination towards social climbing. The Brecknockshire Agricultural Society, the premier society of its kind in Wales of which Harris was a founder member, was another avenue to the society of the gentry. No doubt, his Anglican loyalties and consciousness of social status influenced him against separation, as the result of which Methodism came in for more persecution than it need have had it registered its meeting-houses and licensed its preachers under the terms of the Toleration Act of 1689, but that would have branded them as Dissenters. This course was opposed by Harris who practised religious rites characteristic of a latter-day High Churchman. He even feared that he was doing wrong in establishing societies but fortunately for Methodism he overcame his initial hesitation. Harris never grasped the biblical truth concerning new wine in old bottles.

Harris was a very complex character. A Moravian acquaintance speaks of his ' open, choleric disposition ' and La Trobe noticed his natural impetuosity. Edmund Jones chided him for his passion and intemperance of spirit and Harris's diary frequently contains the phrase ' I was quick to open my whole mind ', usually about someone else's failings. Nyberg's *Journal* which refers to Harris's frequent visits to Bristol comments on his emotionalism and, where he describes Harris's visit to the society to preach in full regimental dress, there is more than a hint of vanity. His sensitiveness about his position as a layman within the movement betrays an inferiority complex. Yet he carried his bid for domination to the point of splitting the Association and even of forming a rival one. Though not solely responsible, Harris contributed more than his share to the friction which arose from a clash of personalities because he tried the patience of his colleagues to the point of gullibility. Women had an attraction for him and for a time he was in the habit of taking his wife around with him until forbidden to do so by the Association, but when he developed an infatuation for Madam Sidney Griffith, the wife of the squire of Cefnamwlch in Llŷn, he ignored the objections of the Association. No one accused him of immorality but when he tried to pass Madam Griffith off as an oracle with prophetic gifts, credibility was strained too far. After 1747 he was certainly subject to ecstasies and dreams which he took for divine revelations. He was tolerated by his colleagues and followers despite his failings because his stature was unquestioned.

He was the greatest dynamic force on the religious scene in Wales and his unremitting zeal and labour were largely responsible for launching and directing the movement. His attention to and skill at organisation secured its permanence and though his loss was keenly felt after the disruption of 1750, the greatest tribute to Harris's work is that the Movement survived this crisis and the organisation showed an amazing resilience and recuperative powers. He forged more contacts with persons and sects of different views than any of his colleagues and exhibited a breadth of view and sympathy which particularly commended him to John Wesley. He was the only Welshman regularly invited to the English Methodist Association which was a select group chosen by John Wesley despite the fact that Harris had rejected Wesley's Arminian teaching and had fallen in line with George Whitefield. He had aspired to forge closer links between the English and the Welsh movements and had acted as a deputy for Whitefield not only in Wales but also in England and in his absence was effectively the leader of the English Calvinistic Methodists. Harris's stature must, therefore, be measured not merely against the background of the Methodist movement in Wales but of the Methodist Movement as a whole.

Daniel Rowland (1713-90)

Next to the year 1735 in importance in the history of Method-ism comes 1737, the year when Howell Harris met Daniel Rowland, Llangeitho, and they decided to combine their efforts. He is reputed to have received his education at Hereford Grammar School which enabled him to enter Holy Orders in 1734 as a deacon and become a priest in 1735. He was appoint-ed curate to his brother who ministered to four churches in and around Llangeitho. He remained in this office until he was cast out of the Church after first serving his brother and then his son. His conversion which took place after he had entered Orders changed the course of his life and henceforth he devoted himself to evangelical preaching. He established such a name as a preacher that Llangeitho became a Mecca for pilgrims from all parts of Wales. Communion Sunday at Llangeitho was a memorable occasion. Whether it was because he was busily occupied at home or from disinclination Rowland did not often travel very far afield as Harris did. In his elegy, William Williams describes the effect which Rowland had upon his hearers. First be featured the tempestuous Law (*Y Ddeddf Dymhestlog*) which caused people to quake with awe and terror. Then he offered a complete and perfect salvation on the basis of Christ's atonement. Rowland's method seems to have changed in the course of time with somewhat less emphasis being laid on the wrath of God and more on His mercy. It is said that the mellowing influence upon him was the Rev. Philip Pugh, Llwynpiod, who ministered to the ' gathered ' church of Cilgwyn. Ironically enough, despite Rowland's great attraction and influence as a preacher, he had but little effect upon Pugh's congregation which steadily moved nearer to Arianism.

In the organisation of the Methodist Movement Rowland's sphere of activity was West Wales where he had particular care of the societies of Cardiganshire and Pembrokeshire. In the latter he had the assistance of Howell Davies whose activi-ties were, however, curtailed because of the opposition of his rector, Griffith Jones, Llanddowror, to his going around preaching. Rowland does not appear to have spent as much time in the organisation and supervision of societies as in preaching, hence the need to depute William Williams to assist him. Although it is claimed that Rowland founded societies as early as Harris, little is known about their location apart from Llangeitho itself. That Rowland's societies were separate and independent from those of Harris leaves no room for doubt since he published his own *Rules for Societies* in 1742 which were in use among them. But even in 1750 Cardiganshire ranked only fifth in the table of societies founded in the South Wales counties and compares unfavourably with areas where Harris was active. Rowland also acquired a reputation as theologian within the movement and it was his pamphlet *Conversation between Orthodox and Mistaken* that precipitated the disruption, an event which has been interpreted as ' a crisis of doctrine '. That he should have been watchful over doctrine is not strange when one bears in mind that nearby was the ' heretical ' church of Cilgwyn. On the question of the need for assurance of salvation Rowland took a more liberal view than Harris and when Peter Williams was being hounded for heresy Rowland took a more tolerant view remembering how bigotry had led to the earlier schism. Rowland had the support of the clerics within the Movement who would have made him General Superintendent of the societies instead of Harris whose support rested among the lay exhorters.

Rowland's personality made a clash with Harris almost inevitable. He was hot-tempered and as the meetings of the Association became more frequent so did the rows between him and Harris. Rowland was as inclined as Harris to authoritarianism and neither was of the yielding sort. Whilst Rowland accused Harris of being ' puffed up ' in pride, Harris retaliated by accusing Rowland of levity and laxity in behaviour, the latter being a matter into which Bishop Claggett inquired without result. That Rowland was an inferior organiser to Harris is also true although it was Rowland who acted as Whitefield's deputy as Moderator of Welsh Methodism. Rowland's *forte* was the spoken word but he also left at least eight prose works and some hymns of little merit. He was the first to part company with the Church and showed less apprehension than Harris about separation. Rowland had less respect for Church conventions, went outside his parish to preach and built a meeting-house for the society at Llangeitho in 1760, three years before he was deprived of his curacies by

Bishop Squires. Thereafter, until his death in 1790, Rowland seems to have confined his activities to ministering to his congregation at Gwynfil Chapel.

William Williams (1717-91)

The third, the youngest and probably best-known of the trio of leaders was William Williams, Pantycelyn, who joined the other two in 1738. Unlike them he came from Dissenting stock since his parents were Independents and he was brought up in that faith. Throughout his life he lived in fairly comfortable circumstances. His education at Llwyn-llwyd Academy must have fortified his Dissenting faith yet it was Anglican orders he entered, an inexplicable event on which he has thrown no light. The turning-point in his career was reached when on his return from school he heard Howell Harris preach in Talgarth churchyard. He abandoned his original intention of becoming a doctor in order to enter the Church and in 1740 was ordained and became curate to Theophilus Evans who was vicar of Llanwrtyd and Abergwesyn. His connection with Methodism was already formed and as early as 1741 a society was meeting at his parents' home and there is every indication that Williams was becoming more and more involved in these activities. This also explains his greater inclination to the Dissenters than either Harris or Rowland.

Williams readily took to itinerant preaching and as early as 1740 Harris saw in him great promise as an evangelical preacher. These peripheral activities displeased Theophilus Evans whose abhorrence of ' enthusiasm ' is well-known and he effectively blocked Williams's path to preferment so that he never advanced beyond the rank of deacon. In 1743 he was made a Moderator (*Cymedrolwr*) at the monthly meeting held at Dugoedydd and in the following year decided to give his whole time to the Movement inasmuch as he was assisting Rowland in supervising the societies of west Wales as well. ' The spirit of Brother Rowland is fallen on Brother Williams ' wrote Harris and evidently the younger was influenced by the older man so that it is not strange that in the dispute between Harris and Rowland that Williams should have favoured the latter. But Williams disliked theological controversy especially in later life when he reflected upon its effect upon the Movement. This forms the

background to his long poem *Theomemphus* where he derides
hair-splitting theology and offers the ' full salvation ' contained
in the Gospel. It manifests Williams's moderate Calvinism
since he eschews the notion that God had willed anyone's
damnation. The Deism and rationalism of the age are likewise
condemned in *Golwg ar Deyrnas Crist* ('View of Christ's Kingdom'), his other long poem in which he defends orthodox
Trinitarianism. But Williams's most practical contribition lay
in the founding and supervising of societies for which he had a
particular genius. He conceived of the society as not only seeing
to the physical needs of its members but also as an instrument
to search out the hidden places of sin and spiritual indifference
and to rekindle zeal.

Williams's name will live as long as the Welsh language
endures if only for the vast number of hymns he wrote. Some
of his English hymns are also well-known. They were written
for use by the societies among whom hymn-singing was as
popular as with the Moravians. His first collection, dated 1744,
was appropriately called *Aleluja* and contained hymns by other
writers as well as himself. The lyrical touches which are so
evident mark out Williams as the herald of the romantic
movement in Welsh literature. His poetic ambition was inclined to the production of the two Christian epics named
above, a novel departure in Welsh literature. *Theomemphus*
was largely autobiographical and throws much light on the
rise and progress of the Methodist Movement. *Golwg ar
Deyrnas Crist* exhibits some acquaintance with scientific and
philosophical as well as theological ideas then current. His
prose work which was the product of later life was the result of
a lifetime's experience and study. His *Drws y Society Profiad*
('Door of the Society of Experience') was a practical approach
to the conduct of societies. In *Ductor Nuptiarum* he ventures into
a discussion of matrimony where he shows sound common
sense, psychological understanding and practical advice. Nor
does modesty prevent him from discussing romantic love in a
way uncharacteristic of his age. Some of his prose works are
polemical in character and written in defence of orthodox
faith against the contemporary heresies which assailed it. His
most ambitious prose work *Pantheologia* was an encyclopaedia
of religions which ventured into the field of comparative

G

religion before it had become the subject of serious academic study. It was written over a period of eighteen years and necessitated a wide scheme of study of the authorities on the subject.

These manifold activities mark Williams out as the most versatile of the Methodist leaders as well as the most erudite. When Harris defected and Rowland confined himself increasingly to his own sphere much of the burden of leadership fell upon his shoulders. He appears to have been a man who was easier to get on with, being free of the tensions which racked Harris and the irascibility which characterised Rowland and it is to him that we owe the fact that Methodism was handed down to a second generation of leaders as a sturdy child.

The Nature of the Movement

Methodism was a movement within the Church and not an attempt to found a new sect. That position was only arrived at when the Church refused to come to terms with it and for the sake of survival the Methodists were obliged to leave it. Welsh Methodism retained the Calvinist doctrine of the Thirty Nine Articles and John Wesley found very few to follow the Arminian path here. Its social outlook was also very similar to that of the Church although it laid less emphasis on social than on moral obligations. It was essentially a ' new spirit ' whose aim was to recapture the pristine purity of the Early Church and to breathe new life into the dry bones of the Anglican religion. The Methodists interpreted literally the command to go out into the highways and the fields to offer salvation. Itinerant preaching was known in Wales from Puritan days and was resorted to here three years before it started in England. The nature of the appeal was emotional and simple ; it was personal and aimed at effecting a change of heart in the sinner. Much was made of the wrath of God and the deliverance that was offered by Christ's redemption. The emphasis on human depravity was in direct contrast to the belief of the rationalists in the perfectibility of Man, the Methodists asserting that man had no powers of regeneration within himself, and that the Grace of God alone could free him from the hold of sin. The change of heart and the acceptance of salvation was the personal experience the Methodists looked for in admitting persons into their societies. Religious observances like church attendance and the partaking of the sacraments were enjoined but the emphasis was laid on personal experience not on outward conformity. It was ' the saving knowledge of the Lord Jesus ' that was the hall-mark of the convert not knowledge of the Bible in an objective way. The effect was visible in personal conduct and in social morality since religion was carried outside the church doors into homes and society.

The stress on personal conduct led to censure of levity of any kind and innocent pleasures like the *'noson lawen'* consequently declined. The stress on rectitude always implicit in Calvinism, was also a reflex action to charges of immorality that were frequently made against the Methodists because of their emotionalism—a charge that was reiterated in the Blue Books of 1847. They have been criticised as other-worldly, alleging that they were more concerned with preparing people for the next world than with people's plight in this. No doubt, they were conservative in outlook and preached forbearance but Methodism was anything but negative. It provided more activity for the individual than anything previously known and gave more opportunity for personal involvement. It also catered for people's gregarious instinct in an age which threw up societies of all kinds. The Methodists realised the layman's need for some outlet in a way which the Church had never done and the societies provided him with a field of activity within a fellowship where lack of education was no handicap. The societies raised their own leaders called ' exhorters ' (*cynghorwyr*) and here again brought out talents that would otherwise lie dormant. Opportunities for leadership were offered at local level in the societies or at higher level in the monthly and quarterly meetings. The advent of the Sunday schools after 1785, to which the Methodists took more readily than anyone, was another field of opportunity that was well exploited. Life with the Methodists was hardly dull and the visit of celebrated preachers who were masters of oratory and drama sometimes brought a touch of theatre into their lives.

The nucleus of Methodist organisation was the society, the first known one being founded in 1737 by Howell Harris at Y Wernos in the parish of Llandyfalle (Brecs.). It is probable that Daniel Rowland was engaged in the same work around Llangeitho from about the same time. After a rather hesitant start, Harris went ahead to organise many societies around Talgarth, several of them meeting in the houses of people of quality. From Brecknockshire Harris extended his activities into Radnorshire and then to Montgomeryshire. For their regulation and in order to achieve uniformity Harris drew up a set of rules by which the societies were divided into bands according to sex if the society was large enough, but it does not appear that the same degree of sophistication in organisation was achieved as John Wesley aimed at. One important division was the gathering of converts into a private society whilst applicants for membership remained on trial for a period in the public society. Entry was not as restricted as with the Dissenters and for this reason expulsion was more frequent since every member's conduct was under constant scrutiny.

The average size of societies was from 10 to 30, females being in the majority and youth much in evidence. Meetings were held at least once a week in private houses and scattered farms until meeting-houses were built. Contributions were levied of 1*d* to 2*d* a week, or more according to means, but the poor were excused. The money went to relieve distress but the number of dependants appears to have been few. Much of the money went to build meeting-houses for the greater convenience of the society and a great deal of voluntary labour as well went into their building. The usual activities of the society were catechising and exhorting but the most important work was receiving testimony. The Welsh language was in common use and this did a great deal to fortify it and to standardise it on the pattern of William Morgan's Bible. In areas which were becoming anglicised like Radnorshire or were already so like south Pembrokeshire, English was the medium. A set of rules was drawn out for the societies at the Llwynberllan Association called *Sail, Dibenion a Rheolau'r Societies* ('Basis, Purposes and Rules of the Societies'), which remained in force till they were superseded in 1801.

The private exhorter (*cynghorwr*) was the person responsible for the conduct of the society and he was assisted by stewards and catechisers; even private disputes were settled within the society. The exhorters were drawn from a wide social class extending from minor gentry to labourers but artisans were most prominent and most had a rural background. Much criticism was directed against their ignorance but, judging by their correspondence, many reached a fair level of intellectual attainment ; there is also evidence of education since many were more proficient in English than in Welsh. This reflects the social character of Methodism, which included many small gentry and prosperous farmers who were often called to act as trustees of the new chapels being built and although Methodism attracted many poor.people they were not much in evidence in the organisation. Superintendents were set over the exhorters but they covered areas as large as counties, Richard Tibbot, who worked in Montgomeryshire, being a typical example. By 1740 there were over forty superintendents almost entirely in South Wales since Methodism had barely penetrated into North Wales as yet. As far as can be ascertained the number of societies founded by 1750 were thus :

Brecknockshire	... 74	Cardiganshire	... 36+
Glamorganshire	... 72	Monmouthshire	... 34
Carmarthenshire	... 71	Radnorshire	... 28
Pembrokeshire	... 59	Montgomeryshire	... 23

Although the societies were local and scattered they belonged to an integrated organisation. They sent representatives to a monthly meeting (*cwrdd misol*) and over that was set a quarterly meeting (*cwrdd cwarter*). Over all these was the Association which became the policy-making body and which took all important decisions after 1740 and approved the exhorters. Thus an integrated presbyterian system was evolved which enabled the Movement to survive the upheaval of 1750. The first Association met at Dugoedydd, near Llandovery, in 1742 and although it contained lay as well as clerical members it was dominated by the triumvirate of leaders to the point of dependence. This eventually posed a problem when the leaders became aged since there were fewer clergy of ' the Methodist way ' in the next generation who could take over from them and this posed a crisis of leadership which was not resolved until Thomas Charles emerged as clear leader.

The Association appointed Howell Harris as General Superintendent of the Societies but the clerical members would have preferred Daniel Rowland. To overcome this situation, each was assigned his own sphere, Daniel Rowland in south-west Wales and Howell Harris in south-east Wales but Harris was reluctant to be confined to any specific area. At the Watford Association, George Whitefield was appointed Moderator which signifies a desire to link the movement in Wales with that in England. The Welsh movement also chose to follow Whitefield's Calvinist theology rather than Wesley's Arminianism and so came to be known as Calvinistic Methodists. Welsh Methodism remained separate from the English movement and the only real link between them was Howell Harris who deputised for Whitefield as Moderator and when Whitefield was on a mission to Georgia, Harris was the effective leader of English Methodism for a time as well. He spent a considerable part of each year in England and complaints were made of his neglecting Wales.

It was on a visit to Bristol in 1739 where there was a Welsh society meeting that Harris met John Wesley and it was he who probably first invited Wesley to Wales. The latter made forty six visits in all but found the language a barrier in most parts which scarcely justified his conclusion that the Welsh were as ignorant as the Cherokee Indians. Wesley showed more judgment and sense in another respect in allowing the Welsh leaders to get on with their work without outside interference and an agreement was made between him and Harris in 1746, probably at Neath, to this effect. The Wesleyan faith thus found very few followers in Wales. A Wesleyan cause was established at Brecon, a town which both John and Charles Wesley often visited, and it was from there that a Welsh mission, surprisingly, under John Hughes went to North Wales and established their first church in the North at Denbigh in 1802. Even less was the influence of Lady Huntingdon's Connexion although it also had chapels at Brecon and Swansea and for a time she maintained a ministerial college at Trefeca. A peripheral contact was made through Harris with the Moravians who established a toe-hold in Pembrokeshire but despite Harris's desire to draw closer to them they were kept at arm's length.

In 1750 the discord which had been growing between Harris and his colleagues led to the parting of ways. Disagreements had arisen at Association meetings at New Inn and Llanidloes and at the Llantrisant Association Harris was expelled. He still had the support of many of the lay exhorters and his influence remained paramount in the counties of Brecknock, Radnor and Montgomery but his attempt to form a rival Association was abortive. Harris's departure gave Methodism a westward orientation since west Wales now became the focus of its activities whilst it lost ground irretrievably in the south-east to the Independents and Baptists and that at the crucial time when economic expansion was about to take place. The number of new causes added in Glamorgan and Monmouth-shire between 1750 and 1800 was small compared with earlier progress made. Little headway had been made in North Wales either after the failure of the early missionary work which started there in 1738. Harris was anxious to press on with the mission, Daniel Rowland less so, and so North Wales got less attention after Harris's expulsion. It was only after the schools of Griffith Jones gained success there that Methodism made any headway and it was the spread of the Sunday schools after 1785 that really opened the flood-gates in North Wales.

Meanwhile Harris had become involved in a new experiment —*Y Cartref* (the Home or Family) at Trefeca—which was a self-sufficient religious community, its members drawn from all parts of Wales and practising a variety of crafts as well as farming some 800 acres. No doubt, Harris had been influenced in this direction by the Moravian communities like the one at Fulneck, which he sarcastically described as ' their grand house in Yorkshire '. It was governed under a strict rule. William Williams tried to heal the breach in the movement realising the great loss it had sustained through Harris's departure. Eventually he was reconciled to his brethren but was never again the power he had been in the early days.

The death of the first generation of leaders increased the trend towards separatism. From 1742 when the first chapel had been built at Groes-wen (Caerffili) more and more appeared especially after 1790. They also came to be used for purposes other than society meetings and preaching. In 1791, the Association at Aberystwyth permitted the society at Gopa-fach

(Tawe Valley) to administer communion in its chapel. By 1798, we hear of baptisms being celebrated in the Methodist Chapel at Carmarthen. The persecution of the Methodists after 1794, in which the clergy were prominent, hardened their attitude towards the Church and reduced resistance to licensing their meeting-houses under the Toleration Act. Exhorters were also becoming dissatisfied since many of them were cast into prison for unlicensed preaching and some left to become Dissenting ministers. Thomas Charles was still reluctant to break with the Church and counselled forbearance but Thomas Jones, Denbigh, was a bolder spirit. He took it on himself to administer communion at Capel Canol, Denbigh, thereby making a breach inevitable. Thomas Charles was won over and in 1811 the Methodists took the long-deferred step of leaving the Church. By that time their organisation was fully fledged and it could be done without upheaval. For some time, however, many clergy were not clear whether they could count the Methodists as their flock or not and Methodists were still obliged to resort to the Church for marriage and burial ceremonies. By 1827, the Methodists had formulated their Confession of Faith which was adopted at Aberystwyth in that year.

The effects of the Revival

The religious revival of the eighteenth century although triggered off by the Methodists was not entirely a Methodist affair as it succeeded in regenerating religious life in every sphere. The effects of it were long-term and although one notices a transformation in progress by the end of our period it was not until the nineteenth century that the full impact of Nonconformity came to be felt. Even so, it was not difficult to recognise that the Age of Thomas Charles was very different from the Age of Ellis Wynne. The one unmistakable sign was the growth in the numbers of the Nonconformist sects as well as the Methodists and all at the expense of the Church. Its loss of membership was most serious amongst the Welsh-speaking lower class which made it appear more and more an alien establishment representative of a privileged class. It also completely identified itself with the reactionary politics of this class as was apparent during the French Revolutionary

War period which did more than anything to crystallise attitudes in this country. The Church was also falling out of touch with developments in areas of economic expansion like Merthyr Tydfil and abandoned the initiative to the Dissenters. While the Methodists were suspected of political disloyalty to the State they could not experiment politically as it would be unwise and they found it necessary to assert their loyalty by such resolutions as that passed at the Bala Association in 1798 which declared that people who criticised the government were unfit to be elders or even members of their societies. Although politically at variance the Methodists were gradually moving nearer to the Old Dissenters.

Too much has been attributed to the influence of Methodism in the eighteenth century since at no time was it sufficiently predominant to have had the influence it is supposed to have wielded. The Baptists and Independents were growing just as quickly and more so in Glamorgan and Monmouthshire after 1750 whilst in North Wales the Methodists scarcely made much impact until late in the century. So it is unrealistic to attribute to them such consequences as political reaction and cultural blight as has so often been done. The slowness of the growth of cultural institutions like the theatre is more attributable to the lack of a civic tradition and economic poverty than it is to Methodist influence. What Methodism did was to provide an alternative attraction to the old folk institutions like the *noson lawen*, which filled what leisure time people had in a creative way and the opportunities provided were free.

The main effect of Methodism was to transform the character of the Old Dissenters from being a narrow, intellectual, exclusive group into a more popular evangelical movement. The only sect they failed to influence was the Presbyterian which, although never numerous, increased its numbers in a Methodist stronghold, Cardiganshire. One consequence was the growth of a Nonconformist conscience which became a powerful force in the nineteenth century but whose effect was less apparent in Wales than in England in the eighteenth century. For example, it failed to inspire much philanthropic endeavour here and what was undertaken was mainly in the field of education. This educational bias was combined with missionary zeal in the founding of The British and Foreign Bible

Society in 1804 with which Thomas Charles was associated from the start, with its aim to provide all the people of the world with a Bible in their own tongue.

The Anti-Slavery Movement failed to draw much response even in evangelical circles, probably because Wales had no direct contact with the problem of slavery as places like Liverpool and Bristol had. It only came to be talked about in Wales after 1789 and one suspects that it was more in the context of the Rights of Man than evangelicalism. The people who spoke out against slavery in Wales were the political radicals and the only obvious link with evangelicalism was Morgan John Rhys. There was, however, a broad religious basis to the movement in Wales, *Y Drysorfa Gymysgedig*, the new journal launched in 1796 for instance, expressing the view that slavery was incompatible with Christian teaching. The Anti-Slavery Movement here was a respectable, middle-class movement rather than a popularly based one and it was from meetings of the gentry and town meetings that the petitions against slavery originated. Clarkson made his only tour in Wales in 1792 bringing with him letters of introduction to the clergy and thus failed to harness the dynamism of Nonconformity to his Movement. No wonder that out of twenty petitions which emanated from Wales only one came from a Nonconformist source at Carmarthen. In 1792, Edward Barnes translated a popular English pamphlet in which he made an outright bid for Methodist support for the Movement. The most that Nonconformity did in Wales on this issue was to awaken the religious conscience which made it more receptive of the anti-slavery propaganda that was circulating. By 1814, it is also noticeable that the leadership of the Movement had passed into the hands of Nonconformist ministers. The Peace Society, launched in 1814 by Tregelles Price as a natural reaction to war weariness, found little support outside Quaker circles, but remained sufficiently alive to be taken up by Henry Richard in mid-nineteenth century by which time it commanded far greater Nonconformist support.

SUGGESTED READING

E. T. Davies, *Religion in the industrial revolution in South Wales*, Cardiff, 1965.

D. J. O. Jones, *Daniel Rowland, Llangeitho*, 1938.

G. F. Nuttall, *Howell Harris, 1714–72*, Cardiff, 1965.

E. Phillips, *Edmund Jones, 'the Old Prophet'*, London, 1959.

G. M. Roberts, *Y Per Ganiedydd*, 2 vols., Aberystwyth, 1949, 1958.

——, (gol.) *Hanes Methodistiaeth Galfinaidd Cymru*, I, Caernarfon, 1973.

A. H. Williams, *John Wesley a Chymru*, 'Darlithiau Tre'rddol', I, 1969.

——, *John Wesley in Wales*, Cardiff, 1971.

Articles:

J. Davies, 'Howell Harris and the Trevecka Settlement', *Brycheiniog*, IX, 1963.

E. D. Jones, 'Some aspects of the history of the Church in north Cardiganshire in the eighteenth century', *J.H.S. Ch. in W.*, III, 1953.

W. M. Merchant, 'Richard Watson, Bishop of Llandaff', *J.H.S. Ch. in W.*, I, 1947.

A. H. Williams, 'The leaders of English and Welsh Methodism, 1738–91', *Bathafarn*, 16–17, 1961–2; 22–24, 1967–9.

7. Anglican and Dissenting Educational Endeavour

Griffith Jones and the Circulating Schools

Griffith Jones (1683-1761) was born of humble parentage in the parish of Pen-boyr (Cards.). He was educated locally before entering Carmarthen Grammar School which was then considered sufficient education to qualify a person for Anglican orders. He did not go to university and his whole life was spent within a day's travel from where he was born. His tastes were simple and he lived very close to the people on whose behalf he laboured with such consideration and sympathy. Being an asthma sufferer, poor health dogged him all his life; he was also neurotic and by temperament gloomy and intro-spective, sometimes irascible. A boyhood dream or ' vision ' convinced him that he was an instrument of divine providence for the regeneration of his people. He was capable of prodigious effort and threw himself with fervour into evangelical preaching and teaching.

He was ordained by Bishop Bull of St. David's who acquired a reputation of saintliness within his own lifetime and had a profound influence over Griffith Jones. In 1710, he moved into the Taf Valley on the borders of Carmarthenshire and Pembrokeshire henceforth to be the scene of his life's work. Here, there was already a long tradition of schooling associated with the activities of the family of Picton Castle into which Griffith Jones was initiated. He is reputed to have taught at a charity school at Laugharne where he lived and had a curacy to which was added the living of Llandeilo Abercywyn. From 1713 he acted as local correspondent of the S.P.C.K. but he had a mind to becoming a missionary with the Danish Mission at Tranquebar in India in which the Society was interested. His candidature was sponsored by Sir John Philipps but when he realised that an outlet for his evangelical zeal lay nearer at hand he changed his mind, and in 1716 received the living of Llanddowror which was in the gift of Sir John. Patron and protégé henceforth worked in complete harmony in serving the needs of their community both spiritually and morally and the ties became closer in 1720 when Griffith Jones married Sir John's sister.

Griffith Jones's first love was preaching which he undertook with such evangelical fervour as was later to characterise the Methodists and which touched off a minor religious revival in Carmarthenshire. This took him itinerant preaching outside his own parish and though he asserted that he never did so except by invitation he was arraigned before the Bishop's court. He was so incensed by this that he intimated to the bishop that it would be better if he spurred the indifferent clergy into action than silenced those who took their work seriously. He was saved from episcopal censure by the intercession of Sir John Philipps but for well-nigh twenty years Jones suffered from the carping criticism of the clergy which was a constant irritant to a man of so uncertain temper. No doubt it did his schools a lot of damage also since many clergy regarded this like his preaching as an unwarranted interference in other people's parochial affairs.

Jones's experience taught him that preaching in itself was not enough and that in order to win souls it was necessary that people should be taught to read the Bible. So, after 1730 his energy was channelled more and more in this direction. It is alleged that it was the visitation of a plague upon his parish in 1730-1 which appalled him so much when he saw so many people dying in ignorance of the Gospel that he decided to open a school, but it is likely that he was so inclined some time before. He took his duty of catechising his communicants before administering the Sacrament seriously and it was this which revealed to him their abysmal ignorance. He even bribed people to come for catechetical instruction by giving doles of bread. It also led to the opening of the school at Llanddowror, probably in the winter of 1731-2 and although it has been suggested that this was a continuation of the S.P.C.K. school in the parish this is unlikely since Jones's school was a Welsh one. It had nothing to support it more ' than what could be spared from other occasions out of a small offertory

by a poor country congregation at the blessed sacrament ',
as he later recalled. By 1736 his experiment was extended to
schools at Llan-llwch, Llansadwrn and as far afield as Defynnog
(Brecs.). Their stated aim was to restore catechetical instruction to the position it had once held in the primitive church
and which formed an important part of every cleric's duty.

He was not entirely satisfied with the existing provisions for
catechetical schools and when Sir John Philipps's death in
1737 placed the responsibility of carrying on the schools
primarily on his shoulders, Griffith Jones responded to the
challenge by making plans to extend literacy on such a scale
as was never before attempted in Wales. The idea of itinerant
teachers was not new, having probably been already used by
Dr. Daniel Williams in North Wales and Sir Humphrey
Mackworth had commended the idea to the S.P.C.K. in 1719.
But no one had ever planned on the same scale as Griffith
Jones contemplated and his was the first organised movement
to emanate from Wales itself, all previous ones having originated in London.

They were unique in another sense inasmuch as they were
the first specifically Welsh-medium schools to be successfully
established, although Stephen Hughes would have wished to
have done so. Jones appreciated the importance of the vernacular and, in a letter to Bishop Otley, was very critical of clergy
who could not preach in Welsh (which included the bishop
himself). He defends his standpoint on the language in *Welch
Piety* which suggests that he had been criticised on that score.
He asserted that his policy was the only realistic one and the
fact that he established some English-medium schools in south
Pembrokeshire absolves him from any charge of bigotry. Jones
had a profound respect for his mother-tongue for its ' simple
honesty ' and its virgin purity, undefiled by ' Atheism, Deism,
Infidelity, Arianism, Popery, lewd plays, immodest romances
and love intrigues ', which surely laid claim to its being the
most chaste of European languages. Whether his theories
were tenable or not the rightness of his judgement rested on the
fact that it was the most practical course to adopt.

The movement spread rapidly in the three south-western
counties and Glamorgan, and pioneer schools were established
in other parts of Wales. The publication of an annual report,

Welch Piety, for the movement's subscribers also gave them publicity. The Report for 1742-3 outlines the procedure for setting up the schools. A church, chapel or empty house would be sought in a convenient place in the parish since money was not available to be spent on building. Public notice of intent to open a school would be given and Griffith Jones would provide a schoolmaster. This preliminary organisation must have depended on close co-operation with someone in a position of influence in the area and the charge of intrusion must thus be treated with caution. Each teacher was provided with the Rules of the schools in Welsh which were to be given all possible publicity. They were accompanied by an introductory letter from Griffith Jones himself which was to be shown to anyone interested and it invited anyone to write to him commenting on the schools and the conduct of the masters. He evidently took precautions against uninformed criticism to safeguard the reputation of his schools.

Schooling had to be free as it was so difficult to attract pupils to school and to ensure attendance ; the duration was also restricted to about three months within the period from September to May when agricultural demands were less pressing. A period of about three months was considered sufficient to teach what was regarded as essentials and so it was in the nature of a crash programme, the utmost being derived from the brief stay of the schoolmasters. Schools often returned to the same parishes but usually to a different part of the parish. The vicar of Meidrim (Carms.) reported that his parish had had a school off and on for about twenty years. Daytime was given over to teaching children but for three to four hours in the evening the schools were open for adults. Griffith Jones asserts that adult attendance was double that of children but although records of child attendance were kept, none exist for adults. The numbers which are given in *Welch Piety* for the years 1737-61 amount to 3,495 schools and 158,237 scholars which are miscalculated and should read 3,324 schools and 153,835 scholars. Even so, there may have been some duplication where a school remained longer than usual in a district and irregularity of attendance suggests that many pupils did not stay long enough to learn to read. If, however, we add but one adult for every child instead of the two which Jones estimated the total would amount to 307,670, which is well-nigh three-quarters of the entire population of Wales at this time, so that his estimate appears to be exaggerated. Even so, it was a sizable achievement if school attendance can be equated with literacy.

Teaching to read was the main work of the schools as finances did not reach to ' writing and cyphering ', and the Bible and Common Prayer Book served as readers. The principles and duties of religion were enjoined and through the Catechism Anglican doctrine was imparted. Catechising was a twice daily exercise so that indoctrination took up a considerable time, but Griffith Jones impressed on his teachers the need for clear exposition so that the children should comprehend and not merely repeat by rote. The promotion of piety was his objective and in this he was at one with Hermann Francke who had established charity schools at Halle in Saxony, an account of which had been published under the title *Pietas Hallensis* which undoubtedly suggested *Welch Piety* as the title of Jones's Reports on his schools. The *Pietas* was translated into English by Böhme, chaplain to Prince George of Denmark, with whom Griffith Jones corresponded. Church attendance was also urged on pupils who were taught to make their responses to the clergyman. Monday morning brought its inquisition about the content of the previous day's sermon and this called for some working relationship between schoolmaster and clergyman.

By 1740 there had been a great increase in the number of schools which shows that their first appearance was greeted with enthusiasm. Then there was a falling-off due to opposition to the schools in some quarters especially from detractors who accused the schools of being Methodist seminaries and the teachers Methodist propagandists. The rise of Methodism influenced the schools in both a positive and a negative way. The genuine interest in religion kindled by Methodism made people anxious to learn to read the Word of God and Griffith Jones garnered a great harvest of such enthusiasts. The taint of Methodism also turned many against the schools and the bitterest critics were Anglican clergy. Griffith Jones had definite connections with the Methodist leaders which all his efforts to explain away could not do convincingly. Jones was

free of sectarian prejudices and accepted help for his schools
from Dissenters and Methodists as his 'great Design' of
offering salvation to people seemed to him to justify. He
availed himself of Methodist and Dissenting meeting-houses to
accommodate his schools and Jones's connection with Howell
Harris, who served for a time as one of his teachers and helped
him to organise schools in South Wales, is well-known. He had
personal connections of some sort with every one of the Methodist leaders and he was also a friend of both John Wesley and
George Whitefield, who regularly preached at Madam Bridget
Bevan's house in Bath which Jones often visited. No wonder
that Griffith Jones was dubbed by his enemies 'the father of
Methodism', although he insisted that all his schoolmasters
should be Anglican communicants and urged them to attend
Church services. Even so, there were known Congregationalists
among his teachers as well as Methodist exhorters including the
hymn-writers Morgan Rhys and David Williams. Hostility
to his schools on account of Methodism was most apparent in
North Wales and the Chancellor of Bangor and eleven clergy
protested to Jones against the intrusion of his schoolmasters
into Caernarfonshire to spread Methodist doctrines and to
undermine the authority of the clergy. This opposition virtually led to the abandonment of activity in North Wales for a
period and it also caused Jones to reconsider his policy. Co-
operation between men of goodwill foundered once more on
the rock of sectarian prejudice and Jones endeavoured to rid
himself of the embarrassment of his Methodist associations. In
1741, he dismissed several teachers for exhorting and the
humiliating conditions to which his schoolmasters were subjected arose from a desire to arrest the decline of the schools
and his anxiety lest they should fail because of popular prejudice.

From 1741, therefore, we can detect a change of policy
directed at removing any obstacle to his design of eventually
establishing a parochial system of schools under the aegis of the
bishops and with the co-operation of the whole body of clergy.
But instead of co-operation Jones was faced by a continued
barrage of criticism which he tried to answer in several numbers
of *Welch Piety*. Some cavilled at the language alleging that the
schools were perpetuating instead of smothering the vernacular.

H

Others, that the poor already had sufficient provisions for religious instruction. To counter allegations that his schools encouraged the spread of Methodism and Dissent, Jones, inconsistently, denounced the Methodists for itinerant preaching and excess of zeal for which he himself stood condemned ; he never acknowledged the Association which the Methodists had formed in 1743. He also made more deliberate efforts to involve the clergy in his work and yielded greater local control of the schools to them. They were invited to inspect the schools and to report upon them and they were given the power to dismiss a teacher and replace him if they so wished. William Morris, writing to his brother Richard in 1749, states that the clergy around Holyhead had insisted on naming their own masters. Some clergy received gratuities for their work until travelling inspectors were appointed later on to visit the schools. Clerical support was more forthcoming after 1745 and this is reflected in the increasing number of schools up to Griffith Jones's death in 1761. The last attack on one of Jones's schoolmasters in Denbighshire occurred in 1746 but by the end of the forties the schools were on the march again in North Wales with co-operation from the clergy.

Between 1750 and 1752 three letters were published which renewed the attack on Griffith Jones. The first two were anonymous and were addressed to George Whitefield and reiterated the accusation that Griffith Jones was responsible for the rise and spread of Methodism and of holding theological views which were similar to theirs. The third came from the pen of the Rev. John Evans, the absentee rector of the neighbouring parish of Eglwys Gymyn and one of the chaplains of the chapels royal. It exhibits a great deal of personal knowledge of Jones and was evidently motivated by personal animus but on what account is not known. It is ironical that Jones's schools which were so given to Anglican indoctrination and his masters grounded in Anglican theology should have been branded as Methodist seminaries. By this time, however, his schools were so well-established that they were not so adversely affected by malicious attacks.

' It is by no means the design of this spiritual kind of charity to make them gentlemen, but Christians, and heirs to eternal life '. For this reason, Jones laid little emphasis on social con-

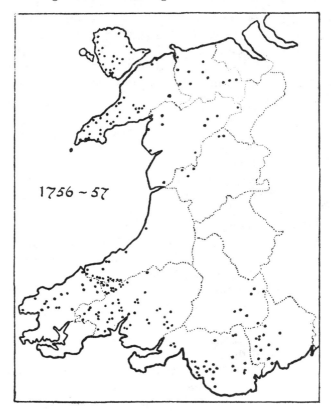

Figure 1
GRIFFITH JONES'S CIRCULATING SCHOOLS
1756–57

(Taken, with permission, from William Rees, *An Historical Atlas of Wales*, Cardiff, 1951)

ditioning and attached more importance to religious devotion in his teachers than sound scholarship. The excessive zeal which led some of them to exhorting was more embarrassing to him than their lack of intellectual qualification. No wonder that they were often derided, ' runaway servants and apprentices' they were called by John Evans, but Jones contented himself that their material and intellectual poverty kept them from the travails of false pride. The pupils also cut their teeth on a heavy diet of pietistical and moral literature supplied by the S.P.C.K. without whose support Griffith Jones could never have satisfied the insatiable demand for reading material in Welsh in the absence of a Welsh press. Some of the material came from Jones's own pen and included a catechism which purported to be ' a compleat Scriptural Body of Divinity ' and which long remained in use as the best of its kind. He was also involved in preparing reprints of the Bible in 1718, 1727, 1746 and 1751 which testifies to the voracious demand of a newly-created reading public. These books were sold to those who could afford to buy and given free to those who could not through the generosity of the S.P.C.K. . This helped Griffith Jones to conserve his funds which could be concentrated entirely on paying his teaching staff.

Griffith Jones claimed that he could teach people to read at a cost of 2s. to 3s. a head as ' it is but a cheap education . . .only the moral and religious branch of it '. But to finance a scheme of such magnitude required a good sum of money and that regularly since his schoolmasters were in regular employment although they were paid only a pittance. £3 to £4 a year is often quoted as their stipend but this is probably too low as their wages were assessed on the number of pupils who were in full attendance at the schools, a strict account of which had to be kept. The task of organisation and finance was thus a heavy burden to be borne by one man. Most of the contributions, other than church collections, came from England and among the donors were eminent scientists of the Royal Society eager to support any experiment designed to banish ignorance. Surprisingly absent from the lists of subscribers in the reports are the names of London Welshmen ; they may well have been too engrossed in their own scheme to establish a school for the children of poor Welsh families in London sponsored by the Society of Ancient Britons and which eventually opened at Clerkenwell. John Evans, Griffith Jones's critic, was a prominent member of the Cymmrodorion and may have influenced others against the circulating schools, an attitude which perplexed Richard Morris, the Society's secretary, in view of Wales's great need. Jones found his firmest friend and most liberal patron in Madam Bridget Bevan, the daughter of John Vaughan of Derllys, who devoted a great part of her annual income to supporting the schools. It was at her home that he died in 1761 and committed the care of the schools to her hands leaving a legacy of £7,000 for the purpose.

The schools continued to flourish down to 1774 despite Griffith Jones's death and Madam Bevan with her intimate knowledge of their organisation proved a good manager. By that time, however, they were well-established and this is attributable to Jones's rare power of organisation and foresight. A man of such compelling vision and genius for ordering things could never have been content with a parochial enterprise and his great achievement was to turn local philanthropy into a national movement. After his death, Madam Bevan appointed two stewards, one in North and one in South Wales to supervise the organisation and pay the masters. The decline which set in after 1774 may be an indication of the schools' success since the number of adults had dwindled perceptibly by then.

Madam Bevan's death in 1779 was a mortal blow since there was no one ready as she had been in 1761 to assume responsibility. Although she left her estate of £10,000 to endow the schools the bequest was challenged by two of her trustees and an action in Chancery was brought. It was not until 1786 that a public enquiry was opened at Laugharne and Carmarthen and not till 1804 that its findings were made known and judgment given that the schools were ' useful and good charities, wisely planned, successfully executed, attended with general and extensive benefit '. A fitting epitaph, for the schools were long defunct. When the money, by then augmented to £30,000, was released from Chancery, a scheme was drawn up in 1807 and implemented in 1809. It provided for circulating elementary schools but on a more established basis and were run on the Bell monitorial system. The Madam Bevan Trust remained in existence till 1854 and its schools were reported on, generally unfavourably, in the Education Report of 1847.

No one will deny the magnitude of Griffith Jones's achievement but historians are by no means agreed as to what it was. Some regard his schools as a retrograde step by comparison with earlier enterprises because of their restricted curriculum. They certainly influenced the thinking of educational pioneers for some time to come and would-be founders of schools still thought along the lines of short-term circulating schools. They had served their day and age well but were no substitute for permanent schools providing a broad-based curriculum. Set against this the fact that they produced a substantially literate nation, probably none more so in Europe at that time. The circulating school movement also provided an intellectual stimulus and laid the foundations of adult education. The success of the Sunday schools was in no small measure due to them and interest in education was kept alive through them. The beneficial effect upon the Welsh language is immeasurable but Griffith Jones's insistence on its use and acquaintance with the prose of the Welsh Bible and some of the classics of religious literature was undoubtedly a tremendous boost to the literary revival and to the *Eisteddfod* dating from the eighteenth century.

Thomas Charles and the Sunday School

The termination of the Circulating Schools with Madam Bevan's death in 1779 removed the only organised provision for schooling in Wales and there were many calls for their revival. William Williams, Pantycelyn, endeavoured to re-kindle public interest by publishing a pamphlet calling for schools to be established similar to those of Griffith Jones. Edward Williams of Oswestry was likewise attracted to the idea of circulating schools in his pioneering work in north-east Wales and the borderland. It is even less wonder that the idea should have dominated the thinking of Thomas Charles who had been born in the parish of Llanfihangel Abercywyn, near Llanddowror, in 1755 and had been taught by one of Griffith Jones's schoolmasters. Griffith Jones was a well-known figure in his neighbourhood and may well have been taken by Charles as his model in life. Stemming from the minor gentry of Carmarthenshire, Charles was able to proceed to Oxford and to take a degree after receiving his early education at Llanddowror and Carmarthen Academy. Among the influences upon his life must be reckoned the broadening outlook of a university education, deficient as it was in his time, as well as the cultural and literary associations of his neighbourhood and in this sense he had the advantage of Griffith Jones. His Oxford degree and background were important to Charles later and saved him from much social ostracism and even persecution.

It also contributed to his self-assurance and ease of relationship with other people and enabled him to move in circles of like-minded people even in England on an equal basis. Following his ordination as deacon (1778) and as priest (1780) he spent practically the whole of his ministry within the Church in three Somersetshire curacies which widened his experience. It was his marriage to Sally Jones who carried on a prosperous business at Bala that brought him back to Wales where he was to embark on his life's work.

Charles's interest in evangelicalism had been fired when he was a student at Carmarthen Academy and from attending Methodist meetings in the town where he was converted by Daniel Rowland in 1773. When he was ejected from the curacy of Llanymawddwy (Mer.) which he held for three months after his marriage he began to interest himself more and more in the activities of the Methodist society at Bala, of which his wife was a member. Bala, with its famous fairs, was then an important commercial centre for a wide neighbourhood and was on the main route between North and South Wales and was rapidly becoming one of the most important centres of Methodism as it took increasing hold over the North. It was the success of the school which he opened at the Methodist meeting-house for the children of the Bala society that impelled him to look further afield and to make work among children his life-task. The success of Griffith Jones's schools convinced him that this was the only practical answer to schooling in Wales. He rejected the idea of Sunday schools of which he was certainly aware by 1785 because he did not think they met with Wales's situation having such a scattered population. Though adopting Griffith Jones's model he introduced some improvements. He gave a good deal of thought to the selection of suitable centres and permitted his schools to remain there for a much longer period of from six to nine months instead of the usual three of the Circulating Schools. He exercised close personal supervision over his schools and gave the pupils a thorough examination before the school was wound up and the master moved on. Although the schools were designed principally for children, Charles was not blind to the needs of adults for whom he always catered, thus establishing his claim as a pioneer of adult education.

The schools were largely self-supporting since the Methodist societies maintained them from the proceeds of collections. Their organisation was not as vast as that of Griffith Jones and was essentially local making unnecessary the raising of a national fund. He thus found an even simpler solution than Griffith Jones's to the financial problem. The progress of his schools was no match for those of Jones, however, and even in 1794 after at least eight years of their existence their numbers could not have exceeded forty. Charles's day-schools were indubitably superior to Griffith Jones's in several respects. His teachers were more carefully selected and although personal piety counted, intellectual ability was not scorned. He satisfied himself of their suitability by gathering them to Bala to be personally instructed by himself. They were paid about £10 a year which, modest though it was, commanded for them some greater status than those of Griffith Jones. They enjoyed another advantage — freedom from clerical supervision, since there is no evidence that they were inspected by any other than Charles himself. In 1786 there were seven schoolmasters in his employ and by 1794 the number had still only increased to twenty. Charles was not beset with the problem of finding sufficient teachers and, in the main, he was well-served by them. They were able to tackle a somewhat broader curriculum than their predecessors although emphasis was still upon reading and learning the Catechism. But Charles was not content with rote-learning and one of the features of his work was that he designed catechisms suitable for children where the emphasis was laid on biblical knowledge rather than upon dogma. He also designed readers for children which were very unlike the pious works laid before a previous generation of children. He was thus one of the first to recognise the specific needs of children in regard to reading material. Writing was also taught in at least some of his schools. It is significant that in the declared aim of his schools knowledge ranked alongside piety—' our point is to diffuse knowledge and promote piety among all ranks '. He showed no less awareness than Griffith Jones had done of the common sense of using the Welsh language for instruction. It is all summed up in his intent ' to teach the children to read their native language correctly and instruct them in the principles of Christianity and nothing more, as the Salvation of their Souls is the only point we have in view '.

The first reference to the idea of Sunday schools in Wales is to be found in a pamphlet published in 1785 by William Richards entitled *A Plea for the reading of Scriptures in Religious Assemblies*. The author proposed that every church and chapel should open a Sunday school for illiterates. They would be denominational and would be staffed by voluntary teachers. The proposal did not bear fruit at that time but the idea had been implanted. By this time, however, Robert Raikes's Sunday schools had been in existence for five years and were rapidly increasing in large towns like Manchester. Others were more impressed with their possibilities than Thomas Charles and by 1786, Sunday schools had been opened in the Oswestry district by Edward Williams who was a Congregational minister in the town. In that year he appealed to the English Sunday School Society for help with the schools ' at least where the English language was in a measure cultivated and used by the inhabitants '. Since the Society was confined to England as its province it could not be of great help but its Chairman was so keen on helping that he set up some schools at his own expense. It is evident from Williams's appeal to the Society that he had set up Welsh as well as English schools and they may well have been in the majority for Williams translated a catechism into Welsh for their benefit. They were, however, confined to this corner of Wales and Williams's enterprise was local in scope. But to Williams as to Charles, Sunday schools were only second-best and inferior to day schools. Where he could he converted some of his Sunday schools into day schools and it is fairly certain that he regarded the one as an introduction to the other.

Another pioneer of the movement was Morgan John Rhys, a Baptist minister of Hengoed, near Caerffili. The plan which he put forward in *Y Cylchgrawn Cynmraeg* in 1793 exhibits a great deal of the influence of the English Sunday school. He urged the need for a national system of Sunday schools in every parish supported by subscriptions which would be used for buying books and paying teachers, paid teachers being a feature of Raikes's schools for some time. There was also a similarity of purpose, namely the reform of the lower classes

and Sabbath observance. In Rhys's favour may it be said that
he no more believed in subordination than he did in indoctrination. He must have started some schools, since within six
months he was urging parents to send their children to them.
It was through his writings that Rhys was to contribute most
to the movement rather than by personal example.

It was with cautious steps and, indeed, extreme reluctance
that Thomas Charles proceeded to establish Sunday schools.
It may be argued that they were forced upon him since he
resisted the idea as long as he could and the first ones he
established were in the nature of a compromise. He may well
have seen the working of the English schools during his sojourn
in Somersetshire which might have persuaded him that they
could not be transplanted to Welsh soil. By 1789, Charles was
reluctantly admitting the existence of Sunday schools in
response to local demands that the day schools should be open
on one or two nights a week, preferably on Sunday ' for those
whose occupations prevented their attending the day schools '.
It is clear that their role was therefore subsidiary to that of the
day schools which continued to exist even where a Sunday
school had been established. Indeed, a Sunday school would
carry on the work after the circulating school had closed and
the master moved on. Charles was still preoccupied with his
day schools at least till 1797 although by this time the Sunday
schools had overhauled them and were gradually pushing them
out of existence. Even after he had been converted to the
Sunday school idea he continued to employ circulating schoolmasters to work ' where none were found willing or able to
set up Sunday schools '.

1797 appears to have been the turning point in Charles's
attitude towards the Sunday schools. He spent a part of that
year in London where he became better acquainted with them
and shortly afterwards he became a correspondent of the
Sunday School Society and Wales was brought within its
sphere. He sought and obtained help from the Society and
under his vigorous leadership Sunday schools and night schools
were set up throughout the country. But, although Charles
owed a great deal to the English movement, the schools which
he evolved bore his own stamp and differed materially from the
English ones. They were also superior to earlier Welsh experi-

ments in this field and were organised on a national scale. They were necessarily denominational since Charles had no support other than what was accorded him by the Methodist societies. The spread of the schools among the Methodists in the North was very rapid and in some localities Methodist churches grew out of the Sunday schools. They also captured the imagination of the whole country coming to be adopted not only by the Dissenting connexions but by the Anglican Church.

The Welsh Sunday school was more democratic in character than its English counterpart. It was and still is controlled by the teachers who, in turn, are chosen from amongst the members. Although the Methodist Sunday schools came under the supervision of the Association its control has always been nominal. For this reason they have been well-described as cradles of democracy for in this sphere at least Welsh people had been long accustomed to ordering their own affairs before they had the opportunity to do so in the political field. It was in character, therefore, that the gospel of social subordination should have found little place in them which shows a difference in outlook from the English ones. In 1809, Thomas Charles noted with satisfaction how the schools had improved the morals and behaviour of the young and although this was a secondary consideration with him he thought it of value to society generally.

The main characteristic of the Welsh Sunday school has always been that it was open to all ages of both sexes and this has helped to instil the idea that learning is a cumulative process which goes on throughout one's life. The method of teaching amongst adults was adapted to this circumstance with discussion being more in evidence than pedagogy. The need for money to run the schools was negligible. They also suited the circumstances of the pupils who enjoyed the benefit of a free education within their spare time. The popularity of the Sunday schools is attested by their rapid spread and by the fact that they brought some colour into an otherwise humdrum existence. The Sunday school festival, known as *Y Gymanfa Bwnc*, brought together schools from a wide neighbourhood to one centre where marathon feats of reciting memorised parts of Scripture were performed in no little spirit of competition and ' weighty men ' won renown for their display of theological argument. It stimulated the intellect, albeit within a narrow field of thought. People acquired the habit of reading, thinking and discussing and the political awakening of Wales was as much the result of this as was its spiritual and educational awakening. The 'Nonconformist conscience' came to be a force to be reckoned with in national life with which even politicians found it necessary to come to terms. The Sunday school was also a cohesive force in society which proved to be a blessing when the mass migration of population took place from the countryside into the industrial areas in the nineteenth century. These people took with them their cherished institutions, the chapel and the Sunday school, which helped to mitigate the problems of settlement in new communities.

The Sunday School Movement in Wales was a success story which was due in large measure to the organising genius of Thomas Charles who presided over its early development and within whose lifetime it had spread to every corner of the country. Its success cannot be measured simply by the number of schools which were opened since even the Education Commissioners of 1847 found them superior to any other provider of education at that time. But instead of the co-operation between Sunday and day-schools which Thomas Charles favoured, the two not only drew apart but even worked against each other. It was in the Sunday schools, rather than in the alien atmosphere of the nineteenth century voluntary schools which ostracised the native language, that the majority of Welsh children found an outlet for their energies, since they accorded more nearly to the temperament of the society from which they had sprung.

The Grammar Schools

It is difficult to estimate the extent of the provision for secondary education within our period. There were probably upwards of thirty endowed schools which contributed either a classical or partly-classical education. About a dozen were survivals from the Tudor or early Stuart periods commonly known as 'Tudor Grammar schools'. By the eighteenth century every county in Wales had some provision for secondary education but most schools were established in the borderland which might be taken as an indication of the economic wealth of these areas or as a symptom of the greater penetration of English influences since the grammar school was a peculiarly English institution. Most of these schools drew from a wide area—we even hear of Irish pupils coming to Friars' School, Bangor—and so boys had to stay in lodgings in town before boarding facilities were developed. Most remained day-schools, however, and never sought to develop a boarding side. They were patronised by the local gentry who often sent their sons there, especially their younger ones ; Ruthin could boast of a future Lord Chief Justice, Lloyd Kenyon, as an alumnus. Cowbridge was equally popular in the South. As landed families became more prosperous in the eighteenth century there was a marked tendency to send their sons to fashionable English schools and interest in local grammar schools correspondingly declined.

The schools were financed from the revenue which accrued from the capital endowment which was invested in land, parochial tithes or loans bearing interest, but whereas property investments augmented in value in the course of the eighteenth century with consequent advantages to the schools, interest-bearing loans became less remunerative to their detriment, as in the case of Hawarden. The master's salary was the first claim on the revenue but where the endowment was sufficiently liberal, provision might be made for an usher, or assistant. The salary of the master was raised from time to time and appears to have kept pace with rising costs especially when so many masterships were coupled with curacies. At Bala and Pengam the eighteenth-century endowments provided money for clothing the poor scholars, known in Bala as ' the blue-coat boys '. In Beaumaris, however, the trustees devoured the equivalent of a writing-master's salary at one feast ! In some instances, such as Llanegryn (Mer.) and Pengam (Glam.), money was provided to enable pupils to proceed to apprenticeships. A fairly common provision was the endowment of scholarships at the Universities for pupils from particular schools. Bishop Henry Rowlands provided for two scholars at Jesus College, Oxford, one from Beaumaris and one from Botwnnog. Friars' School had a scholarship at Magdalene College, Cambridge. The most liberal endowment for this purpose was made at Jesus College, Oxford, by Edmund Meyrick, the founder of Bala School.

The traditional grammar school was an endowed school where Latin and Greek were taught and which usually provided a free education for so many poor scholars. By the eighteenth century the number of 'free schools' had increased often through the generosity of local people who had made money in trade or the professions. Not every school which taught Latin was regarded as a grammar school since many private venture schools had come into existence for this purpose. Standards of scholarship varied considerably. Ruthin, whose statutes were modelled on those of Westminster School, was probably the most ambitious and one of the most successful, comparing very favourably with the best of its kind in England. Not only was Latin taught but the eldest boys were expected to converse in Latin. Greek was also taken to an advanced stage which was extraordinary even for a grammar school.

It is a matter of some doubt how many schools succeeded in adhering to classical standards by the eighteenth century, and the weight of evidence indicates a decline in standards and a watering-down of the curriculum. 'Grammar learning' was usually liberally interpreted and included not only working through Lily's Grammar but also through some prescribed authors whose works were supposed to impart great moral influence. English was little in evidence except for communication, Welsh even less, and so the contribution which these schools made to Welsh culture was negligible. It was the kind of education best suited for a gentleman with its emphasis on manners or Tudor 'civility'. By the beginning of the eighteenth century there was evidently some doubt as to whether this was the kind of education best suited to 'poor scholars' and whether it served any purpose other than for candidates entering the Church. There was a gradual change in the curriculum away from the classics. Llandaff did not appoint a Latin master after 1690 and a number of schools begin to give more prominence to basic skills. The number of classical scholars declined and elementary pupils became more numerous. Some schools developed a lower and an upper school, the latter being reserved for classical scholars.

Complaints were often voiced that founders' intentions were

being ignored as the fee-paying side was developed at the expense of the foundation scholars. In 1708, the trustees of Friars' School ruled that boys must not be admitted for the purpose of learning writing and English and the trustees of Hawarden imposed a test of ability to read the New Testament for admission after the master complained that many boys were being sent to the school to learn the rudiments of English. Attempts to stem the tide were abortive especially when subjects like reading, writing and English were designated as ' extras ' for which pupils had to pay.   Masters found the admission of fee-payers useful to increase their emoluments and their numbers significantly increased in the eighteenth century.   Writing masters were appointed at Friars' from 1708 and at Beaumaris from 1710.   Edward Lewis's endowment for Pengam School which came into existence about 1760, specified reading, writing and casting accounts.   The duties of the master at Meyrick's school at Bala were specified in 1753 as ' teaching reading and writing and the Catechism of the Church of England in the English language '.   This was quite characteristic of the eighteenth-century foundations and possibly exhibits the influence of the charity school movement upon them.   It becomes difficult, therefore, to distinguish between them and elementary schools, and the only differentiating feature often was that some of these endowed schools had a classical side.   By the nineteenth century Latin itself was designated as an ' extra ' at Bala although taught free to the poor foundationers.   No doubt some of the trustees of the older foundations felt that these changes were very remiss, and towards the end of our period attempts were made to revive classical learning, as at Beaumaris in 1783, when new regulations were drawn up which specified the curriculum of study.

Facilities for secondary education which could lead on to university were fairly widespread if less than adequate.   Oxford and Cambridge were still the only universities available although we hear of an occasional Welshman making tracks to Scottish universities before the end of our period.   The generosity of founders of local grammar schools often enabled sons of poor parents to attend the old universities as their registers testify and Oxford drew considerably more than Cambridge. The malaise which lay on the universities in this period was communicated to grammar schools as the academic status of masters and ushers declined and appointments were often made which contravened the statutes in order that the revenue could be deployed to other purposes.

The Academies

The opening of academies in the second half of the seventeenth century was the outcome of two causes. Nonconformists were debarred from the Universities of Oxford and Cambridge which was a blessing in disguise, but they were the sole means of higher education unless one went north to Scotland. The other cause was the attachment which Dissenters had for an educated ministry and since their ministers could not enter universities the connexions had to make their own provision. This emphasis upon a learned ministry characterised the attitude of the Old Dissenters until at least the middle of the eighteenth century when the Methodist emphasis on evangelical fervour brought it into some disrepute. Once established, academies proliferated and were adapted to purposes other than religion. In 1690, the Presbyterians set up the Presbyterian Fund for ministerial education and in 1695 the Congregationalists did likewise, and although they took no steps towards establishing an academy they supported students at an institution already in existence.

The first academy came into being as the result of the ejection of Puritan ministers under the Act of Uniformity of 1662. One of the victims was Samuel Jones who had been a Fellow of Jesus College, Oxford, and who was then vicar of Llangynwyd (Glam.). He opened his academy in his own commodious house at Brynllywarch, near Bridgend, either in 1662 or possibly, 1672. He established a high reputation for learning being, in Calamy's estimation, a great philosopher, a master of Greek and Latin and proficient in oriental languages. In 1690, the Presbyterian Board decided to support some students at Brynllywarch, an example followed by the Congregationalists in 1695. Jones's academy was undenominational and so it remained although it trained ministers of several religious sects. Brynllywarch had won such regard that it was not suffered to die with its founder in 1697, but after that date it was no more than a revered name and the Academy continued its career briefly at Abergavenny under a Congregational minister. It soon returned to the Bridgend area when it was entrusted to the care of Rees Price, the squire of Ty'nton, who ministered to a small congregation at Bridgend and father of the celebrated Dr. Richard Price. After that it made seven moves before finally coming to rest at Carmarthen in 1796 where it had already been twice previously. Its survival was no less than miraculous since it had lapsed more than once and during its sojourns at Carmarthen complaints of indiscipline and even rowdyism were often made to the Presbyterian Board which continued steadfastly to give financial support. More serious were the accusations made concerning the orthodoxy of its doctrine. Thomas Perrot, its master, was an Arminian in his theology and is credited with being the father of Welsh Arminianism. One of his successors, Samuel Thomas, was accused of Pelagianism and it was during his time that the Congregationalists broke away in 1754. Dr. Jenkin Jenkins was an Arian. Religious controversy was greatly heightened by mid-eighteenth century and so denominations which trained their ministers at Carmarthen became concerned over the inconstancy of religious doctrine taught there. It caused the Established Church concern as well since many of its ordinands were trained either at the grammar school or at the Academy in Carmarthen, both of them similarly contaminated.

The disputes over doctrine led to the foundation of denominational academies and Carmarthen remained unique as an undenominational institution. The Baptists had never subscribed to it and from 1732 to 1770 they had maintained an academy at Pontypool which probably made a greater contribution to their English ministry than their Welsh, situated as it was in the borderland. They also relied very largely upon their academy in Bristol and Pontypool suffered from its competition and finally succumbed. A school was re-established at Abergavenny in 1807, later to return to Pontypool and which eventually became the Baptist College of South Wales.

The Congregationalists opened their own academy at Abergavenny in 1754, despairing of Carmarthen's return to orthodoxy. The initiative came from the Calvinists within the connexion and the students were submitted to a confession of faith before being allowed to enter. The academy was

I

moved to Oswestry under Dr. Edward Williams and when he left for Birmingham it passed on to Wrexham where it remained for a quarter of a century.

The Methodists set no store upon book-learning and it was not until the 1830s that they took measures for educating their own ministers. It is true that the Countess of Huntingdon had founded an academy at Trefeca, opened by George Whitefield in 1768 and presided over at first by Fletcher of Madeley whose visits were infrequent. Howell Harris took a great deal of interest in the academy and addressed the students twice weekly. It was not by any means confined to Methodists and students of all Protestant denominations as well as the Church could attend. It was probably unique in requiring proof of religious conversion as a condition of entry. It was uncompromisingly orthodox and the turn-over of masters was inordinately large since the Countess brooked no trifling with Arminianism. John Williams, son of Williams, Pantycelyn, taught there and when he left, the academy moved to Cheshunt. Despite the number of Unitarians who became masters of schools and academies, the denomination never established an academy of its own although there was a very close connection between it and Carmarthen Academy where most of its Welsh ministers were trained.

It should be emphasised that denominational academies were greatly outnumbered by private academies and schools which were the property of the founder and where he alone taught. Many of these masters were Dissenting ministers and as often as not, their schools had some connection with a denomination and frequently prepared ministerial candidates. This was a tradition which started in the seventeenth century, the school kept at Ystradwallter, near Llandovery, being one of the earliest and might, indeed, ante-date 1662. The most famous eighteenth-century example was the school kept by David Davis at Castellhywel (Cards.) which was renowned for its classical education as was the school at Ystradmeurig kept by Edward Richard whose education was too narrowly classical for Lewis Morris to suffer his sons to continue there. The number of private academies and schools increased in the eighteenth century but most of them were ephemeral and did not survive the founder. Nor were they exclusively concerned with ministerial education, the school founded at Caernarfon by Evan Richardson in 1787 turning out an appreciable number of teachers.

The curriculum taught at the foremost academies was a very ambitious one. The classics naturally held pride of place but the chief characteristic of the eighteenth-century academy was the attention given to modern studies. William Williams, Pantycelyn, went to Llwyn-llwyd Academy to prepare himself for a medical career. Logic, mathematics and astronomy were taught at Carmarthen and natural science and conics were later added. When we set against such an impressive curriculum the fact that at most there were only two teachers, one usually designated a classical master and the other teaching theology, it is doubtful whether the students' knowledge of modern subjects could be more than superficial and the syllabus might thus appear to be pretentious. Library facilities were inadequate although the Presbyterian Board did make over sums of money periodically for buying books and equipment and when the academy at Tewkesbury closed in 1721 its library was transferred to Carmarthen.

Elsewhere, provision was much more meagre. Exchange of ideas was made more difficult by the remoteness of many of the schools so that they were little in contact with the outside world. The area which had given security and succour to the early Nonconformist causes were not necessarily the best centres for education. Money was always in short supply although the Presbyterian and Congregational Boards did what they could for their students. Their numbers were usually limited and it was unusual to find more than about a dozen students in residence anywhere. Consequently, the schools hardly kept their masters and the masters were only able to keep their schools by undertaking ministerial work as well. Institutions were kept apart by the hardening of religious differences and the accommodation which was earlier seen at Carmarthen and Llwyn-llwyd, which were attended by students from every denomination, diminished. Carmarthen came to be identified with advanced, even heretical theological views which also bred a radical outlook in politics. It is significant that many of the radical leaders at the end of the eighteenth century were members of Old Dissenting sects and had been in attendance at academies, notably Carmarthen. It is doubtful whether the Welsh academies reached the standards of the best in England, like Warrington, but then their circumstances were very different.

The achievement of the academies must be measured against the difficulties which they encountered. It is evident that many entrants were ill-prepared to embark on secondary or higher education and considering the small number of students the number of misfits was high. Thomas Morgan, a student at Carmarthen, recorded in his diary in 1743 : ' I am very sorry to find that several of my fellow students are not at all disposed to study anything, neither Divinity nor any of the Liberal Arts and Sciences '. These circumstances were bound to depreciate standards and it was not until preparatory schools had come in greater numbers that the situation was somewhat relieved. Language was a major stumbling block. Most of the entrants were habitual Welsh speakers, some of them monoglot, whereas the language in use at the academies was English. It was not until 1796 that realism prevailed when the Presbyterian Board recognised the value of Welsh as a medium of communication when the Carmarthen Academy was reconstituted under David Peter.

The academies and their attendant schools gave an outlet to the pedagogic prowess of some remarkable men, some of them, undoubtedly, the best of their day. Several became masters of English academies such as Shrewsbury, Oswestry and Tewkesbury, which attracted many students also from Wales. The academic standing of the early masters was higher than that of later ones since many of them were University graduates who had been ordained during the Interregnum. By the eighteenth century the academies were obliged to recruit their teachers from amongst their own products. The fact that they were not graduates signifies nothing in the eighteenth-century context but even so the academies also varied considerably in their standards. Many masterships were held in conjunction with the pastorate of a Dissenting cause. Thomas Perrot, who served in both capacities, was the first to receive a salary for his teaching as distinct from his pastorate from the Presbyterian Board in 1725. There was an unmistakable decline in the social origin of the teachers since the early Dissenters were often people of substance and had a standing in their locality. Rees Price of Ty'nton belonged to the minor gentry of Glamorgan and gentry like the Mansels did not consider it beneath their dignity to send their sons to the early academies.

SUGGESTED READING

F. A. Cavanagh, *The life and work of Griffith Jones of Llanddowror*, Cardiff, 1930.
Faculty of Education, University College, Swansea, *Pioneers of Welsh Education*.
D. M. Griffiths, *Nationality and the Sunday School Movement*, Bangor, 1925.
T. Kelly, *Griffith Jones, Llanddowror*, Cardiff, 1950.
R. A. Pritchard, *Thomas Charles*, Cardiff, 1955.
W. M. Williams, *The friends of Griffith Jones*, *Y Cymmrodor*, 1939.
——, *Selections from Welch Piety*, Cardiff, 1938.

Articles:
H. P. Roberts, 'Nonconformist academies in Wales', *Trans. Cymmr.*, 1928–9.
——, 'Yr academiau Anghydffurfiol', *Y Llenor*, 1936–8.
A. H. Williams, 'The origins of the old endowed grammar schools of Denbighshire', *Trans. Denbs. H.S.*, II, 1953.
G. Williams, 'Welsh circulating schools', *Ch. Q. Rev.*, CLXII, 1961.

8. Agriculture and the Land

PHYSICALLY, Wales can be divided into three regions : (1) the highland area or heartland ; (2) the peripheral area around it ; (3) the ingressive areas with access from the east. These physical factors together with soil conditions and climate have determined the practice of agriculture. Pastoral farming was the dominant feature of the first and second areas during our period, with some elements of it apparent in the third. In the first area one would find mountain farms consisting mainly of rough grazing with some meadowland around the homestead. In the second, the upland farm on the *ffridd* lying between 700 and 1,000 feet given to pasture with a little arable but encroaching on the mountain was typical. In the lowland areas the proportion of arable might be as high as one-third, the rest being mainly meadows for hay. Such a pastoral-dominated economy offered much less scope for change than an arable economy and to describe the change that happened as a ' revolution ' is a misnomer. The advance of change from east to west was slow and its speed rarely exceeded a mile a year. Mixed farming was a feature of the better areas with dairying prominent, the surplus milk going to rear calves whilst farms near a market or port produced butter and cheese. Mrs. Anne Evans who farmed Highmead in the Teifi Valley made from £42 to £112 annually between 1781 and 1796 from the sale of butter and cheese and it was generally reckoned that most tenants could clear their rents in this way. Carmarthen was an important dairy market with merchants resident there and dairy produce left its port in quantity for Bristol and London. Thomas Johnes of Hafod (Cards.) found that he was too remote from a market to produce cheese commercially and people in his situation had to rely on the rearing of store cattle for their livelihood.

The Cattle Trade

Cattle-rearing was still more important than sheep-rearing

in the Welsh economy. Cattle were sold for fattening at from six months to three years to the Midlands, to Leicestershire and Northamptonshire especially and to the southern counties of England. Fairs around London like St. Bartholomew's and Barnet's were their eventual destination and London relied largely upon Wales for its meat. Pembrokeshire sent cattle directly by water to the West Country and Bristol. Some Welsh drovers settled as graziers in Leicestershire and Northamptonshire to reap the profits that could be made from fattening cattle which doubled their value. Some 30,000 beasts passed through Herefordshire alone from the Welsh summer and autumn fairs which is some indication of the volume of the trade.

The *porthmon* (cattle dealer) was thus a key-figure in the economy. Reports about his integrity varied ; he was execrated by Ellis Wynne and Twm o'r Nant as a brawling, dishonest fellow. Dealers had to obtain a licence to trade from Quarter Sessions and only married men could apply, but Cardiganshire J.P.s complained of a number of unlicensed dealers in 1763. Cattle were taken on trust, sold at the distant fairs and the farmer was paid on the dealer's return. Many dealers, however, borrowed money to have capital to trade and it is known that in Denbighshire and Radnorshire the Receiver of the King's taxes lent them money from the revenue and pocketed the profits. Loans were usually short-term and procured on the security of bonds, the dealer paying his debt to the Bank of England or some other London house which was a safeguard against being robbed on his travels. In Llŷn, a partnership of four was reputed to have an annual turn-over of £16,000. With their experience in financial transactions it is not strange that several dealers turned to banking, Banc yr Eidion Du (Black Ox Bank) at Llandovery, and Banc y Ddafad Ddu (Black Sheep Bank) of Aberystwyth and Tregaron originating with them at centres long associated with the cattle and sheep trade. Drovers collected beasts in vast flocks and herds which were driven on the hoof to their destination along trackways often known as ' Welsh way '. Adam Smith noted that ' live cattle are perhaps the only commodity of which transportation is more expensive by sea than land '.

Enclosures

By the eighteenth century much of the lowland was already gathered into compact farms. It cannot be ascertained how widespread strip farming in the open field was outside the Norman-occupied lands of the Vale of Glamorgan and Pembrokeshire where the nucleated village also appeared. Its survival was also noted in parts of Wales where its origin was more likely to be Welsh than Norman as at Llan-non in Cardiganshire. Partial consolidation of such holdings had taken place but the process was still in operation and not complete by the end of our period. Though consolidation of strips was a less conspicuous feature of the enclosure movement in Wales than in England there are instances, as at Tre-grug (Mon). where parliamentary Acts were used for the purpose of redistribution of strips. Redistribution by private agreement was more common and evidence survives in estate plans as at Fonmon manor in Glamorgan.

The traditional Welsh pattern was more diffuse with dispersed farms being a feature of the landscape with an occasional hamlet. The process of enclosing had affected the arable areas first and foremost since vast areas of pastoral and marginal land remained unenclosed, half of Cardiganshire being described as ' champion ' till the 1790s. The main impetus to enclosure was the greater profitability from higher food prices. Even before the outbreak of war in 1793 our production of corn was barely sufficient for our own needs and bad harvests between 1795 and 1800 and 1808 and 1812 caused the government to fear that the country might be faced with starvation. The result was inflated prices and although the price of corn was generally lower in Wales than in England, it was sufficiently high to be a strong incentive to cultivate more, especially in the richer farming areas where wheat was grown, though marginal land was also put under the plough that had never been cultivated before. The price of meat did not rise as much as the price of corn and so the incentive for pastoral enclosure was not as great. The most compulsive reason for enclosure was population pressure since the population of rural areas had been increasing at only a slightly lower rate than that of urban areas. The shortage of land to go round caused people to settle on the marginal land, and the *hafod* or *lluest* which had been the summer home of that part of the family which moved to the hills with their cattle and sheep came into occupation all the year round. Even so, the increase of the agricultural area did not relieve the pressure on the land.

Welsh farming units were small and it is not strange that this should have led to engrossing by which several farms were joined to form a larger unit. This process affected rented farms more than freeholds since it was the deliberate policy of some landlords. This was often accomplished simply by letting more than one farm to a single tenant and as early as 1815 Gwallter Mechain (Rev. Walter Davies) forecast the probable social effects of a dearth of farms, one result of which was late marriages. Contrary to his notion, the larger farms were usually the lowland farms where engrossing had taken place, not the upland farms.

The commonable waste which was largely unenclosed down to 1800 came to be divided up into compact farms which were outliers of lowland farms and even became independent units. The process was achieved by dividing the common between those farmers who had rights of grazing upon it, farmers usually taking the part of the common on which their animals had traditionally grazed. The small farmer often received so little land by an enclosure award that it was scarcely worth the expense of enclosure nor did it adequately compensate for loss of common rights especially when he was left to rely entirely on his own holding. Since common rights were attached to farms in the parish and since they could be converted into holdings, lords of the manor and farmers in courts leet strenuously opposed squatting on the common. It was in the eighteenth century that the *tŷ un nos* (one night house) enters into folk-lore the traditional belief being that if a person could erect a house on the common overnight with smoke pouring out of its chimney in the morning this established a claim to occupation. The Crown began to assail squatters in Cardiganshire before the end of the eighteenth century and lords of the manor, like Sir W. W. Wynn in Arwystli, did likewise. The same lords who resisted the encroachment of squatters encouraged their own tenants to take in parts of the mountain into their farms by extending their boundaries. The enclosure commissioners dealt with the problem of squatters by acknowledging occupa-

tion for 21 years as constituting a claim otherwise their land
was apportioned with the open land. Cottages also lost rights
of fuel on the common although sometimes a turbary was set
aside in some Acts.

Most eighteenth century enclosures were effected by private
Acts of Parliament, the first in 1733, but by 1795 only 13 had
been passed involving some 28,596 acres, mostly in border
counties. Between 1801 and 1815, 76 Acts were introduced
involving some 200,000 acres, but some of these Acts were
retrospective and some were never fully implemented. They
dealt in the main with commonable waste rather than arable
and typical of the enclosures of the Napoleonic era were the
ffriddoedd lying between 700 and 1,000 feet on the upland
fringes. One instance is Fforest Fawr in Brecknockshire where
about 40,000 acres were enclosed under an Act of 1808. The
prominence of the marginal land in these enclosures rather
confirms that the lowland areas had already been enclosed.
Marshes, like Traeth Mawr between Caernarfonshire and
Merionethshire were recovered from the sea and though some
reclaimed marshes were capable of improvement in general
they were areas of low productivity and as the Land Commission Report of 1896 pointed out the expressed intention of
improving the land was not always borne out.

The consent of the owners of 2/3rds to 4/5ths usually of the
acreage of a parish had to be given before an Act could be
proceeded with. Where an estate owned much of the land the
consent of the landlord and the tithe impropriator was often
all that was necessary. A Bill was rarely opposed by a parliament of landowners and interested parties often sat on its
committee stage. Commissioners were named in the Act and
they were paid £3 a day to do the necessary work and so were
not disposed to hurry matters. Few of them were Welsh and
most were stewards of local estates who had the necessary
expertise in surveying. They were naturally biased in favour
of landowners but there is little evidence that they made
unjust awards since they were generally careful towards
legitimate claims. The claims of persons who held by custom-
ary right rather than by legal title might be over-ridden and
where claims were unproven the presumption went in favour
of the lord of the manor. The land was surveyed preliminary

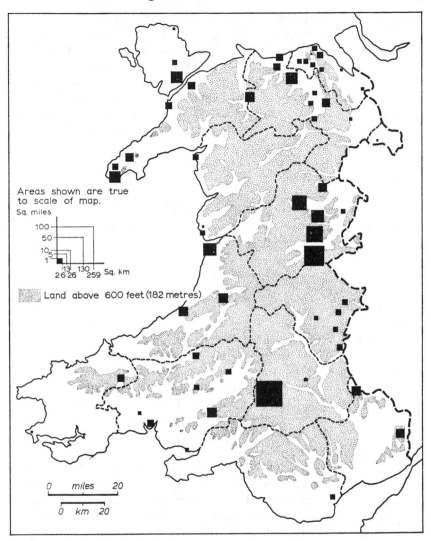

Areas shown are true
to scale of map.
Sq. miles

100
50
10
5
1
|13 130
2·6 26 259 Sq. km

Land above 600 feet (182 metres)

0 miles 20

0 km 20

FIGURE 2

ENCLOSURES AUTHORIZED BY ACT OF PARLIAMENT, 1793–1815

(Source: I. Bowen, The great enclosures of common lands in Wales, London 1914)

(Map by kind permission of Professor David Thomas and Mr. Christopher Lewis)

to an award and some of it might be sold to defray costs which thus fell more lightly on the beneficiaries ; in some instances tithes were also redeemed. The legal costs and costs of enclosing have been estimated to average about 25*s.* an acre in England but there are several instances where this was exceeded in Wales. Objections might be made to Quarter Sessions but these were usually futile and where an award was as unpopular as that relating to Mynydd Bach (Cards.) in 1812 resort to force was not uncommon.

Whilst many of the lesser gentry had gone down in the social scale because of adverse conditions at the end of the seventeenth century the greater gentry enlarged their estates on an unparalleled scale. Some capital was spent by them to buy land in order to achieve more compact estates and some landowners even exchanged land to their mutual advantage as was done between the Hafod and Trawsgoed estates in Cardiganshire. Marriages were used for the purpose of family aggrandisement, the Wynnstay family thus acquiring estates in most of the counties of North Wales. Estates which devolved upon heiresses often suffered eclipse if an heiress married into a greater landed family, often English, as happened on successive occasions in Merionethshire. Landowners were the principal beneficiaries from parliamentary enclosures as well and they encouraged, even pressurised their tenants to enclose open land adjoining their farms. Along with an increase in acreage went an increase in their rentals especially in conditions of wartime inflation. The increase in rents of some Welsh estates was less than the national average increase of 90% whilst in other cases it trebled as it did on the Trawsgoed estate. Landlords were able to meet rising costs by putting up rents where farms were let on annual tenancies but less quickly where they were let on leases. Some estates were encumbered with heavy mortgages to which eighteenth century landlords had had increasing resort and settlements on various members of a family could prove a heavy drain.

Rents were the most important source of landed income, estates being regarded as units of ownership rather than units of production ; complaints of rack-renting were already being made before the end of our period. Rents hardly ever came down even when farming was depressed, landlords preferring to give rebates or extended credit rather than lower rents. Leases were longer and more readily granted in the South than in the North but tenants thereby often had to undertake obligations that fell on landlords elsewhere especially in regard to buildings ; leases also tended to perpetuate antiquated customs like heriot. After 1790 the number of annual tenancies increased especially in the North whereas in other parts 21 year leases were regarded as the happy medium which gave tenants sufficient stability to encourage them to improve their holdings.

Improvements

Wales had a fair number of ' spirited proprietors ' who provided the impetus for whatever improvements that did occur. Some kept home farms to provide the necessities of their household and these were often run on progressive lines as model farms in the hope that it would lead tenants to emulate them. Thomas Johnes of Hafod, author of *A Cardiganshire Landlord's advice to his Tenants* was in touch with the new husbandry through contacts with persons like Arthur Young and the Scotsman, Dr. James Anderson. The improvement of grassland was one of the major preoccupations since only thus could sufficient fodder be raised to increase stock-rearing. Edward Corbet of Ynysymaengwyn drained and improved marshland at Tywyn (Mer.) which enabled him to let the land at between 30*s.* and 40*s.* an acre instead of 9*d.* as hitherto.

Crop husbandry was given almost entirely to cereal growing which, through constant repetition, impoverished the soil. The type of cereal was determined by farming conditions, wheat in the most-favoured areas, rye in the poorest ; this was also reflected in the diet of the population. Yields were generally poor but bad harvests brought matters to a crisis in the years 1798-1800. This caused the Board of Agriculture to institute inquiries throughout the country which left us some valuable contemporary Reports on the state of agriculture. It appears that the potato was the only root crop commonly grown and its acreage was increasing by 1815 because it became a major item of the poor's diet. The introduction of a four-year rotation on the ' Norfolk ' model of turnips, barley, clover and wheat was restricted mainly to the ingressive areas where clover and turnips had been introduced and even there turnip cultivation did not exceed 5% of the arable acreage. Improvements in animal husbandry were also the work of progressive land-owners who had the capital to buy pedigree stock which gradually improved the animals bred by their tenants as well. Improvement of stock was one of the reasons which made enclosures necessary. Thomas Johnes was in correspondence with prominent English breeders like Collings and Bakewell and was responsible for the appearance of merino sheep in Wales. Edward Corbet was the foremost cattle-breeder in North Wales and his cross-breeds were as hardy as natives but much heavier ; his sheep fetched 19*s*. against 13*s*. for others while his cows sold at twice the usual price.

The greater economy that was attendant upon drill husbandry was almost unknown in Wales where even a scythe was only to be seen in wheat-growing areas ; threshing was done by flails and winnowing by the wind but threshing machines were beginning to make their appearance by 1815. Thomas Johnes was responsible for introducing the lighter Rotherham plough with curved mould board into his district and variations appeared elsewhere such as the Lomax plough which had arrived in North Wales by 1800. Local blacksmiths were encouraged by agricultural societies to manufacture ploughs suited to the needs of their areas. Provision was made in some enclosure acts for the construction of roads, and wheeled carts came increasingly to replace sleds and pack-horses. The horse made its appearance in farm-work earlier in the North than in the South where oxen continued in use for ploughing into the nineteenth century.

Labour was abundant in rural areas so wages remained low even during the French Wars, 11*d*. to 1*s*. being common in North Wales where there was little competition for labour ; this was a strong disincentive for investment and improvement. More and more labourers became entirely dependent on wages which fell far behind prices and caused great destitution. Mobility of labour was usually confined to short distances and farmers were careful not to employ outsiders for a full year as this would entitle them to a settlement within the parish. Neighbourhood groups working co-operatively provided the extra labour needed for shearing and threshing whilst extra help at harvest time could be had from cottagers who repaid

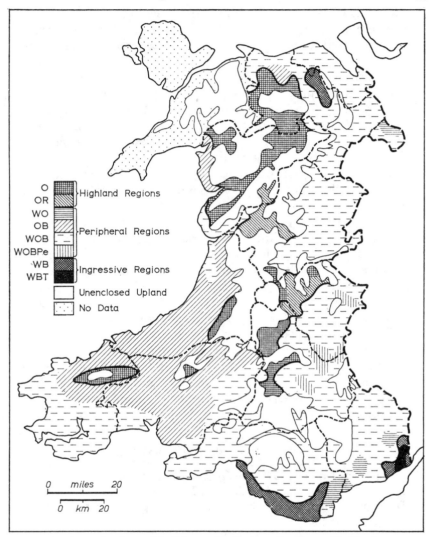

O: Oats; R: Rye; W: Wheat; B: Barley; Pe: Peas; T: Turnips

FIGURE 3

CROP COMBINATION REGIONS, 1801

(Source: P.R.O., H.O.67, 1·6, 12–13, 21–2)

(Map by kind permission of Professor David Thomas & Mr. Christopher Lewis)

any obligations to a farmer by harvest service. In the wheat-growing areas of the Vale of Glamorgan the more prosperous farmers hired seasonal gangs from as far afield as Cardiganshire.

Agricultural societies were formed by progressive landowners for the purpose of furthering scientific agriculture. The Brecknockshire Society was the first, founded in 1755, followed by that of Glamorgan in 1772 and those of Cardiganshire and Pembrokeshire in 1784. They awarded premiums to farmers for growing new crops like turnips and held competitions to encourage craftsmanship in ploughing and hedging. Experiment was their keynote in a frontal attack on tradition and reaction.

The landlords were the principal benefactors from enclosure but the benefits declined proportionately down the farming scale. Large farmers in the better areas profited from higher grain prices but these had to be offset against higher rents. The introduction of commercial methods by estate agents or stewards drew complaints before the end of our period, protests against the Wynnstay stewards being voiced at Llangadfan (Monts.) at least half a century before Samuel Roberts raised a protest at nearby Llanbryn-mair. Protests were also voiced in the ballads of the period and it is no wonder that outbreaks of violence were common after 1790 particularly in areas like Cardiganshire and Caernarfonshire where commons enclosure had proceeded far.

SUGGESTED READING

D. Jenkins, *Thomas Johnes o'r Hafod*, Cardiff, 1948.
P. G. Hughes, *Wales and the Drovers*, London, 1943.
D. Thomas, *Agriculture in Wales during the Napoleonic Wars*, Cardiff, 1963.
D. Thomas, *Cau'r tiroedd comin*, Lerpwl, 1953.

Articles:
D. Baker, 'An eighteenth century drover', *J. Mer. H. and R. S.*, VI, 1972.
B. G. Charles, 'The Highmead dairy, 1778–97', *Ceredigion*, V, 1964.
M. Davies, 'Field patterns in the Vale of Glamorgan', *Trans. Car. Nat. Soc.*, LXXXIV, 1954–5.

A. H. Dodd, 'The enclosure movement in North Wales', *B.B.C.S.*, III, 1926.

H. Edmunds, 'History of the Brecknockshire Agricultural Society', *Brycheiniog*, II, 1956.

G. E. Fussell, 'Glamorgan farming,' *Morgannwg*, I, 1957.

D. W. Howell, 'The economy of the landed estates of Pembrokeshire', *W.H.R.*, III, 1967.

J. M. Howells, 'The Crosswood Estate, 1647–1947', *Ceredigion*, III, 1956.

W. Linnard, 'Thomas Johnes of Hafod—Pioneer of afforestation', *Ceredigion*, VI, 1970.

W. B. Minchinton, 'The Agricultural returns of 1800 for Wales', *B.B.C.S.*, I, 1964.

O. Parry, 'The financing of the Welsh cattle trade', *B.B.C.S.*, VIII, 1935.

C. Thomas, 'The Corsygedol estate during the Age of Improvement', *J. Mer. H. and R. S.*, VI, 1971.

——, 'Merioneth estates, 1790–1850', *ibid.*, V, 1967.

D. Thomas, 'Arthur Young in Wales', *B.B.C.S.*, XX, 1964.

H. M. Thomas, 'Margam estate management', *Glam. Hist.*, VI.

J

9. Economic Developments

THOUGH the eighteenth century witnessed an unparalleled economic growth which is usually described as the ' Industrial Revolution ', it should be borne in mind that industrial development had been gradually proceeding since at least the sixteenth century. After 1760, however, growth was more pronounced in both speed and extent though we should remember that the great expansion still had to await the nineteenth century. Developments in Wales mainly occurred in the metal industries, coal and slate as landlords hastened to exploit the resources of their estates. There was no comparable development in textiles to what occurred in the North of England. Economic growth was made possible by the expansion not only of the domestic market through the development of transport and communications but also of overseas trade. Another important factor was the attraction to Wales of entrepreneurs, mainly from England, who brought both capital and technology, though native entrepreneurs were by no means inconspicuous. Early industry had been sufficiently diffuse as not to leave many marks on the landscape but eighteenth-century developments made for greater concentration, urbanisation and even pollution. For the purpose of simplification, industrial development has been discussed under the headings of different industries though one should bear in mind that many of the developments referred to were contemporaneous and were often interrelated.

The Lead Industry
Lead mining which had received a boost in Queen Elizabeth's reign virtually came to a standstill during the Civil War but activities were resumed at certain centres soon after 1660. The resumption of the Mines Royal monopoly in 1660 aroused a great deal of opposition from landowners and the Society was subjected to a great deal of harassment. In 1688, the Society of Mines Royal and the Mineral and Battery Works combined

and formed a subsidiary company to work the mines of Cardiganshire and Merioneth. Cardiganshire was more exploited by the monopoly company than Flintshire because its ore was rich in silver. A rich find was made at Esgair-hir in 1690, and in 1693, Sir Carbery Pryse of Gogerddan fought a test case against the Crown to determine a landowner's right to work minerals on his own property and obtained a favourable verdict. Parliament, which was always sensitive to the rights of property, brought in an Act in 1693 which empowered landowners henceforth to exploit their own minerals provided precious minerals were made available to the Crown. Sir Carbery was unable to exploit his success personally and so formed a company ; henceforth this became the more usual form of proceeding rather than by private development. At his death in 1694 his shares were purchased for £14,000 by Sir Humphrey Mackworth whose Mine Adventurers are regarded as an important stage in modern company development. It was a joint-stock company raising capital by selling bonds although Mackworth's methods had many of the elements of a lottery. Its shares were advertised in London and a glowing prospectus was issued which led to great public speculation and an attack on stock-jobbers by Defoe. Raising money was a problem in such a remote place and Mackworth attempted to solve it by setting up a local bank until the government put a veto on bills of credit by private banks. The Company was beset by other difficulties as well, having to provide accommodation and food for the workmen and a school for the children. In 1708, a House of Commons inquiry was instituted into the Company's affairs and Mackworth was found guilty of ' notorious and scandalous frauds ' which reduced the Company's activities considerably after 1710.

Speculation revived in the thirties, a rich vein being found at Darren Fawr in 1731 which was worked by a Flintshire company. The Cwmsymlog silver lode was rediscovered and the frenzy of speculation led some landlords to encroach on Crown lands so that the Crown was obliged in 1746 to appoint a steward to safeguard its own and in 1752 Lewis Morris was appointed as his deputy. There ensued a long battle between local landowners and Crown officials which culminated in an attack by a hired mob on Esgair-mwyn, a rich mine which

Morris worked for the Crown, Morris being taken prisoner and held in Cardigan goal for six weeks. There ensued a long wrangle over his stewardship and by political jobbery the lease of the mine was granted to Lord Powis. Chauncey Townsend, a Swansea industrialist, was active in the south of the county working a mine at Llanfair Clydogau which yielded 87 ounces of silver per ton. Thomas Bonsall had much success in working the Nanteos leases till the French Revolutionary War virtually brought activities to a standstill in Cardiganshire.

Flintshire was a centre of comparable importance and there some of the landed gentry, Grosvenors, Mostyns, Hanmers, Pennants, augmented their family fortunes through lead-mining. Several rich mines were developed around Halkyn Mountain where mining costs were lower than in Cardiganshire and easy access to Dee ports reduced transport costs. From about 1702, the Quaker Company, one of the most reputable in the business, acquired control over about twenty mines which were efficiently managed with a view to long-term development. The Company had its own smeltery at Gadlys and between 1703 and 1744 sent 430,604 ounces of silver from there to the Royal Mint. Activities declined as the century wore on but the Company was still active down to 1792. Sir George Wynne of Leeswood made a lucky strike at Halkyn in 1728 which made his fortune whilst the Prince Patrick mine is reputed to have yielded a million pounds in thirty years. 'The process of extracting lead from flint', it was reported, 'has turned out so profitable as to create a baronet (Wynne), give rise to esquires, and add grandeur to the equipages of noblemen'. Although activity in Flintshire was curtailed after 1792 the recession was not as serious as in Cardiganshire and in 1812 Grosvenor made another lucky strike on Halkyn Mountain when so many others were lapsing into bankruptcy.

Mining in Denbighshire was centred on Minera where there was a great influx of Cornish and Irish miners in the 1740s. In 1761 a rich find was made there and another at Llanferres in 1762. The Myddeltons were most prominent among county families engaged in mining. John Wilkinson, the ironmaster, extended his interests by acquiring control of Minera in 1783. He tried to weather the French Wars by manufacturing lead pipes but mounting stocks caused him to desist. Transport costs militated against developments in Montgomeryshire in the eighteenth century but following an important find at Llangynog in 1692 a mine was successfully worked there which passed into the control of the Powis family in 1725. Mining was started at Dylife also after 1770. Small mines were opened in Caernarfonshire at Llanengan and Penrhyn-du in Llŷn and at Llanrwst and Penmachno but the yield was not considerable. Merioneth attracted an unusual speculator in the Englishwoman, Elizabeth Baker, and mining was attempted at Llanfrothen, Llanelltud and between Tywyn and Machynlleth. The Rhandir-mwyn level in Carmarthenshire proved a lucrative source for the Cawdor family who established a smeltery at Carmarthen to process its output. Llantrisant mine in Glamorgan which came into the hands of the Bute family in 1770 at one time employed over 500 men. Lead mining was thus widespread but the chief centres were Cardiganshire and Flintshire.

Under-capitalisation was a recurring weakness in the industry. In the post-monopoly period capital was provided mainly by landowners who acquired it from agriculture or from rents. But there was seldom enough for extended operations and they looked to a quick return on their outlay hoping for a lucky find to make the undertaking self-financing. Technical difficulties and unstable prices often meant that the gentry could not hold out for long and operations were frequently suspended giving the industry a very chequered history. So, landlords had to change their policy, and many of them turned to leasing out their mineral rights in return for royalties on the ore raised. One-tenth was considered a normal royalty but one-seventh might be demanded if prospects were bright. It did not pay to drive too hard a bargain as lessees might react by looking for short-term gains instead of ploughing back profits to provide more capital. Most of the mining companies came from England especially the North and in several instances their managers who supplied the technical skills set up on their own. The Quaker Co. which operated in Flintshire was one of the best organised in the business, investing in long-term development and even in research. Some firms, like the Quaker Co., had their own smelteries and profits from smelting were often put into mining ; the Flintshire smelters did so in Cardiganshire. There was always a number of small men on the fringe of the industry who obtained ' take-notes ' from landlords and worked a mine on a partnership basis, paying royalties. This was usually a sign of prosperity in Flintshire but the contrary was the case in Cardiganshire.

The industry provided employment for a great number of people but many were also partly engaged in agriculture which had the effect of depressing wages, since workers were not wholly dependent on them. Skilled labour had to be imported mainly from the North of England at first and later from Cornwall. Skilled men were often bound to their employers by long-term contracts until a sufficient pool of skill was built up with local labour. The work was often hard and unattractive and Mackworth was obliged to hire convicts to meet his labour needs. Immigrant labour was usually mobile and went where work was available but English settlement in Denbigh and Flint had a marked anglicising effect on communities. This was not as apparent in Cardiganshire since much of its outside work-force came from Flint. When the lead industry declined at the end of the century many miners left it for the iron mines. Managerial positions were almost invariably held by Englishmen.

Wages in the industry were low because there was little competition for labour except in the north-east where higher wages might be got. Elsewhere 1s. a day was a common wage for a miner and 6d. for a labourer around 1700, rising in summer to about 14d. to keep miners from absenting themselves at harvest time. Piece-work was general and short-term contracts were made with the men so that they could be adjusted if too advantageous. A weekly subsistence was paid with a final reckoning about every six weeks by which time miners who had a bad bargain might be in the Company's debt for candles and gunpowder. Women and children were hired to pick ore, the former at 6d.—9d. a day, the latter at 4d.—8d. . The Quaker Co. was exceptional in relating wages to the cost of living ; it was more usual to tie them to the price of lead. Conditions of work were generally bad ; mines were badly ventilated because, in the absence of gas, companies spent little on it. Flooding also frustrated mining and in

Flintshire it was often complained that there was too much water down below and too little above where it would be useful for washing ore and driving mills. Shift work of no more than eight or even fewer hours was imperative in such unhealthy conditions which reduced life expectancy to around forty. In remote places the miners had to live in barracks going home only at week-ends. They were dependent on truck-shops for supplies and some masters like Thomas Bonsall in Cardiganshire were accused of exploitation. The Mine Adventurers were singular in having a welfare scheme but it is doubtful if it was ever effective. Unemployment was endemic as trade fluctuations were recurrent.

Improved techniques like the use of adits for drainage made developments possible in the seventeenth century but put up mining costs. Pumps operated by hand or by horse gins and later by water power had to be used for draining deep mines. Steam engines were early in use in Flintshire, Newcomen's engine being erected at Hawarden soon after 1712 and the Quaker Co. installed one at Trelogan in 1731 but their extravagant consumption of coal added to costs. John Wilkinson installed Watt-Boulton engines, for which he made cylinders, at Minera in 1783 and afterwards at Mold. Flint and Denbigh could exploit their coal resources but Cardiganshire was dependent on water power for which long and expensive leats had to be constructed. Great improvements were also made in smelting methods which were very crude before 1700 and far behind Dutch practice. The coal-fired reverberatory furnace was introduced at Neath by Mackworth and in Flintshire by Dr. Edward Wright. Mackworth also converted the charcoal-burning furnaces on the River Dyfi to coal which was brought as ballast in ore-ships returning from Neath. The introduction of Lyddall's patent in Flintshire increased the yield of silver from the ore and in the case of Cwmsymlog ore the yield was raised to 65 oz. a ton. Cardiganshire, lacking the advantages of Flint, sent its ore first to Neath and then to Swansea. The acquisition of Cardiganshire mines by Flintshire smelters diverted supplies to centres at Holywell, Mostyn and Mold which had access to Dee ports and the coalfield. Smelting outpaced mining in Flintshire; hence the need for securing Cardiganshire supplies.

The industry was beset by transport difficulties because many mines were so remote. Wheeled transport only came into use instead of mules and pack-horses in Cardiganshire after 1760. The use of carts caused rutting of roads whose repair added to expenditure. It was difficult to get carriers at all at certain times of year and some landlords like Lord Powis made it obligatory for tenants to do carriage service in their agreements. Navigable rivers were used where available, the Dyfi, Conwy, Dee and Severn being so used. Sir Humphrey Mackworth deepened the River Nedd and cut a canal from it to his works. Sea transport was cheapest ; it was reckoned that it cost 5s. a ton to transport ore six miles from Esgair-hir to the River Dyfi whereas it could be carried from Dyfi to Neath by sea for 1s. a ton.

The availability of markets and good prices were incentive factors in development. Prices rose after 1660 and by 1750 even poor ore fetched £11 a ton, the best £24. Local needs were usually the first call on production but the great expansion of the domestic market is a feature of the eighteenth-century economy, with Bristol and London becoming important markets for lead. Cardiganshire depended on Swansea smelters and Bristol merchants for an outlet for its product since it did not develop direct overseas trade. Flint and Denbigh traded with Chester merchants and lead exports from the port of Chester came mainly from these sources. Ancillary industries became increasingly important in the profitability of the industry ; calamine, for instance, which was worked in connection with lead, being used for brass-making and some of the leading brass manufacturers were attracted to Holywell for this reason. These ancillary developments helped the lead industry in Flintshire in the harsh trading conditions of the end of the century. The United States embargo of 1780 hit the trade badly but not as much as the French Revolutionary War when prices fell to £8 a ton at a time when costs were rapidly rising. The Berlin and Milan Decrees virtually closed continental markets and led to the closing of mines with low output and high costs leaving only a few survivors in the more favourably-placed areas.

The Copper Industry
The copper industry was the most important of the metal

industries in Wales until it was superseded by iron. Although this had happened by the end of our period the Welsh iron industry did not assume the same degree of importance in world trade as the Welsh copper industry had done. It reached its zenith before the end of the eighteenth century but there was a long aftermath during which some parts of the Welsh copper industry remained important. The mining and smelting of copper were really two separate activities and although inter-connected, the smelting part of the industry tended to become more and more independent of the Welsh copper miners.

The Acts of 1689 and 1693 which ended the monopoly of the two Elizabethan mining societies gave a boost to the industry but because copper was not found as often or in the same quantities as lead it did not give rise to the same prospecting mania. It was sometimes found in conjunction with lead as at Esgair-fraith, Goginan and Cwmystwyth in Cardiganshire on which Neath depended in its early days. The only big copper find was made on Parys Mountain which was big enough to need capital beyond the means of private developers. In 1761, the old Roman workings were re-discovered on the eastern side of the mountain on Sir Nicholas Bayly's land ; copper was also found on the western side which was held on a joint lease by Bayly and William Lewis of Llysdulas. Bayly already owned a mine at Penrhyn-du in Llŷn which he leased along with his interest in Parys Mountain to a Macclesfield Company. In 1768, the great find was made ; a dispute between Bayly and his co-tenant, the Rev. Edward Hughes, who had married the Llysdulas heiress, led to a protracted lawsuit in which Thomas Williams, a Llanidan solicitor, acted for Hughes. He not only mastered the case but also gained an insight into the working of the industry and entered into partnership with the Rev. Edward Hughes and John Dawes to form the Parys Mine Co. . The death of Sir Nicholas Bayly led his successor Lord Uxbridge to terminate the Macclesfield Co.'s lease and to found the Mona Mine Co. with Thomas Williams who was also appointed manager.

Until then the copper industry had been dominated by Cornwall and, inasmuch as the Cornish master-smelters were fewer in number than the mine-owners, they were able to dictate terms. In the 1770s, Anglesey began to bid for a share in the market and Thomas Williams had to do battle with the Associated Smelters who were hand-in-glove with the Cornish miners. He upset the equilibrium of the copper industry and broke Cornish domination by undercutting prices and exploiting the advantage which cheaper production in the newer mines of Anglesey gave over the older Cornish ones. The Cornish smelters had to come to terms and an agreement was reached to share the home-market between them and to adopt a common pricing policy. The monopoly of the Associated Smelters over the Cornish mines was broken and he marketed their product on a commission basis, thus establishing by 1788 a virtual monopoly of the supply of copper to the market. The years 1788-92 were the heyday of his power and they coincided with peak production in Anglesey mines. In 1799, Williams admitted that he controlled capital to the extent of £800,000. Thereafter, Williams's fortunes waned as Anglesey production diminished, the decline of the Parys mine being more serious than that of the Mona.

It has been asserted that Williams acquired a monopoly over Cornish marketing in order to bolster his declining fortunes in Anglesey, but the opposite is the case since the Cornish miners were not slow in reading the signs of the times and abrogated their agreement, returning to a free market in which, with their production increasing, fortune was on their side in contrast with Anglesey. Wales's share of Britain's output of 7,500 to 8,000 tons a year was about 3,000 tons in the mid-eighties ; by 1799 it had declined to about 1,000 tons. Production at the Mona Mine reflects the situation in Anglesey :

| 1792—1,058 tons | 1797—800 + tons | 1799—484 tons |
| 1793— 823 tons | 1798—716 tons | |

Britain's output was still increasing, the Anglesey short-fall being made up by Cornish production. The Mona Mine had been borrowing capital instead of ploughing back profits with Lord Uxbridge drawing over £2,000 in duty ore alone in 1789. In 1811, he let the mine to a company of which he remained a partner. The association of the Williams family with the industry in Anglesey ended with the death of Thomas Williams in 1802. He had been a unique entrepreneur in his time since no one had ever acquired such control over a single industry as he did which gave Wales a dominant place in the world copper market. He also diversified his interests over mining, smelting, manufacturing and chemicals. He was undoubtedly a monopolist and was accused by rival interests of exploiting his power, accusations which arose because Williams had successfully attacked their own monopoly. Wales's part in copper-mining diminished after 1800 although smaller mines were being worked at Drws-y-coed, Llanberis, Aberglaslyn, Tremadoc and the Great Orme at Llandudno.

Copper smelting became a separate industry which by the end of the eighteenth century was coming to rely less and less on the production of Welsh mines. Neath developed as an early centre under Sir Humphrey Mackworth who carried on smelting and refining at Melincryddan, receiving its ore mainly from Cardiganshire. From 1684, Mackworth was using coal for smelting, a supply of which and of clay for furnaces was found locally. Neath was equally well-placed to receive ore from Cornwall but Swansea developed as a rival and eventually eclipsed Neath. In 1717, Dr. Lane started smelting at Llangyfelach outside Swansea and in 1727 the work was taken over by Robert Morris who gave its name to Morriston ; after 1727, the White Rock works were also in operation under Lockwood and Co.. Swansea, like Neath, had plentiful supplies of coal available and it was soon apparent to the Cornish mineowners that a saving of about 40% could be made by smelting at Swansea rather than carry coal to Cornwall. The ore-ships on their return from Swansea carried coal as ballast which was in increasing demand for driving steam pumps. Chauncey Townsend erected new plants at the Middle and Upper Bank Works which helped to make Swansea's share of copper output the largest in the world. In 1750, it was producing about 50% of Britain's copper needs, by 1799, 90%. Brass was also manufactured and Swansea assumed the place which Bristol had formerly held in copper and brass manufacture. Thomas Williams acquired control of the Upper and Middle Bank Works and diverted some of the Anglesey supply there. The expansion of the industry at Neath and Swansea occurred partly because the burgesses were not as concerned about pollution as Liverpool which caused companies like the Roe

Co. to move out and settle at Neath, although Robert Morris was obliged to go outside the borough to Morriston to set up his works.

The Parys Co. set up furnaces at Amlwch but for roasting ore rather than smelting so that transport costs could be cut. Most of the Mona product went to St. Helen's (Lancs.) and the Parys Co. built furnaces at Ravenhead close to the Sankey Canal and cheap coal and also close enough to exploit the Liverpool slave trade. Thomas Williams entered the copper and brass manufacturing industry which was dominated by Birmingham and Bristol merchants, establishing the Greenfield Copper and Brass Co. at Holywell which catered for the Navy and also produced green vitriol and sulphur which gave an impetus to the chemical industry there. He made an agreement with Mathew Boulton and the Cornish copper interests to open joint warehouses at London, Liverpool and Birmingham and to take advantage of the great increase in demand and diversification of use. Williams had to do battle with the established merchants which was reminiscent of his fight against Associated Smelters and in order to clear his name of allegations made against him obtained a parliamentary commission of inquiry before which he testified. It became clear that the merchants' complaints were attributable to a falling-off of trade in wartime rather than to any restrictive practices Williams indulged in. He had successfully sought Navy contracts against them when ships came to be clad with copper sheathing, an experiment which only succeeded because Williams was able to make copper bolts to secure the sheets for which he obtained a monopoly. Success in this field offset the fall-off in trade during the French Wars ; the East India Co. and the slave-merchants also followed the example of the Navy and Williams secured a substantial part of their trade especially from Liverpool which he supplied from Holywell. In the course of the sixty years after 1750 the Welsh export trade in copper increased seven-fold ; it showed some spurts during the Seven Years and American Wars and a recession at the end of the latter when America threw open its markets. It soon recovered with the growth in naval and industrial demands.

	Wrought	Unwrought	Total
1750	7,056 cwts.	1,690 cwts.	8,746 cwts.
1760	11,918	279	12,197
1770	24,951	—	24,951
1780	34,691	12,599	47,290
1785	29,587	12,332	41,919
1806	46,954	—	46,954
1810	57,366	814	58,180

Welsh copper exports, 1750–1810. (Source: A. H. John,
Industrial Development of South Wales, p. 111)

The copper industry was organised into a few large units and because of their size they drew but little on local sources of capital which came in the main from the copper and brass merchants especially of Bristol and London. Smelting at Swansea was started by Bristol and London merchants and the fact that these firms were well-established and had capital resources enabled them to weather trade recessions although these were fewer than in the lead industry. Thomas Williams set up banks at Chester, Bangor and Caernarfon in order to finance his enterprises.

The mining industry found plenty of labour locally for the semi-skilled tasks of open-cast mining and 1,200 were employed in Anglesey by the 1780s. During the French Wars numbers declined and by 1809 only 600 were at work. The number of smelters employed in Wales increased throughout the century and by 1770 there were 500 at work in Swansea and about 100 in Anglesey. Since skill was needed for smelting, Humphrey Mackworth had been obliged to import technicians who trained local labour and by the end of the century a sufficient pool of skilled labour was available so that migration was confined to short distances such as from Neath to Swansea. Skilled men had to enter into long-term agreements in the early days which might even extend to a lifetime and they were required to swear oaths of secrecy and not to divulge the ' mystery ' of their trade. Long-term contracts lost favour by the end of the century because they restricted mobility and meant that employers had to pay wages at times of trade recession. Wages in mining were only sufficiently high in Anglesey to draw labour away from agriculture and 10*d.* to 14*d.* a day was

average for a miner. While Anglesey miners were earning 8s.
a week in 1791, Cornish miners earned from 7s. 6d. to 10s. 6d. ;
discontent was mounting in the island and broke out in riots
in 1815. Piece-work prevailed in mining, sub-contractors
hiring the labour. Wages of South Wales smelters were lower
than those in Lancashire and this was one reason why some
firms moved there as Roe and Co. did from Liverpool to
Neath. Combinations of labour developed earlier in this
industry in South Wales than in any other and in 1795 smelters
at the Mines Royal Works at Neath successfully struck for
higher wages as did the Birmingham Copper Co.'s workers
at Swansea in 1798. Both the mining and the smelting branches
of the industry were particularly fortunate in being able to
take advantage of sea transport. Amlwch which was no more
than a creek was developed into a small port by improvements
made between 1782 and 1785 and by a parliamentary bill of
1793. The success of Neath and Swansea was in no small part
due to the fact that they were ports within a short distance of
the coal-field.

The iron industry

Iron mining and smelting was widespread in Wales and
furnaces could be found in almost every county to supply local
needs. The industry had moved into south-east Wales from
the Forest of Dean and the well-known family of ironmasters,
the Hanburys, had already arrived in Monmouthshire by
1600. Chepstow, a river port, developed a considerable export
trade. In 1666, the Hirwaun works was opened and by 1700
the Melingriffith furnace had been established outside Cardiff.
These early works needed timber supplies for charcoal smelting
and local poets often complained of the denuding of wooded
valleys. Furnaces had to be portable to follow timber supplies
and this limited their capacity, their average annual output
being around 100-150 tons. They often used inferior iron ore
mined locally, Abraham Darby's furnace at Dôl-gun, near
Dolgellau, being quite typical. Many charcoal-fired furnaces
remained in operation till the end of our period although
superseded by technical advances.

Significant developments were apparent soon after 1700 in
which the Welsh gentry played a prominent part. Charles

Lloyd of Dolobran, a Quaker and friend of Abraham Darby, had already erected a country forge at Mathrafal near his home and acquired control of Bersham works where he un-successfully experimented with Darby's methods between 1700 and 1720. The South Wales gentry were further stimulated by Sir Humphrey Mackworth's example to exploit the re-sources of their estates. The Mansels of Margam owned ironworks and the original lessee of Lord Windsor's land at Dowlais where such spectacular developments were to take place was Thomas Morgan, the squire of Ruperra. Thomas Lewis of Newhouse, Llanishen, and Thomas Price of Watford were among the partnership of nine who formed the original Dowlais Iron Co. in 1759. Social compatibility ensured co-operation in sharing out timber supplies and fixing prices of iron before local fairs. The amount of capital which could be deployed from land was not, however, adequate for post-1750 developments and landowners were relegated to the role of lessors of mineral rights rather than of ironmasters in their own right.

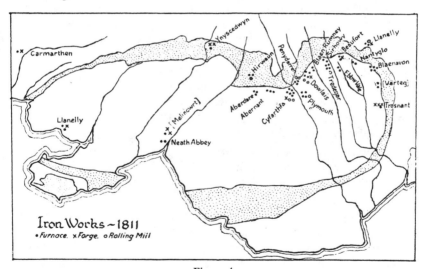

Figure 4

IRON WORKS
1811

(Taken, with permission, from William Rees. *An Historical Atlas of Wales*, Cardiff, 1951)

The entrepreneurs in the industrial phase of development were almost invariably English. Some Welsh landowners formed business partnerships with English capitalists but the role of the capitalist grew in importance whilst that of the landed proprietor diminished. English ironmasters took over some existing forges, Thomas Pratt acquiring the works at Tredegar and Machen in 1732 and Thomas Maybery the Brecon furnace and the Pipton forge in 1753. Thereafter, entrepreneurs were attracted from the old English centres as large-scale developments occurred. From 1753 Bersham began its long association with the Wilkinsons who came from Furness ; in 1759 the Dowlais Iron Co. was formed on the basis of a partnership of nine, many of whom were English merchants; in 1765 Anthony Bacon, a native of Whitehaven, arrived in Merthyr Tydfil to establish the famous Cyfarthfa works which was enlarged in 1767, and in his wake the Homfrays and the Crawshays followed.

The most spectacular developments occurred on the north-eastern rim of the coal-field where iron ore was found along with coal suitable for smelting, building stone for buildings and limestone for lining the furnaces. Works were concentrated within a narrow belt extending from Hirwaun in the west to Blaenafon in the east. Prospectors also met with a readiness on the part of landowners who owned the mineral rights to grant long-term leases at low rents when the future was yet very uncertain. Anthony Bacon paid only £100 rent per annum to Lord Talbot of Hensol for his lease in 1765 but when it came to be renewed there was a sharp increase. Bacon exploited this readiness of landlords to grant leases and acquired leases over land which he sub-let to ironmasters like the Homfrays. The prospect of a long tenure encouraged the lessees to establish large and permanent units and to organise on a long-term basis and by 1815 eight big concerns were established on the north-eastern rim of the coalfield.

Many of the ironmasters were technologists who came to Wales as managers but after a while acquired partnerships and the more thrustful often bought out the other partners as Richard Crawshay did at Cyfarthfa. The connection between entrepreneurship and Dissent has long been established. The brothers John and William Wilkinson were educated at a

Dissenting academy and John came much under the influence of his brother-in-law, Dr. Priestley. There were several Quaker families of ironmasters like the Lloyds of Dolobran who were natives or the Homfrays and Harfords who came from outside, and inter-marriage with English Quaker families was common. The Guests were Wesleyans whilst the Crawshays were among the very few Anglicans. Inter-marriage with the Welsh gentry caused many of the ironmasters to forsake their early religious allegiance as they set up dynasties which rivalled those of the landed class.

The units of production in Wales were large from the start, larger even than Midlands' plants, so requiring more capital. Since there was no money market and little surplus capital to be had in Wales it had to be sought outside and the great inflow of capital is an indicator of the high rate of development. Blaenafon apart, little of this capital originated in the Midlands. Most of it was supplied by Bristol iron merchants and even linen drapers ; out of the nine original Dowlais partners, four came from Bristol and in 1776 Bristol merchants also took over Melingriffith. London was the other main source, Anthony Bacon and the Crawshays, for instance, being active in its trade. Richard Forman, another London merchant, provided capital for Homfray to work the lease on Penydarren. High profits were earned and much of them were ploughed back to increase productive capacity. Thus capitalisation increased spectacularly ; that of Cyfarthfa rose from £14,370 to reach £104,000 by 1798 and £160,000 by 1813. Blaenafon capital amounted to £250,000 by 1816 and that of Tredegar to £100,000 by about the same time ; even the smaller works reached the £100,000 mark. The result was the rapid expansion of the number and productive capacity of units. The personal nature of the capital market was a notable feature, much of the money being raised among relatives and friends. The gentry often provided short-term loans on bonds or mortgages to meet temporary needs which was very useful before banking was developed. They also in some instances opened coalmines to meet the needs of the iron industry as the Wynns and the Myddeltons did in Denbighshire. Otherwise, landed capital was confined after 1750 to providing fixed capital in the form of sites and buildings which were let on lease.

K

The labour supply came from contiguous areas of Glamorgan and Brecknockshire, at first by short-distance migration, and thereafter from the remoter counties of Cardigan, Carmarthen and Pembroke. Much of it was seasonal with rural workers spending up to seven months of the year at the ironworks, returning home for sowing and harvesting. The labour force remained Welsh for some time and Heath Malkin noted that even after 1800 the workmen of Merthyr were mainly Welsh-speaking. Migration from the English border counties to the eastern part of the coalfield was on the increase but settlement thinned out as one moved westward. What labour was drawn from the Midlands was mainly of skilled men especially in foundry work and they were often provided with houses which went with the job. Houses clustered around the works which gave Merthyr Tydfil the appearance of a scatter of villages before the in-filling process began. Iron-masters had to organise food and fodder especially in times of shortage and some set up 'truck' shops, a practice the Crawshays eschewed. When medical facilities were provided they were financed by deductions from wages. English technicians trained a pool of skilled local labour and inasmuch as the works were new there was a quick response to new techniques although they already tended to be labour-intensive.

Ironworks employed labour on a big scale, the work force at Cyfarthfa reaching 1500 probably by 1800 but certainly by 1810. Labour was organised on the sub-contracting method whereby a sub-contractor undertook part or the whole of the process of production, hired and paid his own men in return for an agreed sum on tonnage produced. This was a transitional stage in industrial management but it served the purpose of ironmasters who were primarily merchants rather than in-dustrialists. Mining was also sub-contracted, agreements whereby a contractor agreed to deliver x tons of clean ore at the ore bank over a period of 12-18 months at a sum around 5s. a ton plus bonus being a norm. Skilled labour constituted about 30-40% of the work force which was very high. Smelters, puddlers and forge-men were the élite and often commanded house, firing and drink for special work. Pay was graduated according to skill, a mine-breaker earning about 5s. a week as against 10s. for a founder in the early days. Finermen and hammermen served long apprenticeships and were thereafter tied for a number of years with a view to ensuring a supply of skilled labour or to prevent a works' secrets being taken elsewhere. By 1800, this practice was in decline as the labour force was adequate and masters resented paying men in slack times if they were on long contracts. The number of ancillary workers was also high, upwards of 200 being needed to service a blast furnace. A piece-work system or a time plus bonus system generally operated but labourers were paid by the day, 1*s.* a day being normal in 1756 rising to 2*s.* 6*d.* by 1796. The wages of furnace-keepers ranged between 22*s.* 6*d.* and 27*s.* by 1805 because wages had risen during the French Revolutionary War and were as high as if not higher in South Wales than in the Midlands. Combinations of workmen appeared early in South Wales thé agitation usually starting with the better-paid workmen ; in 1810 the Dowlais puddlers struck for a whole month against reduction of wages. Discontent led to a link-up with the Luddites after 1813 from which time friction between masters and men increased and was aggravated after 1815 by a trade slump.

Large-scale organisation was a feature of the Welsh iron industry from the start of the industrial phase, some works developing into big complexes. Between 1790 and 1800, the Cyfarthfa works with its greater forge capacity absorbed the pig-iron production of Hirwaun, Plymouth and Dowlais as well as its own. Small works were often worked in conjunction with larger ones as Hirwaun was with Cyfarthfa, light work being farmed out to them. After 1800, Dowlais and Plymouth developed their own forges and became more independent. There was a high degree of integration also inasmuch as the ironmasters were owners of coal mines, tramroads, canals and, in some instances, tinplate works to squeeze every possible advantage out of their leases. The management of such large complexes was often unwieldy and as with labour organisation passed through a transitional stage. The Dowlais partnership was jointly responsible for management until John Guest was entrusted with the sole management in 1767 and eventually became a partner and sole owner. Most of the undertakings started as partnerships with each partner receiving his share of production for sale but control usually passed to the more thrustful ones who had an eye to modern managerial techniques. Combinations of masters were not popular in Wales until 1802 when the South Wales Ironmasters Association was formed which held quarterly meetings to discuss prices and matters of common interest.

The developments of the second half of the eighteenth century were only possible because of the great advances made in technology. Darby's method of using coal (1709) for smelting came into general use after 1750 and enabled the industry to settle down and grow in suitable locations. Coke-smelting was used from the beginning at Merthyr and Dowlais where many of the technical advances were made. The Cort process, the most important single invention, was speedily adopted by Crawshay who borrowed some of Cort's workmen to teach his own and from Cyfarthfa the practice spread to Penydarren and elsewhere. It is claimed that a comparable process was being contemporaneously developed by Peter Onions at Merthyr. Whatever, the process was in such general practice by 1790 that it came to be known as the ' Welsh process '. By it, pig-iron could be refined to bar by puddling in a reverberatory furnace and then rolling, with a consequent increase in production of a better quality product with greater economy. There was a succession of minor improvements such as the insertion of an iron floor to the furnace by Homfray instead of sand and better blast-furnace techniques. Successful experiments in engineering led to a great release of industrial productivity especially in connection with steam power. John Wilkinson's new method of cylinder boring not only improved the accuracy of cannon but also helped Watt and Boulton to perfect their steam engine. Wilkinson established a close connection between his Bersham works and Boulton's Soho Works in Birmingham which was interrupted by the discovery that Wilkinson was pirating the patent and building his own engines for his mining ventures. A great increase in the number and capacity of plants was evident by 1815, Cyfarthfa with Hirwaun having 13, Dowlais 12 and Beaufort 11. The capacity of furnaces reached 1,100 to 1,250 tons of pig-iron per annum which was seldom realised, Cyfarthfa's output in 1814 being 9,600 tons. Improvements in smelting spelt the doom of local iron-mines whose ore was inferior; the cost of transporting imported ore from the ports to the works at the head of the valleys in the long run led to their undoing.

With commercial production the industry soon outgrew its local significance when only the surplus of local needs found its way to outside markets like Bristol. The industry was greatly stimulated by the recurring wars of the eighteenth century which created demands for munitions and thereafter created markets in developing colonies. Wilkinson's Bersham Works and Bacon's Cyfarthfa Works were really munitions factories in wartime casting guns and shot under government contract. Bacon also developed commercial contacts with the American colonies and the East India Co. The ironmasters successfully re-deployed their production during the ten-year respite from war after 1783 when the industrial uses of iron were exploited for a variety of purposes such as bridge-building, after the construction of Ironbridge in 1779, or machine-building for the ever-expanding textile trade. Commercial interests dominated the Welsh industry whose output was handled by Bristol and London merchant houses which were always sensitive to changes in the market. The Cyfarthfa management chafed against control by their London house which they found very frustrating in time of booming trade if convenient during a slump. The Crawshays only sold locally or at Bristol if there was a glut on the London market. There was little attempt to contact Midlands manufacturers directly or to establish export contacts except through the trade. The development of ancillary industries like the well-known foundry at Neath Abbey was also neglected, tinplate works being the one exception.

The development of transport facilities was crucial to the industry's success in such remote situations and was taken in hand by the ironmasters. Bacon was the prime mover in improving the road from Merthyr to Cardiff via Caerffili in 1767 ; the Crawshays promoted the Glamorgan Canal which was opened in 1794 and the tramroad from Penydarren to Navigation House was the work of the Homfrays. The opening of the Ellesmere Canal likewise proved a great boon to the Bersham and Brymbo works. By 1811, about 150 miles of tramroad was in existence mainly for the purpose of connecting iron-works to canals.

Tinplate

The tinplate industry migrated into Wales from the Forest of Dean in the late seventeenth century but thereafter the most significant developments in it were to take place here pioneered mainly by the Hanbury family who settled at Pontypool. Improvements in the quality of their product assisted by mid-eighteenth century wars which cut off continental supplies enabled the Welsh industry to capture the home market from German manufacturers. Edward Lhuyd noted in 1697 that the Hanburys were using a process for rolling plates which came into more general use by 1728 and they were also responsible for introducing greater standardisation. Many works were attached to iron forges as at Caerleon, and in the case of Melingriffith an iron forge was converted by its Bristol owners into a tinplate works, drawing its supply of pig-iron from the nearby Pentyrch works and later from as far afield as Bristol and the Midlands. The area between Pontypool and Cardiff formed one centre but by 1750 another had developed west of Swansea at Ynys-pen-llwch, Cydweli and Carmarthen. The last two works were owned by Robert Morgan who, after 1759, concentrated his production at Carmarthen by enlarging his works with the aid of Bristol capital. A works existed at Llechryd in south Cardiganshire which supplied the needs of local tinkers who made most of the domestic utensils in use. Bristol and London ironmasters were the main providers of capital because this created another market for iron especially after 1763 when production of munitions ceased. Increased production of iron reduced prices and stimulated tinplate production which reached 80,000 boxes in 1805 of which 50,000 were exported which shows how completely the Welsh product had supplanted the German in European markets. Welsh technology by experimentation and practice promoted improvements in pickling and tinning which made its product superior to any other. Wages compared more than favourably with those in other industries, the workmen being paid as a group on their production. The Melingriffith workers, though paid less than those of Caerleon about 1760, were often provided with houses and medical attention. By 1815, out of 26 tinplate works known to exist, 13 were situated in South Wales, 11 of them in the counties of Monmouth, Glamorgan and Carmarthen which were to give the Welsh industry a clear lead in the nineteenth century.

Coal

Although it had an importance of its own, the fate of the coal industry in the eighteenth century was closely tied to that of other industries as well. Coal was used for fuel where seams were found near the surface and a coastal trade in it grew up from Neath and Swansea to Bristol and West Country ports. Flintshire mines likewise exploited the Chester market. By 1688, coal formed 90% of Welsh exports but this was only because it had so few rivals. After 1712, there was a remarkable increase in exports to the Irish market not only from South Wales ports but also from Flintshire and for some time this remained more important than the foreign market. Developments in inland transport created an expanding market and landowners were not slow to develop their coal resources to meet it. The names of Mackworth, Mansel, Myddelton and Owen (Orielton) are conspicuous among the early entrepreneurs but their active participation declined as it was less risky to lease their rights in return for rents and royalties. Coal was used in the seventeenth century for smelting non-ferrous metals but it was its application to iron-smelting after 1709 that greatly augmented the demand for it which accounts for developments in the Taff, Cynon and west Monmouthshire valleys. Metal-working at Holywell and Mold stimulated Flintshire mines and at Minera and Bersham the Denbighshire ones. Cort's invention of 1783 was a powerful stimulus and ironmasters and smelters opened their own mines, some of them going over entirely to coal production as the demand grew. By 1800, the coal industry was already freeing itself from dependence on the metal industries as we enter the age of steam and Newport was the envy of South Wales ports because it was exempt from coal duties on shipments to the eastern part of the Bristol Channel. The industry was well-supplied by local labour and since there was no call for high technical skill there was little call for outside labour. The introduction of steam-engines especially the Watt-Boulton ones improved mine-drainage enabling deeper mines to be sunk to tap the lower seams. Much road and tramroad construction was done to solve the transport problems of the industry.

Slate

The slate industry both by origin and character is recognised as the most Welsh of all industries. Already by 1688 a million slates were exported from Wales but it was the expansion of the domestic market that is significant within our period. House building and urbanisation were going on apace, mostly outside Wales, and the Welsh industry was well-placed to exploit the urban development of northern England. Liverpool and Chester were its most important markets but London also absorbed much of its product. The Irish market was also expanding and came next in importance to the domestic one. Improvements in communication which reduced costs as well as opening up new markets were an important factor in development.

The main developments occurred in Caernarfonshire on the seaward side of Snowdonia and within a short distance of the coast. By 1793, Caernarfonshire was producing about 60% of Britain's slate and this expansion affected remote areas like Llangollen and Glyn Ceiriog in Denbighshire and Llangynog in Montgomeryshire which supplied slate to contiguous areas of England though beset with transport difficulties. Quarrying was also long-established in the Prescelly Mountains but there was no comparable development there to Caernarfonshire. It was at Bethesda on the Penrhyn estate that developments along industrial lines were first attempted after the estate came into the hands of the Pennant family by marriage in 1765. Small scale quarrying by quarrymen in partnerships had been going on before, ' custom of the quarries ' being paid to the Penrhyn estate but, although this took a good slice out of the profits of quarrymen, it yielded little in royalties to the estate. Richard Pennant decided on a more business-like approach and in 1768 he reduced the number of leases to 54 granted for 21 years at various rents and laid down rules for methodical working. The slate was to be delivered on the quay at Abercegin where the slate-reeve would dispose of it and settle with the undertakers.

The royalties collected by the estate in 1782 still only amounted to £90 because the quarrymen lacked the capital for large-scale development and could ill-afford to spend money on unremunerative work. Pennant bought out existing leases for £160 and set about to organise the quarry as a single undertaking. He also built a factory to manufacture slates for school use which found a ready market in Liverpool. To establish a quarrying monopoly in the district he took out leases on neighbouring Crown lands. Prospects bade fair until the outbreak of war and Bethesda achieved an output of about 15,000 tons in 1794, equivalent to 60% of Caernarfonshire's output. The imposition of a 20% duty on coastal trade was a crippling blow and it arrested house-building in Liverpool and London, especially the latter as the duty became heavier according to the length of the journey. Risks at sea had to be covered by insurance which added to costs. Recession set in after 1794 but Pennant had enough capital to enable him to utilise the slack time for reorganising the quarry, introducing gallery working, laying down tramroads and in 1813 building a slate mill with sixteen frames. The quay at Abercegin was also enlarged and renamed Port Penrhyn. The years after 1803 witnessed some revival of trade and by 1808 a profit of £7,000 was being shown. The year 1814 was again a period of recession but it was temporary and when post-War trade did revive Bethesda was well-placed to exploit the great back-log of housing which had accumulated during the War. Above all, Pennant had demonstrated the advantage which capital resources gave.

| 1782— 1,000 tons | 1794—15,000 tons | 1808—20,000 tons |
| 1793—11,000 tons | 1796— 8,000 tons | |

Output of Penrhyn Quarry in selected years.

Pennant's example was more tardily followed by Thomas Assheton Smith of Faenol at Llanberis where small-scale quarrying had also been carried on. Developments were arrested by transport problems and even by 1793 output had only reached 2,650 tons. Smith granted a 21 year lease to a company of three in 1788 known as the Dinorwic Slate Quarry which made a systematic survey and trials and set 40 men to work on eight separate faces. By 1796 about 120 men were employed and output was up to about 3,600 tons. When the lease expired in 1809 Assheton Smith joined the company on a half-share basis and also derived a royalty of ⅛th of the output.

The market was on the up-swing by then and from 1809 to 1828 with the exception of 1814 an average profit of £8,750 was netted. Nantlle Valley was a third centre of the industry in Caernarfonshire where the tradition of slate quarrying by small partnerships was well-established and persistent. In a dispute between the Glynllifon estate and the Crown agent after 1790 the quarrymen took the part of Lord Newborough because the Crown exacted higher rents than they had been accustomed to pay to the estate as Crown lessee. In 1800 the Crown set the quarries on a 31 years lease to a partnership which formed the Cilgwyn and Cefn Du Slate Co. which also obtained leases for quarrying in the Ffestiniog area of Merionethshire where slate mining had started after 1765. Nantlle was well-placed to take advantage of Caernarfon as a port and was not as beset with transport problems as Dinorwic. It had a major share of the trade with Ireland, Caernarfonshire sending as many as four million slates to Dublin alone in 1748 and thereafter the market greatly expanded. This market was not so badly affected by the French Wars or the slate tax and so Nantlle did not suffer as great a set-back as the other quarries and remained profitable even after 1812. In 1793, about 47% of Wales's output went to Ireland and most of it came from Nantlle.

Capital for development was found mainly within Wales, the most conspicuous entrepreneurs being landlords like Pennant (later Lord Penrhyn) and Assheton Smith. Pennant had sufficient means without recourse to borrowing or forming a partnership and whereas some of it was derived from land the family was also connected with West Indies trade. His ownership of the land and the port facilities gave him complete control over the situation and a high degree of integration. Assheton Smith moved from the position of lessor of mineral rights to a half-share in a partnership and finally assumed control of the undertaking. Pennant and Smith were free from the limitations of a lease and therefore could take a long-term view. They were also favoured by an upward swing in the trade-cycle after a temporary recession at the outbreak of war. Capital for working Dinorwic was originally raised by a partnership but this remained the practice throughout at Nantlle where slate merchants, lawyers, landowners, bankers

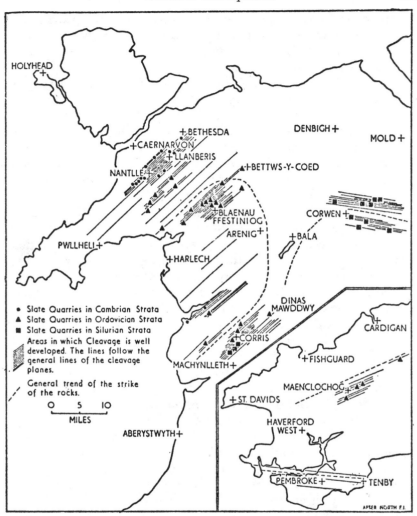

Figure 5

THE DISTRIBUTION OF SLATE QUARRIES
AND OF CLEAVED ROCKS

(Taken, with permission, from E. G. Bowen (editor), *Wales*, Methuen, 1957)

and quarrymen participated. Nantlle quarries were worked on a lease, however, which led to more intensive working and more mechanisation than at Bethesda and Dinorwic which were more labour-intensive.

Improvements in transport and communication were just as important in improving the future of the industry as the great boom in house-building. Dinorwic at first had no usable road ; after being ferried across Llyn Padarn the slates were borne by pack-horses to Caernarfon and such was the transport from Ffestiniog to below Maentwrog. In 1788, a road was laid from Llanberis to Caernarfon and in 1790, Lord Penrhyn built one from Bethesda to Bangor. This enabled broad-wheeled carts to be brought into use which provided many local farmers with another prop to their livelihood. The cost of transportation remained high and sometimes exceeded production costs ; land transport cost as much as twice that of the sea-voyage to Liverpool. Breakages were also common and reduced profit margins. The cost of transport by road from Bethesda was reduced from 5s. 3d. a ton in 1788 to 4s. in 1796 and at Dinorwic from 10s. to 6s. 6d. Despite the War and the slate-tax the proportion between transport cost and cost of production came down progressively especially in the case of Bethesda after 1801 when a tramroad was built from the quarry to the quay at a cost of £5,000, reducing the cost of transport to 1s. a ton. Further, it enabled 100 tons a day to be moved with fewer breakages ; the other quarries built tramroads to convenient ports later. W. A. Madocks developed the harbour facilities at Portmadoc by building *Y Cob Mawr*, an embankment to control the Dwyryd and Glaslyn rivers, in 1807, and enlarging the quay which was finished in 1815 and which became the port for handling Ffestiniog slate.

Local labour was plentiful and most of the quarrymen also worked small-holdings. They worked in gangs each negotiating its own ' bargain ' with the setter, a monthly subsistence being paid with a quarterly reckoning known as *tâl mawr* (big pay). Wages in the industry increased for a day labourer from 10d. in 1790 to 1s. 4d. in 1794 at Dinorwic and skilled quarrymen by the day from 1s. 6d. in 1801 to 2s. 6d. in 1811. Piece-work rates reflected these trends but the recession of 1814 caused an all-round fall. Quarrymen very early formed benefit clubs to ward against accidents and injury which were all too common. Marketing organisation was advanced by standardising the size of slates which were given the name of duchesses, princesses, ladies etc., with a steady increase of concentration on the larger sizes to reduce roofing costs.

Quarry area	Coastwise traffic	To Ireland	Total	Number employed in 1796
Dinorwic	1,930 tons	720 tons	2,650 tons	120
Bethesda	6,640 tons	4,360 tons	11,000 tons	350 (500 in 1794)
Caernarfon (mainly Nantlle)	1,990 tons	5,990 tons	7,980 tons	560
Merioneth	200 tons	300 tons	500 tons	
Other	1,800 tons		1,800 tons	

Table showing the relative output of quarries in 1793 and the employment situation in 1796.

The Woollen Industry

The woollen industry figured next in importance to the cattle trade in Welsh rural economy but by comparison with some English districts the gross output was small. Whereas its value for the four counties of Merioneth, Montgomery, Monmouth and Pembroke in 1747 was estimated at £100,000 that of Yorkshire at that time amounted to £2,371,940. Along with Denbighshire these were the principal clothing counties each specialising in a particular type of cloth although Pembrokeshire reverted more and more to selling wool. It was in the boroughs that early developments within the industry occurred in South Wales and there are many references to it in the records of Cardiff and Caerffili but by 1700 it was declining as a town-based industry and Carmarthen's attempts at reviving gild control proved abortive. In North Wales it was a rural craft from the beginning. Welsh clothiers produced for the English market and border towns competed for their trade. Oswestry was the original centre but the Shrewsbury Drapers succeeded in attracting the trade to their town and managed to retain control over it till the end of the eighteenth century. In his poem, *The Fleece* (1757) John Dyer describes the ' Northern Cambrians ' carrying ' their labours on pygmean steeds ' to Shrewsbury upon whose shearmen Welsh clothiers were entirely dependent for the finishing processes which they themselves could not do for lack of capital and they needed quick returns and a secure market. From Shrewsbury Welsh cloth was exported through London to the continent. South Wales cloth found an outlet in Bristol where the Shrewsbury Drapers kept a factor to buy it up. By 1700, Welshpool was developing as a depôt and the Shrewsbury Drapers were obliged to go there to buy the cloth rather than lose their supply.

After 1770 a breach was made in the Shrewsbury monopoly, Liverpool merchants sending factors to North Wales to ' forestall ' the cloth either at local fairs or even at the loom before the Shrewsbury Drapers could get it. Liverpool merchants developed Barmouth as a depôt for the export of Merioneth webs and in 1776 it was estimated that £40,000 worth of webs and £10,000 worth of stockings were exported from there annually to Liverpool, Chester and London for the American and West Indian market. The outbreak of war in America in 1776 was a temporary reverse but that of the French Wars in 1793 was a permanent one. Factors kept by the Shrewsbury Drapers in Welsh towns saved the clothiers a long journey to market but they met with mounting competition from Oswestry, Chester, Wrexham and Welshpool.

The prosperity of the period 1776-93 is reflected in the exports of cloth from small ports like Aberdyfi and Derwen-las on the River Dyfi. Some factors set up as drapers on their own account and were often known as ' Welsh Drapers '. Their role was that of middle-man who paid for the cloth when it was ready and supplied wool to the clothiers or cash if necessary to keep the craftsmen in production. They supervised the manufacturing and finishing processes and thus emerged as an employing class; the craftsmen, however, lost their independence and were reduced to wage-earners. The clothier-manufacturer who was so prominent in Yorkshire was uncommon here but there were a few like Peter Price of Pennal, near Machynlleth. The family was the traditional unit of production but even that was not wholly committed since agriculture was carried on as well. Lack of capital retarded organisation and very few cottagers were able to set up as manufacturers on an industrial scale. Nevertheless, the Welsh cloth industry was moving towards greater independence of the English drapers by the end of our period ; the setting up of a market hall at Welshpool in 1782, whose trade by 1816 amounted to £65,000, was a step in that direction.

The organisation of the industry remained loose and the producers scattered till the end of the eighteenth century which made it difficult to evolve any integrated industrial complex. Yarn was spun by cottagers since an outlay of about 5s. was all that was needed for a locally-made spinning-wheel and about 6d. for hand cards and these were sufficient to put the women and children to work. Wool could either be bought at local fairs or gathered from hedges where sheep had strayed; farmers also allowed cottagers to collect loose wool at shearing time. In many instances weavers provided wool at from 5d. to 8d. a lb. . Spinning-jennies did not appear in Wales till after 1795 and these needed factories to house them. Weaving was men's work and farmers often hired servants for their skill at this trade. A loom cost upwards of £2 and so it was farmers mainly who could buy them ; weaving-sheds (*tai gwŷdd*) were often attached to a farm and sometimes, a dye-house. The work was, however, seasonal when farm work was slack. Yarn could be bought at markets like Dolgellau and Machynlleth. Fulling was done at mills and the frequency of the name ' pandy ' suggests that they were well-distributed and within reach of most home-producers. These became the first factories into which machinery was put increasingly after 1790. Some corn mills were converted to factories because they were harnessed to water-power. One of the earliest factories in North Wales was that at Dolobran which was converted from an iron forge in 1789. Spinning-machines were added to the looms together with a dye-house using vegetable dyes.

Montgomeryshire was the first county to successfully develop the industry on factory lines in the Severn Valley towns, and in Llanbryn-mair and Machynlleth. Flannel was the staple product which was prepared for the Shrewsbury market. Until about 1800, the putting-out system flourished, the industry remaining a complement to farming, it being usually reckoned that about half the rent could be made from flannel working. The introduction of machinery after 1790 enabled the industry to begin to develop independently. By 1800 it was noted that

there were 40 water-driven carding machines in the county
and factories capable of doing all the manufacturing processes
were developing. Aikin refers to ' infant factories ' at Newtown
in 1796 and by 1810 they were equally apparent at Llanidloes.
Although there were no large establishments employing labour
there were many people involved and a proletariat class was
beginning to emerge.

The scale of the industry in Merioneth was smaller and it
was directed to the production of webs which were rough in
texture and used by the Army for clothing ; it was also exported
to America to clothe slaves.   There were many scattered
fulling-mills in the county but after 1740 we see a concentration
at Dolgellau where there were at least 15 fulling-mills by 1800.
Carding and spinning were cottage industries, the yarn being
sold at Dolgellau and Machynlleth markets to weavers and
craftsmen-clothiers like Peter Price of Pennal who were
dependent on cottage spinners.   Dolgellau became a centre
where factors settled and fulfilled the role of an employing
class. Carding machines were installed at Mallwyd and Pennal
in 1798-9 and, after initial opposition, at Dolgellau after 1801.
The Rev. Walter Davies established that £48,000 worth of
webs were produced annually in the county but he under-
estimated the number of fulling-mills. The knitting of stockings,
caps and gloves was general and from £200 to £350 worth was
sold weekly at Bala market. The factors were known as ' Welsh
hosiers ', Gabriel Davies of Bala being a good example. The
stocking trade also flourished at Llandovery and Tregaron
especially with the growth of industry in South Wales.

The cloth industry figured less prominently in Denbighshire
and was mainly centred around Wrexham and the Ceiriog
Valley where undyed and undressed webs were produced as
in Merionethshire. John Mostyn of Segrwyd did, however,
set up a factory at Denbigh which at its peak employed 800
hands.   Cotton manufacture also appeared in Denbighshire
at Llangollen but it was Holywell in Flintshire with its four
mills that became the Bolton of Wales. About 1800, W. A.
Madocks set up a short-lived woollen factory at Tremadoc
with 60 looms which produced army cloth and several carding
machines appeared at Beddgelert after 1805. In South Wales
the cloth industry was in decline by the end of the eighteenth

century and efforts to revive it were abortive. Caerffili was still largely dependent on its textile production for employment and both there and at Llandaff there were noted stocking fairs. The Glamorgan Agricultural Society set up a factory at Bridgend in the 1780s which was unique in possessing an Arkwright water-frame but its profitability declined after 1807. The Brecknockshire Agricultural Society encouraged English weavers to settle in the county and set up spinning schools with paid instructors. The decline continued nevertheless and Brecknockshire followed the example of Pembrokeshire in exporting its wool. The industry gave much incidental employment throughout the country to carpenters, coopers and blacksmiths, John and Robert Davies of Llanbryn-mair being good examples of country craftsmen who turned to building machinery for what became a national market necessitating the setting up of an additional works at Carmarthen.

SUGGESTED READING

J. P. Addis, *The Crawshay dynasty*, Cardiff, 1957.

D. J. Davies, *The economic history of South Wales prior to 1800*, Cardiff, 1933.

A. H. Dodd, *The Industrial Revolution in North Wales*, Cardiff, 1971.

J. R. Harris, *The Copper King*, Liverpool, 1964.

J. G. Jenkins, *The Welsh woollen industry*, Cardiff, 1969.

A. H. John, *The industrial development of South Wales, 1750–1850*, Cardiff, 1950.

W. J. Lewis, *Lead mining in Wales*, Cardiff, 1967.

J. Lindsay, *A history of the North Wales slate industry*, Newton Abbot, 1974.

W. E. Minchinton (ed.), *Industrial South Wales*, London, 1969.

D. M. Rees, *Mines, mills and furnaces*, London, 1969.

W. Rees, *Industry before the Industrial Revolution*, 2 vols., Cardiff, 1968.

B. B. Thomas, *Braslun o hanes economaidd Cymru*, Caerdydd, 1941.

Articles:

W. H. Chaloner, 'John Wilkinson', *History Today*, I, 1951.

J. W. England, 'The Dowlais Iron Works, 1759–93', *Morgannwg*, III, 1959.

J. D. Evans, 'The uncrowned iron king', *N.L.W. Jnl.*, VII, 1951.

L

H. G. Jones, 'Llandudno copper mines in the eighteenth century', *B.B.C.S.*, X, 1939.

W. H. Morris, 'Kidwelly tinplate works', *Carms. Ant.*, V, 1964–9.

A. N. Palmer, 'John Wilkinson and the Old Bersham Works', *Trans. Cymmr.*, 1897–8.

R. O. Roberts, 'The development and decline of the copper and non-ferrous industries in South Wales', *Trans. Cymmr.*, 1956.

C. D. J. Trott, 'Coal mining in the borough of Neath in the seventeenth and early eighteenth centuries', *Morgannwg*, XIII, 1969.

M. I. Williams, 'Economic and social life in South Glamorgan, 1600–1800', *Morgannwg*, III, 1959.

——, 'A contribution to the commercial history of Glamorgan', *N.L.W.Jnl.*, IX, 1955, XI, 1960, XII, 1961.

10. Transport and Communications

Roads

ROAD administration was still governed by a statute of 1555 which placed the responsibility 'on the parish as a whole and on every individual thereof'. The parish vestry annually appointed an unpaid surveyor who was obliged to act or be liable to a fine. Quarter Sessions supervised the vestries holding them to their obligations and special highways sessions were regularly held to discharge this duty. Statute labour of six consecutive days was still enforceable on parishioners who also had to provide their own tools, horses and carts ; personal attendance was excused by the sending of a substitute. Commutation of labour service to a money payment was permissible by the eighteenth century and was in force at Wrexham as early as 1721 but farmers in Merionethshire and Pembrokeshire found labour service easier than finding the cash equivalent. Forced labour was nevertheless unpopular and was the cause of the neglect of the roads. J.P.s and high constables could present neglected roads and bridges before Quarter Sessions and if the Grand Jury found a ' true bill ' the parish responsible had either to make amends or be fined and it was not until the surveyor had issued his certificate that it was discharged. A Highways Act of 1691 laid down standards of road construction and empowered parishes to levy a rate but this course was seldom adopted. After 1764, Glamorgan levied a standard rate of 6d. in the £ in lieu of labour service and after 1766 appointed surveyors, the Cardiff Trust paying theirs as much as £40 a year. Bridges very early became a county matter and *ad hoc* committees were often appointed to deal with them. Repairs were generally done by contract labour and the increasing product of rates enabled many stone bridges to be built in the latter half of the century following William

Edwards's ultimate success in spanning the Taff at Pontypridd in 1755.

Contemporary reports describe Welsh roads as execrable, Valentine Morris of Piercefield calling those of Monmouthshire ruts and the much-travelled Arthur Young agreed that they were only matched by the badness of the inn accommodation found along them. Travel was so difficult before 1750 that the gentry felt cut off from social intercourse in their own locality which made their stay on their estates virtually an exile. The needs of trade were just as poorly served and even in the borderland ' pygmean steeds ' were virtually the only means of carrying goods. The steady growth of industry after 1770 was the greatest spur to road-building, and industrialists joined with gentry and innkeepers in pressing forward ; the owners of the Dublin packet and the Irish Parliament were also interested in improving communications with Ireland. The initiative was taken by the gentry in most areas and improvements were often financed by private subscriptions, the gentry of Monmouthshire, for instance, spending big sums on road repairs which had been raised thus. Most activity was to be seen in the borderland, along the main routes to Ireland through North and South Wales and in the newly developing industrial areas. Anthony Bacon was the first industrialist to build a road to connect his ironworks at Merthyr with Cardiff in 1767. When the Cynon Valley road was put in hand in 1803 ironmasters were still the prime movers behind it. Quarry owners like Lord Penrhyn and Assheton Smith built roads in North Wales from Bethesda to Bangor and Llanberis to Port Dinorwic in 1782 and 1809 respectively. Parliamentary Acts for the construction of canals and tramroads sometimes also provided for roads as in the case of the Aberdare Canal Act and several Enclosure Acts made similar provision.

Turnpike Acts relating to Wales belong to the second half of the eighteenth century and even a populous and expanding county like Glamorgan had only obtained eight Acts by 1800. The turnpiking of roads did not, however, relieve parishes through which they passed of their responsibility and they could still be presented before Quarter Sessions for default. Parliamentary permission had first to be sought to create a trust usually by a petition from the gentry, clergy and freeholders, the cost of the Act being borne by the trust. The object was to improve the roads by making users pay and so the trusts were allowed to erect gates and toll-houses and to raise their capital by borrowing on the security of the tolls. The trusts were local bodies and often parochial in their outlook resenting in particular the increasing flow of through traffic which used their roads. The number of trusts proliferated very soon and road bonds were regarded as a good investment. The existence of many of them was rendered precarious by over-borrowing, the interest thus becoming a considerable drain on revenue since road bonds were expected to yield 5%. Tolls were often auctioned to the highest bidder, so charges were variable and there was no limit to the number of gates which could be erected.

The trust operating between Wrexham and Shrewsbury from 1752 must be reckoned amongst the earliest. The needs of the woollen trade soon led to turnpiking the roads between Welshpool and Shrewsbury and Oswestry but when Robert Owen left his Newtown home in 1781 he still had to walk as far as Welshpool to meet a coach. Similar activity followed in Flintshire after 1756 and Caernarfonshire after 1759. Turnpike roads did not appear in Merionethshire till after 1775 but by 1800 North Wales had about 1,000 miles of turnpike roads and the trusts had come to be organised on a county basis. Glamorgan was a different case because since 1764 it had been organised into five turnpike districts based on Cardiff, Cowbridge, Bridgend, Neath and Swansea which made for very fragmented organisation. Monmouth had been one of the pioneering South Wales counties and by 1815 about 25% of its roads were turnpiked.

The increase of Irish traffic through Milford Haven and Holyhead by the end of the century called for road improvements. The General Post Office urged improvements on several Quarter Sessions which raised much animosity against it since the mails paid no tolls. Areas through which the main roads passed were gradually waking up to their importance and in 1789 the South Wales Association for Improvement of Roads was formed on a voluntary basis. Its principal concern was the east-west road and in 1790 it caused a survey of the road to be made along its whole length through South Wales.

It also appealed to local gentry for co-operation and even presented negligent parishes before Quarter Sessions Due to its initiative this road was reported to be in excellent condition by 1796 and Arthur Young rated it as third of all the roads of England and Wales.

Developments along the Holyhead road were even more significant and cast their influence on road development in Wales and elsewhere. The merits of a road to Holyhead via Shrewsbury had been argued against those of the Chester road and the issue was a matter of consequence to either town and especially to its innkeepers. By 1808, the G.P.O. had finally chosen in Shrewsbury's favour and the road continued thence to Capel Curig, Bangor and Holyhead thus avoiding the perilous passage of the River Conwy and the hazards of Penmaen-mawr. The Menai crossing was still dangerous and as early as 1785 a committee of local gentry had considered the feasibility of a bridge. In 1810, Thomas Telford was commissioned to make a survey and report and in 1811 a parliamentary committee recommended the building of a bridge but a bill to that effect was not introduced till 1819. Even more significant was the making of a grant of £20,000 by the Government in 1815—the first ever towards road-building—and ten commissioners were appointed to supervise its spending. A further consequence was the bringing of the whole road from London to Holyhead under a single administration and the advantage of this was soon realised elsewhere.

There can be no doubt that the condition of the roads was greatly improved by 1815 mainly through the activity of the turnpike trusts and leading to a great increase of wheeled traffic much of it originating from the Irish routes. In 1776, the owner of the White Lion in Chester began a daily service to Holyhead by flying post-chaise at a fare of two guineas ; in 1779, the landlord of the Raven and Bell, Shrewsbury, provided a service from that town which in 1780 went through to London. From 1784, the G.P.O. began to operate mail coaches through North Wales and from 1785 through South Wales, the daily service by coach via Chester replacing the post-boy until it was switched to Shrewsbury in 1808. In that year a weekly coach service was inaugurated between Shrewsbury and Aberystwyth via Newtown which was increased to two coaches a week during the season to cater for the traffic to the seaside. Cardiff was well-supplied with services to London by 1796 with connections for Bristol, Bath and Milford Haven. The cost of coach travel was high, a short journey from Cowbridge to Cardiff costing 12s. in 1786 and one from Swansea to Bristol £1. 10s. but increased traffic brought reduced fares whilst journeys were shortened by higher speeds of travel made possible by metalled roads. Coaching services called for posting and stabling facilities and so inns grew up along the main routes, several being found in Cardiff near the west gate where the road left the town. Wagon services for freight became more frequent after 1780 when a wagon service began to ply between Chester and Bangor and by 1790 a stage wagon operated directly from London to Holyhead. *Y Wagen Fawr* was a familiar sight in Montgomeryshire bearing bales of flannel to market.

Water transport

A considerable volume of traffic was water-borne inasmuch as a number of Welsh towns were situated on estuaries or navigable river reaches, Chepstow and Carmarthen being virtually inland ports. River navigation was possible on lengthy stretches of the Wye and Dee and at high water the River Severn was navigable to shallow-draught boats to Pool Quay which gave access to the Bristol Channel to the lime and slate quarries, woollen and agricultural products of Montgomeryshire. There was much coastal traffic around Wales's long coastline and especially between South Wales and the West Country and in 1737 Lewis Morris was commissioned to draw up navigational charts of our coast. By the end of our period there was a great increase in both the number and tonnage of ships with the increase in Irish and overseas trade. Several small ports had fishing fleets which provided seasonal employment for many. Increased trade called for better harbour facilities in old ports and a few new ports like Portmadoc were coming into existence which also supported a modest ship-building industry in which much local capital was invested. By the end of our period the greatness of Swansea, Cardiff and Newport as ports of world importance was already being laid and each was connected to its hinterland by canals.

The earliest canals were cut in the western part of the coal-field to carry coal to local industry. Humphrey Mackworth built a canal to his Melincryddan works between 1695 and 1700 which could accommodate ships of 100 tons. In 1768, Sir John Glynne cut a canal across Saltney Marsh to carry coal to the River Dee and after 1769 several short lengths were cut in the Swansea-Cydweli area. It was the needs of the iron industry which prompted canal building which at that time seemed the natural solution to its problem although Wales was not ideal for it. Ironmasters were thus prominent in pioneering them but so also were some landowners anxious to develop their estates, several canals being built for agricultural purposes.

Most of the great projects were launched in the decade between 1790 and 1800 and included the Glamorgan, Neath, Monmouthshire and Swansea canals which were authorised in that order. Between them they provided 77 miles of water-way at a capital outlay of £420,000. The following table, after Hadfield, will show the situation reached by 1815 :

	Miles of narrow canal	*Miles of river navigation*
1760		$75\frac{3}{4}$
1770	5	,,
1780	5	,,
1790	12	,,
1800	$143\frac{1}{2}$	$74\frac{1}{2}$
1810	$145\frac{1}{4}$	,,

(Source: Charles Hadfield, The Canals of South Wales and the Border)

They carried iron mainly from the works to the seaports, and food and fodder in reverse. Two families of engineers were involved in most of the Welsh canals, the Dadfords and the Sheasbys, the elder Dadford having been an associate of Telford. The canals were built in difficult terrain along river valleys posing great problems of engineering and later of operation, the Glamorgan Canal reaching a summit of 550 feet necessitating 52 locks, some with a fall of 10 feet which was much greater than normal. Water shortage from drought in summer, frost in winter and constant repairs to locks occasioned frequent stoppages. Freighters provided their own boats of

20-25 tons but they could seldom be loaded to capacity. Friction between partners and operators added to physical difficulties. The canals did not coalesce into a network, the Neath and Swansea canals being the only ones which were linked and that not till 1824 ; a tramroad projected to link the Neath and Glamorgan canals did not materialise.

The Glamorgan Canal was the first and biggest of the canal ventures at the end of the century. Authorised by an Act of 1790, the stretch from Merthyr to Newbridge (Pontypridd) was opened in 1793 and by 1795 it was open to Cardiff. Its total cost was £103,600 or £4,145 a mile which was higher than the Neath Canal at £2,857 and the Aberdare Canal at £3,745 but lower than the Monmouthshire Canal at about £10,000 a mile. Money was raised by subscription shares there being 71 subscribers in all involved in the Glamorgan Canal with the Crawshay family foremost. The Glamorgan Canal was singular in limiting dividends to 8% inasmuch as the interests of the users predominated over those of investors. The result was low tolls, those for iron coming down from 5*d.* to 2½*d.* a ton by 1809 with the greatly increased traffic and the cheapness of transport ensured the continued use of canals well into the railway age. The congestion at the sea-lock in Cardiff indicates that the Canal was worked to capacity and provided all concerned with a better return than any Welsh canal.

Jealousy of existing canal interests prevented the creation of a viable network in north-east Wales, and the branch of the Ellesmere Canal which was built to the quarries beyond Llangollen left the ironworks of Bersham and Brymbo and the collieries of Ruabon isolated. This Canal is probably best-known for the fine aqueducts which Telford built at Chirk and Froncysyllte which were triumphs of engineering combined with aesthetic beauty. The Montgomery Canal was commenced in 1797 to join the Ellesmere system but it was not completed till 1819. With a higher capital outlay than any Welsh canal the returns were also less inasmuch as it served a mainly agricultural purpose.

Tramroads

Canals would have been impracticable in many places had they not been serviced by a network of tramroads which increased their catchment area. Most were constructed between 1790 and 1811 again to serve ironworks mainly, about 150 miles being laid in South Wales alone. By their means the Hirwaun-Aberdare area was linked to the Neath Canal. It was the high-handedness of the Crawshays which caused Homfray to build the Penydarren tramroad from his works to Abercynon, thus duplicating the Canal service. Most of the tramroads were to be found in Monmouthshire and were built by the Canal companies and freighters. South Wales had a tramroad network which was rivalled only by that of Tyneside. In North Wales tramroads were built independently of canals except for that which linked Ruabon with the Ellesmere Canal. Lord Penrhyn linked his Bethesda quarry with the quay at Abercegin by tramroad and Llanberis was similarly linked with Port Dinorwic.

Two epoch-making events are connected with the story of Welsh tramroads. In 1804, Richard Trevithick brought a steam engine he had been experimenting with at Coalbrookdale to Penydarren where it was put to draw wagons carrying 10 tons of iron and 70 persons along the tramroad to Quakers' Yard and this event inaugurated the railway age. In the same year the tramroad from Swansea to Oystermouth was opened to carry passengers and thus provided the first passenger train service in the world.

Banking

Finance for economic growth posed a serious problem because Wales was far-removed from financial centres, and some time passed before it could generate sufficient capital from within. A growing economy and an expanded labour force necessitated more money in circulation. The earliest banking enterprise was that of Humphrey Mackworth in connection with the Mine Adventurers which was shortlived. Country banks began to appear in the second half of the eighteenth century, *Banc y Llong*[1] being founded at Aberystwyth in 1762 and the better-known Brecon Old Bank by Walter Wilkins in 1778. Developing industrial centres like Wrexham and Holywell also became banking centres. Some banks were pioneered by industrialists like Thomas Williams

[1] Ship Bank

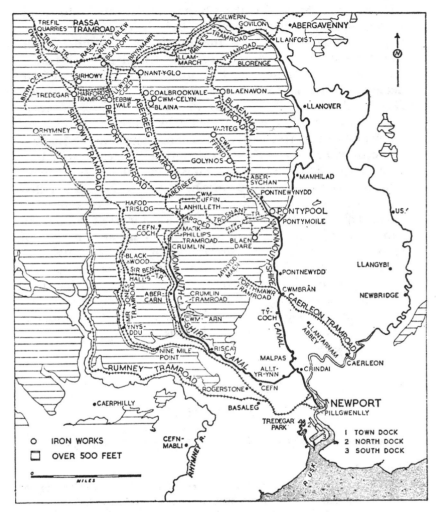

Figure 6

The MONMOUTHSHIRE CANAL AND ITS TRAMROAD
CONNEXIONS

(Taken, with permission, from C. Hadfield, *The Canals of South Wales
and the Border*, Cardiff 1960)

who was associated with the Chester and North Wales Bank (1792) with branches at Bangor and Caernarfon. William Pugh, a country squire, was the founder of a Newtown bank which helped finance the Montgomery Canal. John Wood, a lawyer, was the founder of the first Cardiff Bank. Cattle dealers, like David Jones, were responsible for *Banc yr Eidion Du*[1] of Llandovery (1797) and *Banc y Ddafad Ddu*[2] of Aberystwyth and Tregaron which issued notes bearing the imprint of an ox and a sheep respectively. Dealers engaged in the London cattle trade had accounts at banking houses there ; since bills of exchange drawn on London houses were the most common form of currency it is not surprising that dealers who handled so many of them should turn to banking. The success of these banks depended largely on the creditworthiness of the owners and many of them succumbed during financial panics as in 1810 and 1814-16. They suffered from lack of capital and reserves, concentration of investment in too narrow a field and lack of liquid assets. Nevertheless, local banks like that of Brecon helped finance some canal undertakings but it was outside concerns like the Harfords of Bristol which contributed to larger enterprises in the iron industry.

[1] Black Ox Bank
[2] Black Sheep Bank

SUGGESTED READING

C. Hadfield, *Canals of South Wales and the Border*, Cardiff, 1967.

Articles:
J. C. Davies, 'The origin and history of the Turnpike Trusts in Monmouthshire', *Presenting Monmouthshire*, II, 4, 1967.
A. H. Dodd, 'The roads of North Wales, 1750–1850', *Arch. Camb.*, 1925.

11. Social Life

Our period witnessed a great natural population growth, slightly higher in the first half in North Wales and in the second half of the eighteenth century in South Wales, although the situation differed from county to county. If we accept the questionable pre-census estimates shown below, down to 1670, North Wales showed a higher increase than the South and after a slight decline to 1700 it recovered thereafter. Cardigan, Flint and Montgomery had higher than average percentage increase and showed greater density changes as well. Although there were several hundreds in South Wales with a population density of over 100 per square mile there were none with over 150 by contrast with 5 in Anglesey. After 1801, the hundreds of the south-east show higher than average increase because of the attraction of population to the ironworks and this trend

Population

	Est. total 1670[1]	%age of whole	Est. total 1700[2]	%age of whole	Est. total 1750[2]	%age of whole
N. Wales	160,461	44	158,000	38	209,600	42
S. Wales	210,647	56	248,200	62	283,200	58
Total	371,108	100	406,200	100	492,800	100

	Census 1801	%age of whole
N. Wales	252,785	43
S. Wales	334,343	57
Total	587,128	100

[1] Based on Hearth Tax Returns, 1670; see L. Owen, *Trans. Cymmr.*, 1959
[2] Statistics compiled by John Rickman and published in Census Returns, 1821

was to change the whole population pattern thereafter. The increase was attributable to migration, mainly short distance, rather than natural growth, with its consequent effect on rural areas. Between 1801 and 1811, 47 out of 89 hundreds showed a decrease of over 10% in the number of agricultural workers and two counties, Merioneth and Radnor, showed a net loss of population despite natural increase.

Population increase was also attended by social change. In 1660, Wales was still made up of a number of communities with strong local loyalties, social and family ties and each with distinctive characteristics which made for a varied cultural tradition. The community was virtually self-supporting in an economic sense and looked after its own whether for charitable or educational purposes. Although there was a deep attachment to the past the eighteenth century was a formative period during which new economic and social forces were beginning to remodel society. Society was traditionally divided into 'bonedd a gwreng' which represents an upper and a lower class. 'Bonedd' was not the exact counterpart of the English aristocracy since it sported no titles and at first the approach of the Welsh gentry to English titles was a very tentative one. Lineage had been the established criterion but the creation of economic wealth and the rise of a moneyed class was to advance rival claims to the leadership of society by 1815. 'Gwreng' or 'gwerin' also began to have a new meaning as attachment to and dependence on the soil diminished. The change was necessarily gradual since early industry was mainly rural but by 1815 the industrial proletariat had come into being. In between these classes a new class had interposed itself whose claim to recognition was economic and which included captains of industry, professional men, shopkeepers, merchants and prosperous farmers. Society was becoming more complex but the subtleties of class difference remained, a certain element of élitism even entering the ranks of Dissent. The newer social elements stood for orderliness and organisation which militated against the frivolity of fairs and holidays as much as did Methodist austerity. Greater social mobility which accompanied improvements in communications extended the possibilities of organisation in every direction and gradually eroded the isolation of communities.

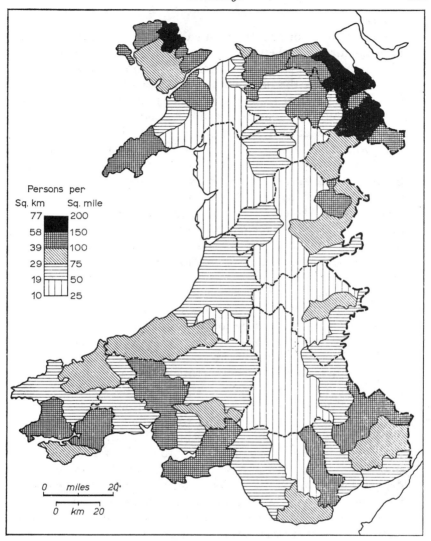

FIGURE 7

POPULATION DENSITY, 1801 : by hundreds

(Source Census 1801)

(Map by kind permission of Professor David Thomas and Mr. Christopher Lewis)

The Gentry

Ellis Wynne commented satirically on the obsession of the Welsh gentry with their lineage but social change was to make his comments less apt by the end of our period. It was apparent by his time that the habits of the gentry were changing away from the old traditions and ideals. Deep-seated attachment to the old families remained but the *parvenus* of the Civil War period were regarded with more reserve. The possession of land was the distinctive feature of this class and the size of their estates came to count for more than lineage. They lived by their rents and their rent-rolls increased with the rise in land values and as the process of estate building advanced. Legal devices like entail gave an added measure of protection to estates against the incidence of spendthrift heirs by making the incumbents tenants for life rather than outright owners. This enabled sustained growth although many estates were heavily encumbered with mortgages. Setting out money on mortgage was one means whereby property could be acquired since if a mortgagor defaulted the mortgagee could foreclose. More land was acquired by marriage than by purchase and so marriages were calculated to enhance family fortunes.

The aristocratic element was not prominent in Wales and although there were some aristocratic estates they only formed small parts of larger English complexes as in the case of the Duke of Beaufort and the Earl of Pembroke. Baronets and squires were more numerous and were influential in their own neighbourhood since they were resident whilst the peers seldom were. Some owned enough property to qualify for a peerage ; such were the Wynns of Wynnstay and the Morgans of Tredegar. The number of families with incomes of over £3,000 a year was, however, much fewer than of those with incomes of £1,000 plus who formed the backbone of the squirearchy. Moreover, their number increased at the expense of those of £500 and above as the minor squires were more sensitive to the economic stringency of the Restoration period with its added burden of taxation as well. There was little to choose between many minor squires and yeomen except that they were rentiers not farmers. Thus many old-established small estates ceased to be independent units especially when an inordinate number of them devolved upon heiresses. Many old family names disappeared except where the new incumbents expected to derive advantage from adopting them ; in marrying into the Tredegar family the Goulds adopted the name of Morgan thus concealing the breach. Some heiresses married into the peerage and this might well have awakened the interest of the Welsh gentry in acquiring peerages by the end of the eighteenth century, which was not apparent earlier. A new type of '*bonedd*' had arrived and no one would have mistaken the Stuarts of Cardiff Castle for the old gentry of Glamorgan with whom they were often at odds. Differences were no doubt accentuated by the growing infusion of wealth into many upper class families ; the Rice family of Dinefwr received a peerage and a substantial fortune by marriage with a London banker almost at the same time. Wealth became more obtrusive with the advent of nabobs like William Paxton or Richard Pennant into county life. More acceptable were those families who came to the fore by the success of their founders in professions like the law, the Trevors, Jeffreys, Williams (Llanforda) and later the Kenyons, all from the north-east, being such conspicuous examples.

The prosperity of landed families was usually reflected in building programmes the volume of which was much greater in the eighteenth than in the seventeenth century. It did not produce Palladian mansions on the scale of the English ones but houses like Leeswood were modest examples of the classical style. Georgian-style houses are not numerous but fairly well-distributed in Wales though earlier styles, like that of Queen Anne persevered well into the eighteenth century. Few great architects are known to have worked here but their styles were copied by knowledgeable gentry some of whom, like the first Lord Newborough, were amateur architects. There were works of reference they could consult with whose aid they were able to instruct local craftsmen. Their buildings often reflect personal taste rather than contemporary fashion, Thomas Johnes courting both the classical and the Gothic style in his houses at The Priory, Cardigan and at Hafod. Many old houses like Powis and Chirk Castles were restored and added to often resulting in a complete architectural mix-up. There was hardly a definitive Georgian period of architecture in Wales but the contemporary vogue of landscape gardening resulted in many of the fine parks which surround country houses and

M

' Capability ' Brown himself worked on the grounds of Cardiff Castle.

The management of estates became more professional with the employment of stewards and they were run on a commercial basis. This more mercenary attitude was deplored by popular critics like Twm o'r Nant and Jac Glan y Gors who remembered the old type of squire with affection. For a number of reasons greater pressure was exerted on tenants and the situation is summed up thus by Twm o'r Nant :

> Rhwng cyfraith stiwardied a balchder gwŷr mawrion,
> Mae tenant i'w ganffod fel rhwng diawl a'i gynffon.[1]

Some landlords were interested in the new scientific agriculture and some planned for their heirs, Sir Edward Lloyd of Pengwern and Thomas Johnes of Hafod embarking on large-scale tree-planting. Management was not entirely a male concern since households were expected to be self-sufficient and this depended on the skill of the lady of the house in running the dairy, brewhouse and laundry as Mrs. Anne Evans of Highmead (Cards.) did with such success.

The country gentlemen adapted to the new age and were alert to the advantage of developing the resources of their estates. In Cardiganshire and Flintshire they were pioneers of the lead industry, in Pembrokeshire they worked coal and in Glamorgan started ironworks. Few of them launched into large-scale industry and they became content to act as lessors of land and mineral rights drawing rents and royalties which substantially increased their income whilst leaving the risks to more experienced industrialists.

Contemporary critics condemn the gentry for dissipating their wealth ; the introduction of the sporting gun and the breeding of pheasants made sport a pastime of gentlemen and resulted in the severities of the game laws which became an added tenant affliction. These new interests diverted many gentlemen from patronage of culture. In the early eighteenth century they had been prominent as patrons of education and the S.P.C.K. owed much to them. They were prominent in the subscription lists to books and had many dedicated to them.

---

[1] Between steward-made laws and the vanity of great persons, a tenant is caught between the devil and his tail.

By the 1760s however, William Vaughan of Corsygedol was probably unique amongst his class in being able to meet the bards on their own terms. Literary squires were not a rarity. Thomas Johnes of Hafod was an erudite translator of French chronicles ; Thomas Pennant of Downing acquired a European reputation as botanist and zoologist ; John Lloyd of Wigfair was a scientist who had set up a laboratory as well as a library. The tradition which Robert Vaughan of Hengwrt had created as collector of books and manuscripts was still alive since the possession of a fine library was often regarded as the hall-mark of a gentleman but the contents too often remained unused except by an occasional wandering scholar. The old type of squire patronised the harp, as William Bulkeley of Brynddu still did ; the new might patronise the theatre like Sir Watkin Williams Wynn II did in adding one to his great house. Collecting paintings and *objets d'art* seems to have been fairly general among this class judging by the number which have survived in their houses to this day.

From the evidence of inventories the standards of comfort improved over the century. The homespun products of local craftsmen were rejected for furniture from London workshops or at least from Chester and Bristol. Where that was not possible pattern-books were shown to local craftsmen who copied Sheraton chairs they had never actually seen. Mahogany superseded oak and even walnut and panelling gave way to wall-paper. Standards of living described by Dineley as plain also changed with more sophisticated tastes in food and the habit of tea-drinking became universal. Hospitality remained liberal and visits to neighbouring houses running to short stays became habitual and often gave rise to excessive drinking. Balls were held at Christmastide and during the week of Great Sessions in the county town. These were often occasions for riotous conduct, the subject of acid comment by Twm o'r Nant, and the printing of rules of decorum was not done without need. The gentry spent longer periods away from home, in London when Parliament was in session which necessitated renting a house there with visits to Bath during the season. They followed the social round and lived up to their station often with dire consequences to the finances of their estates. Gambling was a weakness of the age and an occasional Welsh squire like Sir Herbert Lloyd of Peterwell dissipated his whole estate at the gambling tables. Some Welsh gentry were even to be found amongst the fashionable fringe represented by the *dilettanti* and the *macaronis* whose concern for dress and appearance was as great as that of the ladies who were becoming increasingly conspicuous in society. The only way that the expense could be met was by squeezing all that was possible out of their property. This strain was ultimately communicated to their tenants who not only disliked being milked but resented the way of life which their rents supported and of which the old gentry would not have approved.

The primary concern of any country gentleman was his own ' country ' which signified his own county or nearer neighbourhood. This was his natural element in which he revelled, to which a seat in Parliament was merely an adjunct. The gentry monopolised all offices of local government of note and nominated their followers to lesser ones. The younger gentry were expected to cut their teeth on county government discharging the duties of J.P. before they aspired to higher things like a seat in Parliament. The office of Lord Lieutenant was the prerogative of the premier family in the county whatever its politics and he was the leader of county society. The office of High Sheriff declined in importance as the expense attendant on it increased in the eighteenth century until it came to be avoided. With the abolition of the Council of the Marches in 1688 and the decline of the attraction to Ludlow, the Quarter Sessions and Great Sessions acquired more importance as the volume of business transacted there increased. Attendance at Quarter Sessions had priority even over attendance on Parliament, and long absence from Westminster was often excused if a gentleman was active in the affairs of his county. Attendance at Great Sessions had the added attraction of being a major social occasion. Although the number of J.P.s had steadily increased the number of active ones was often low because some were incapacitated and others were absentees; this imposed severe strain on those who had to deal with business ranging from care of roads and bridges, relief of the poor to administration of the county gaol. Nevertheless, they opposed diluting the Commission of the Peace by admitting people of lower social rank, exception being made of the clergy. This is not strange when they transacted such business as tax assessments with their own interests uppermost in mind. Keeping down the poor rate was a major consideration in administering poor relief so that persons were not allowed a settlement in the parish unless entitled which often resulted in dire hardship to unfortunates. Many J.P.s in times of hardship like the 1790s did administer wisely and with humanity when large-scale shortage and poverty was only relieved by their initiative in bringing in corn supplies. There were also less sensitive souls whose first reaction was to resort to suppression of unrest by the military which again indicates the chasm that was opening between them and their social inferiors.

The Middling Sort
A middle class hardly existed before the eighteenth century but began to evolve in the course of it. It was an urban phenomenon which accompanied the growth in size and importance of towns and was more advanced in some parts of the country than in others. The increase of trade was notable and was centred on towns and small ports. Shopkeepers and merchants became settled parts of the community replacing the travelling packmen, Carmarthen with its river port and Wrexham with its numerous small industries becoming centres for merchant houses. The Common Council of Cardiff had a significant commercial element in it in 1731 and this element was still prominent in 1789. From its early days of growth the ' shopocracy ' had been prominent in the life of Merthyr and most of the commissioners in the Court of Requests were shopkeepers. They acquired property and provided a counterbalance to the domineering ironmasters. Factors in the woollen trade set up their small factories in towns like Dolgellau. Cattle-dealers established banks at centres like Llandovery and Tregaron where they did most business.

Professions became more numerous in the course of the century. The clergy held a place in society second only to the squirearchy to which they were closely allied although there is little to support the idea of the fox-hunting parson in Wales. The clergy were drawn from a wide social range. Some were of the gentry class and were the principal beneficiaries of lay patronage in the Church. At the other end of the scale was the

poor curate risen from the lower class and surviving on a
pittance. Discrepancy in learning and attainment stood out as
between a scholar like Dr. Wynne of Bodewryd who stemmed
from the squirearchy and the humble curate who was barely
literate. The law was regarded as a respectable as well as a
lucrative profession but to rise to its pinnacles needed a substantial measure of education usually ending at the Inns of
Court. The Recordership of a corporation was often the door
to a parliamentary seat and that was the high road to preferment. Even country attorneys who were numerous in towns
like Carmarthen reaped the benefits of increased business with
land transactions, marriage settlements and wills stemming
from the landed class ; the development of industry at the end
of the century also created its own kind of business and litigation. At this level, a measure of education at a local grammar
school followed by an apprenticeship to an established attorney
was all that was necessary and law practices were often hereditary.

In maritime areas the Navy provided careers as the correspondence of the Morris Brothers testifies but the Services were
seldom means by which a poor lad could climb the social
ladder since they were controlled by patronage. Medicine,
originally a lowly profession divided between the physician-
apothecary and the barber-surgeon, gradually gained in
respectability. There was no prescribed course of study and
young men prepared for it by serving an apprenticeship as to
any other trade. When David Samwell became a ship's doctor
in 1775 a brief appearance before the Royal College of Surgeons
was sufficient to certify him as competent. It was experience
that qualified him to become a surgeon on the ' Discovery '
under that most exacting master, Captain Cook. The fact that
Smollett's Surgeon Morgan in *Roderick Random* was a Welshman
suggests that Welsh doctors were numerous. By 1800 the Royal
College of Physicians and Surgeons had laid down courses of
study which took young Welshmen to Dublin if they lived
close to the sea, or to Edinburgh which led in the field of medicine. Some Welshmen distinguished themselves at Guy's
Hospital by 1800, notably Sir Noah Thomas from Glamorgan
who attended on George III.

Teaching was a lowly profession though masters of grammar

schools had social standing and were well-paid ; not so their ushers who often had to hold curacies to help out. Under the terms of most endowments both had to be University graduates. The teachers in charity schools were paid from the endowment or charged fees which had to be low to attract pupils ; they often held parish offices as well to make ends meet. Many of them were ill-educated and often turned to keeping school because they were unfit for anything else. Banking was a new profession as yet and the rise of industry called for professional servants as well as technologists and technicians and in a new town like Merthyr they soon became prominent in civic life. Land agents and surveyors came into their own in the second half of the century when many estates were surveyed for the first time. Lewis Morris saw in this profession a sufficient opening to set up in practice on his own account. Numerous Enclosure Acts involved a great deal of surveying and mapping and although many surveyors came from outside some were Welsh land agents. The Hopcyn family served the Margam estate for at least three generations and it was common for fathers to bring up their sons to their professions. John Nash must have been one of the earliest professional architects in Wales during his stay at Carmarthen, most builders being expected to supply their own plans and speculative building was well under way in the new towns. The development of transport and communications called for innkeepers, boarding-house keepers at resorts and postmasters.

The growth of a middle class was conducive to civic spirit and worked towards liberation from landed influence in towns. Unfortunately, it was not counterbalanced by the growth of a prosperous class of freeholders in the country as the economic dependence of the farming community on the landed class increased rather than diminished.

The Lower Orders

In his survey of population in 1696 Gregory King included the labouring poor amongst those who depreciated the nation's wealth on the grounds that their income was not always adequate to their needs and needed supplementation usually from parish funds. If this was true of England it was more so of Wales where income per head was generally lower since most people were still dependent on agriculture till the 1780s. The ' lower class ' covered a wide social spectrum of artisans, labourers and people unable to support themselves. At least a section of the farming community belonged to it for although the lot of the large farmer was improving there was little to choose between that of a small farmer and a farm labourer's. The pressure on land also diminished his prospects and in upland areas where transhumance was still practised the *hafod* came into permanent rather than seasonal occupation.

The farm labourer hired his services by the year or half year either renewing his contract or moving to a new place in May or November. Single labourers usually lived in, a loft over the outbuildings serving as their dormitory. Although they might be hired for the job of ploughman or carter there was no strict division of labour and in winter-time men-servants did the weaving. Married labourers usually lived out and drew much of their due in kind but the number of tied cottages was inadequate to their needs. On a large farm women servants were as numerous as men and they invariably lived in.

Craftsmen who congregated in villages and towns were also dependent on agriculture since they provided for the needs of the countryside around. They migrated from farm to farm living in while the job lasted. Many workshops specialised in particular products and ' schools ' of craftsmen were identified with certain towns and were patronised by gentry. A system of apprenticeship was still in being for crafts though it vanished from the small factories which finished cloth or worked leather. Persons with itchy feet followed the drovers on their long journeys and even maid-servants joined their company to go as far as London to do seasonal work or enter domestic service. The sea provided employment for many, in fishing during the season and in coastal traffic at other times.

Two developments were apparent by the end of the century ; first, the congregation of workmen in unprecedented numbers in works and mines, and second, the growth of the proletariat. It was the development of the metal industries that was responsible for this, particularly the iron industry. Though many still lived on small-holdings and others worked seasonally, more and more were becoming entirely dependent on their wages.

Wages rose steadily and by the third decade of the eighteenth century were governed mainly by the market since the fixing of wages by Quarter Sessions had lapsed. Arthur Young noted that 1s. a day was a labourer's wage in Glamorgan in 1768 and by 1793 7s. a week was being paid in Brecknockshire ; 8d. a day was still the winter wage in Merioneth and 1s. in summer. Fluctuation occurred between areas, and wages in good agricultural areas could be from 10s.to £1 a year more for a man or maid-servant than in poorer areas whilst competition from industry in some counties forced agricultural wages up somewhat. Down to 1770 wages at least kept pace with prices but thereafter tended to lag behind and after 1790 real wages suffered a drastic cut as prices outdistanced wages. A ploughman's wage was £5 and upwards plus keep in 1794 and a dairymaid's a little less ; during the wartime period the Rev. Walter Davies reckoned that wages rose about 30%. But wages responded to the market less slowly than prices which was to the advantage of farmers ; nor was the pace the same throughout the country.

Prices rose steadily to 1750 but thereafter more sharply and after 1790 soared upwards. The main indicator is the price of wheat and although there was little wheat grown or consumed in Wales the price of barley and oats kept pace with it. War, blockade and the population rise contributed to it but the main cause was the poor harvests from 1793 to 1795 with their drastically reduced yields. Welsh farmers in general were not severely hit because they concentrated on stock rearing not on cash crops. The price of meat was steadier but lower than grain and although it was lower in Wales than in London, it doubled during the war period. The consumption of meat by the poor was low, its place being taken by salted bacon and fish if at all. Complaints of *drudaniaeth* (dearness) were common and were echoed in popular verse for even salt rose in price with wartime taxation and the poor consumed more of it than anyone else. In the *Case of Labourers in Husbandry* (1795) the Rev. D. Davies, the Welsh rector of Barkham, quoted three family budgets from Denbighshire and two from Merionethshire each showing a deficit.[1] Virtually all the incomes were consumed on food which was mainly bread and milk foods

[1] See p. 224

with meat being completely absent. This was the lowest
possible diet and the increasing consumption of potatoes is
another indicator of extreme poverty. The steep rise in the
poor rate points to more dependence on poor relief, and in the
four North Wales counties other than Anglesey and Caernarfon
the poor rate quadrupled between 1775 and 1785, almost a
decade before real hardship set in. The situation was not as
bad in areas of developing industry and Sir Frederick Eden
in his *State of the Poor* (1797) quotes a Monmouthshire labourer's
budget where his wife spent 4*d*. a week on tea and sugar
though here again meat was absent.

When so many families lived so near the starvation line the
meagre earnings of the women and children of the household
made a big difference. A hard week's knitting might provide
less than 2*s*. profit and even a sociable evening in the form of a
noson wau (knitting night) was turned to advantage. The
custom of *gwlana* (wool gathering) provided enough wool to
make cloth and though all clothes were homespun they became
more colourful as time went on. Travellers commented on the
distinctive fashions of dress in different localities. Legs were
clad in worsted stockings and feet in clogs, children running
barefoot in summer.

Housing conditions in most areas were squalid, the expression ' habitations of wretchedness ' being the general tenor of
comment. Houses were built by those who needed them and
were often the product of communal effort in the absence of
capital. Many of them were *tai un nos* (one night houses) built
overnight by squatters and so makeshift in construction and
appearance. Roofs were thatched with rushes, floors were of
mud, windows unglazed and smoke from peat fires added to
the gloom and pungent smell. The Rev. Walter Davies describes
them thus : ' One smokey hearth, for it should not be styled a
kitchen, and one damp litter cell, for it cannot be called a
bedroom, are frequently all the space allotted to a labourer,
his wife and four or five children ... Three-fourths of the
victims of the putrid fever perish in the mephitic air of these
dwellings '. Arthur Young describes some Pembrokeshire
cottages as no better than Irish cabins. Better housing and
more picturesque was found in the Vales of Clwyd and Glamorgan and in Montgomeryshire. Many farmhouses were built

in the eighteenth century often embracing dwelling-house, cowshed and hay-loft under one roof in traditional manner but the 1801 Census indicates that outside areas of industrial development very few cottages were being built. Rents rose during the Revolutionary War period, a Cardiganshire labourer paying £2 2s. a year out of his earnings of £8 for a cottage and place to keep a cow. The Rev. Walter Davies reckoned that rents were 300% too high. Standards of comfort were primitive and inventories testify that household contents ran only to the bare necessities of furniture ; pieces of furniture were so valued that they were specifically named as bequests in wills.

Life expectation for the poor fell much short of 50, even shorter in occupations like lead-mining. Infant mortality was high and if one survived birth there was still a high risk to the age of 5. Infant mortality did come down after 1780 only to rise again during the hard times after 1793. Resistance to disease was so low that any epidemic took a heavy toll. Medical facilities hardly existed apart from the ministrations of self-designated country doctors like the Rev. J. R. Jones, of Ramoth. A belief existed even among members of the Royal Society that inoculation was early practised in Wales, probably the ' cow pock ', but high mortality rates lend it little support. We hear of inoculation against small-pox in Haverfordwest in 1775 and in 1779 Sir Watkin Williams Wynn had the poor of Ruabon inoculated by a Bala doctor. Public dispensaries appeared in towns before the end of our period but no hospitals are known to have existed.

Pauperism attracted little attention in the early eighteenth century and what there was could usually be met out of charity. *Cymorth* (aid) was an institution which still survived for the relief of individual paupers by private donations. *Cardota* (begging) was general, the poor going from door to door begging for bread and victuals and charity school organisers complained that it interfered with child attendance. Collections were made in church and by Dissenting causes and sometimes a portion of the church mise was set aside for poor relief. Charity was recognised as an obligation on the part of the better-off and even industrial concerns like the Anglesey copper-masters made donations of as much as £354 to a flour fund

for the poor. Organised relief was, however, lacking until
comparatively late within our period, Monmouthshire being
virtually the only Welsh county to implement the Elizabethan
poor law system in Stuart times. Poor rates had been introduced to Wrexham by 1729 but were unknown in Anglesey
and Caernarfonshire until about 1760 and after 1770 hardly
any parish could avoid a levy, but only the more populous
parishes appointed overseers in addition to churchwardens.
The provision of workhouses where paupers might be set to
work was not implemented till the 1730s and some were
equipped with looms and spinning-wheels. An Act of 1792
enabled 80 parishes in Montgomeryshire and the borderland
to join together to build a House of Industry at Forden which
could house 500 but it was found to be more expensive than
providing outdoor relief. During the French Wars some
parishes laid out money on corn purchases to ward off starvation ; others paid the rents of paupers and for this reason
paupers were regarded as desirable tenants. It is difficult to
find instances of wage supplementation on the Speenhamland
model but the decline in the standard of living of the poor
after 1750 and the rise of the poor rates strongly suggests it.
The statistics for the rural parish of Meifod (Monts.) are
illuminating. In 1701, its poor and church rate combined
amounted to only £39 ; in 1761, a poor rate of 6d. in the £ was
levied and the expense was £91 ; by 1800, the rate had risen
to 6s. 6d. in the £, the expense to £1195. Parishes put all kinds
of obstacles in the way of people from obtaining a settlement
within the parish ; farmers hired servants for short terms and
squatting on the common was discouraged. More money was
often spent on litigation concerning settlement cases than would
have relieved the persons concerned. Pauper children were
boarded out as apprentices and farmers were often obliged to
take them ; this constituted a pool of cheap labour since very
few were taught trades. In Amlwch, the regulation that
paupers should wear a patch with a large P was revived in
1794.

Some attempts at self help were made by or on behalf of the
poor ; friendly societies caught on after 1750 and by 1800 there
were 5 in Wrexham and 3 in a small town like Machynlleth.
Contributions were about 6d. a month and benefits were drawn

at times of sickness and death. There were savings societies in Cardiff about 1750 and in 1789 a prospectus of one was published in Caerffili to which contributions of 6d. a week were proposed ; such societies appear to be unknown in North Wales at this time.

The violence of the working class has attracted more attention since riots were sporadic throughout the century especially in years of shortage like 1794-6, 1798-1800 and 1812 but there are several earlier instances. Almost all were food riots, spontaneous in outbreak and short-lived in duration and they were usually directed against farmers and merchants who were suspected of creating artificial shortages for profiteering. They appeared in rural as well as industrial areas but miners and weavers were very prominent and so were women. They seldom led to looting and when corn was commandeered it was shared and paid for at what was regarded as a fair price. It does not appear that there were any demands to raise wages. Enclosure riots involved the small farmers mainly and these had appeared as early as 1791 on Hirwaun Common and in 1812 at Llanrhystud (Cards.). Working men, artisans and small farmers took part in the emigration of the 1790s and emigrants left from parts of the country like Caernarfonshire from which few had gone before. The opening of mines and quarries in the U.S.A. offered prospect of good wages even for labourers who had no stake in the land they were leaving behind.

Rural Life

Country life was vigorous and colourful, its pattern determined by the seasonal round of agriculture around which traditional customs had grown. There was very little leisure apart from what was offered by Christmastide and saints' days and two important dates in the farming calendar, *Calan Mai* and *Calan Gaeaf*[1] which had their distinctive observances and appropriate carols. Circumstances were so hard that even social life had its utilitarian ends and work often had its lighter side. Farming was labour-intensive and a farmhouse was a social institution. For farming tasks such as harvesting which required more labour than usual the labour force could be

[1] The Kalends of May and the Kalends of Winter

augmented by the *medel gymorth* when all those who were under an obligation to a farmer for having the use of horse and cart or for being allowed to plant potatoes in his field returned it by the recognised number of days of harvest service. Many who were under no obligation were ready to help in order to share in the merriment since home-made *cwrw bach* or *diod fain*[1] flowed freely and harvest home was attended by a good supper. The last sheaf harvested was *y gaseg fedi* which was borne into the farmhouse against opposition from within and dancing in the barn rounded off the end of harvest. Some farm work like reaping and ploughing was done to the rhythmic singing of work songs. Sheep-shearing was organised on a communal basis each farm having its allotted day on which the neighbourhood assembled to help.

Marriages were attended by a certain ritual which was designed to give the young couple a start in life. After a dowry had been settled the families on either side engaged the services of a *gwahoddwr* (bidder) who went from house to house announcing the impending marriage, inviting guests and reminding people of any *pwyth* (obligation) to either family. *Pwyth* was dutifully returned and on the wedding day the young couple received all manner of useful gifts which were necessary for setting up house and in the course of the day goods up to £40 or £50 in value might be received. Social critics maintained that this institution made it too easy for young people to get married ; it is certain that the age of marriage was lower in the eighteenth than in the nineteenth century. Funerals also had their observances. The *gwylnos* (wake-night) started as a religious observance but it became an occasion for revelry. Guests brought food and drink and on the funeral day a collection was made to defray expenses. What strikes us is the facility with which events were turned into social occasions to bring some colour into an otherwise drab existence and how these customs served a social purpose to help those who were in need.

Gŵyliau mabsant ('saints' days') were faithfully kept because they were the only holidays that could be expected. They started as religious festivals and this remained a feature in Anglesey but in general the revelries took over. The church

[1] Small beer

was still the centre of life and the churchyard the venue of most activities. When local loyalties were so strong it is not surprising that rivalry between parishes should be equally so. Games like *cnapan* and *bando* were communal games which offered the opportunity to put skill and strength to the test. Sabbatarianism was not observed and fairs were often held on Sundays to avoid interfering with work. Following morning service the rest of the day was given over to merriment. A contemporary verse gives a characteristic description by a reformed sinner :

> Er dechrau f'oes, nid oes mo'r gêl,
> Bum lawer Sul mor siwr a'r sêl,
> Yn trainio bowl, yn trin y bel,
> Mewn poen a thrafel arw,
> Coetio a bobio a neidio wnawn
> A gwario a gawn am gwrw.[1]

Social critics were bemoaning the frivolity of the age long before the Methodists took over.

Folk customs like morris dances were still upheld in the Vale of Glamorgan according to William Thomas, the diarist of Michaelstone-super-Ely, and from Easter to September *taplasau haf* formed summer revelries. A *twmpath dawns* ('country dance ') was held in one or other village of the Vale throughout the summer and fiddlers and harpists earned a living by them. The diarist, himself puritanically inclined, took some comfort from the fact that these customs also appeared to be declining. The *Mari Lwyd*[2] remained a Christmastide custom in the Vale of Glamorgan longer than anywhere else albeit.

Although fairs had primarily an economic purpose since it was there that most people obtained their needs from travelling pedlars they also had their entertainment side. The ballad-singer was always in attendance singing and selling ballads and sometimes a travelling troupe played an interlude.

Cruel sport like cock-fighting was a popular attraction and often the only sport in which all classes still joined. Cock-

[1] Since youth I have spent many a Sunday, I cannot deny, playing bowls or ball, in pain and travail often ; playing quoits and bobbing and leaping and spending what I had on beer.
[2] A Christmastide observance wherein a horse's head bedecked with ribbons was paraded.

fighting was at its greatest popularity in George III's time and the fact that it had its ' Welsh Rules ' and that the principal contest was called the ' Welsh Main ' signifies its prominence in Wales. Gentry and even clergy kept fighting cocks and cockpits were to be found in churchyards as well as in the yards of inns. Contests might be held between rival country-houses such as are spoken of by Elizabeth Baker, the Dolgellau diarist. They were often held in conjunction with horse races during ' wakes week ' which usually fell between Easter and Whitsun.

Rural crafts could be a communal activity ; the *noson wau* was a night spent in knitting while the men-folk either made baskets, ropes or, more romantically, love-spoons. The blacksmith's forge or cobbler's shop was a place for foregathering and there the craft of the *cyfarwydd* (story-teller) was much exercised on ghost stories and the like which fed the credulousness and superstition of the age with beliefs in various portents of death. Although punishment of witches was abolished by an enlightened age in 1736 belief in them persisted and many a farmer with a sick animal on his hands or a farmer's wife who could not make butter feared they were under the spell or evil-eye of some old crone and hastened to the *dyn hysbys*, who was the local oracle, for relief. As enlightened a man as Lewis Morris believed in fairies alleging that the little men called ' knockers ' had been very busy directing the miners to a rich lode of lead at Esgair-mwyn.

The Towns

Eighteenth century Welsh towns were small in size and population, urbanisation and the emergence of large towns only beginning to make their appearance by the end of our period. Each county had five or six towns or extended villages, Radnorshire rather less and Glamorgan more. They were the centres of communication and serviced a wide rural area whose economic life they so often reflected. Natural growth accounts for a rise of 50-100% in the population of most of these towns in the course of the century and increased economic activity was beginning to attract immigrant population.

Towns of military origin had evolved as administrative centres. County towns were the venues of the Court of Great Sessions twice annually (the Assizes in Monmouthshire), their sessions lasting up to six days. Quarter Sessions met four times a year alternating in some counties between two towns and there parliamentary elections were held which could last up to three weeks. All these occasions were attended by social functions and as William Bulkeley noted, many of the gentry were in town ' not for any business there was but to dance in balls and feasting which were every night '. It is no wonder that towns where country business was transacted should become centres for attorneys and professional men whose services were in increasing demand as economic life developed.

There were indications, however, that corporate life was in decline. Some towns had fallen under the control of small cliques who managed civic affairs in their own interest and as the commissioners who inquired into the state of municipal corporations intimated were 'not altogether free from suspicion ' of appropriating borough property which had disappeared in unexplained circumstances. Carmarthen had a very tempestuous civic history inasmuch as there were two rival corporations claiming control until the Grenville Act of 1765 resolved the matter. Even so, corporation property had to be mortgaged to defray the expense of the Act. Some corporations existed merely for the purpose of returning members of Parliament and development was often arrested in the interest of maintaining political control. Policy in regard to admission to burgess rights differed widely ; in Cardigan which enjoyed exemption from tolls on its trade the privilege was enjoyed by a great many whereas in Swansea which was already a thriving town admission was deliberately restricted so that few enjoyed the benefits and had the effect of preventing the town from realising its economic potential. Some towns had yielded to the control of local magnates who might in some instances be a lord of the manor as the Duke of Beaufort was in Swansea. The most enterprising residents often disdained to knuckle under to the lord's local minions and so were often denied any responsibility in the government of the town.

The accounts and impressions of contemporary tourists indicate that towns were undergoing change though architecturally and from the standpoint of town planning Welsh towns do not compare favourably with some English or even Irish towns that were developing at this period. The volume of

N

Georgian architecture in Wales is small because its economic development occurred later ; it is, however, fairly well-distributed. Brecon has several Georgian streets and Malkin describes it as ' one of the best-built in Wales in point of accommodation for persons of fortune and condition . . . the number of spacious and modern-built houses is greater in proportion to its size than perhaps any town in Wales '. It was already a town of contrasts since the streets occupied by the poor are described as ' very mean and often ruinous '. The small town of Montgomery has retained its Georgian character best of all because little expansion has taken place there since. Developments were afoot at Milford from the time that Nelson discovered the great potential of the Haven as a naval anchorage and dockyard, and due to the enterprise of Charles Greville who acted as the local landowner, Sir William Hamilton's agent in planning the development of the town. An Act was obtained in 1790 and the early buildings in the town are Georgian in style. Georgian houses are to be found in Beaumaris, Ruthin, Haverfordwest, Aberystwyth, Cowbridge, Chepstow and Monmouth though whole Georgian streets and crescents are hard to come by.

Carmarthen, being a prosperous port and distributive centre for a large area, was the largest of the old towns and Dafydd Thomas in *Hanes Tair Sir ar Ddeg Cymru*[1] states that its houses were fair and the bagpipes were heard at fashionable weddings oftener than anywhere in Wales.[2] Another traveller described it as ' one of the most wealthy and polite towns in Wales ' with some good private houses belonging to neighbouring gentry who lived there during the winter months. George Whitefield confirms this view and the actor-manager Masterman uses the word ' urbane ' to describe the society of Carmarthen and Swansea which must have been unusual for a Welsh town of this period. It offered many diversions which often proved too much for the theological students who attended the Academy there. But though some of them dissipated their time at cards others might resort to the reading room to read the *Gentleman's*

---

[1] ' The History of Wales ' Thirteen Counties '.
[2] Teg yw'r tai sy'n Nhref Caerfyrddin
O Heol Awst i Stryd y Brenin ;
A'r bagpipes sy'n amla'n canu
I'r Priodasau mwya'ng Nghymru.

Magazine or to attend lectures in Science which is not to be wondered at when we remember that the Academy's tutors had friends in the Birmingham Lunar Society.

Monmouth probably captures the atmosphere of a Georgian town more than most Welsh towns combining prosperity derived from a rich agricultural district with elegance conferred by some fine town houses lining its broad streets. The gentry sought genteel pastimes even in the country and enterprising innkeepers provided assembly rooms where fashionable dances and balls were held and which were barred to social inferiors. Abergavenny and Monmouth had assembly rooms and one of the Mackworth correspondents tells us that the fashionable assemblies at Neath were superior even to those of Swansea. Horse-racing became a popular pastime for the gentry and racecourses appeared outside several towns. Race-meetings lasted a whole week at Llandrindod and even at less fashionable places like Tywyn (Mer.), Llanberis (Caerns.) and Newmarket (Flints.), they were attended by all kinds of genteel diversions.

Wrexham was unrivalled in North Wales for its size, prosperity and appearance and the bard had some justification in describing it as the largest in Wales and possessing a fine steeple.[1] Fashionable balls were common at Denbigh and Twm o'r Nant denounces them for debauchery. The fashionable institution of the coffee-house appeared not only at Wrexham and Denbigh where it was named after John Wilkes but as far afield as Bala and Dinas Mawddwy.

Two trends in urban life became apparent by the end of our period, first the desire for economic expansion and second, the growth in civic pride. Growing prosperity increased the resources of corporations and this manifested itself in secular buildings. Till the eighteenth century money had mainly gone into ecclesiastical buildings and this form of beneficence continued in the form of church repairs, re-roofing, laying stone-floors and installing pews rather than in the building of new churches. The growth of Nonconformity led to the building of chapels in some numbers before the end of the century. More unusual was the deployment of money for building town and guild halls which depended at least in part on private

[1] Glwys yw Gwrecsam, teg ei chlochdy,
Dyna'r dref sydd fwya' yn Nghymru. (D. Thomas)

munificence. The guildhall at Carmarthen was built with the aid of a patron, John Adams ; Montgomery town hall also dates from this period and the building of market halls had already commenced in the towns of the Severn Valley before the end of our period.

Corporations were slow to become amenity-conscious. Few towns could rival Caernarfon in 1673 from Richard Bloome's account : ' The streets are regular though the buildings are not and exceedingly well-paved. It is the only place in Wales I have seen so . . . Most of the Welsh towns have the two faults of narrow streets and bad pavements '. Cardiff would have confirmed this opinion since one hundred years later virtually every street in the town was presented before Quarter Sessions as being in need of attention on account of obstructions, nuisances and disrepair. Civic enterprise obtained in 1774 an Act of Parliament for Better Paving and Lighting of its streets under which 26 street commissioners were appointed but they were very inactive since it was still reported in 1800 that only three streets had been paved. In 1775, five oil lamps were erected but even in 1820 some streets were still candle-lit. It was not till 1809 that Swansea came to appoint a body of commissioners whilst the inhabitants of Merthyr were still threatening to indict their vestry for neglect of their streets in 1813.

Very important to urban development was the improvement of communications between towns and especially with London. By 1765, Brecon was connected to London by a post-coach and by the turn of the century Cardiff had a daily coach service to London. This encouraged the opening of inns in towns along coach routes which also served the purpose of posting stations where horses could be changed. They were also frequently used as post-offices where commodities from household goods to S.P.C.K. Bibles were left for collection. Innkeepers began to tout for trade and inserted advertisements in local papers. A traveller could stay at the best hotel in Neath for five shillings a week and three shillings for his servant with hay and grass for two horses at 12*d*. a night. By 1800 most towns had post-offices which served the countryside around and by 1807 some areas had a daily delivery of mail ; a letter put on the mail coach in London could reach Cardiff on the same day.

Much transportation was seaborne and river ports as well as small coastal towns owed their prosperity to this fact. The expansion of agriculture, seasonal fishing and the development of industry in their hinterland contributed to their prosperity. Aberystwyth, for instance, profited from mining developments nearby and the town came largely under the control of mining speculators towards the end of the eighteenth century. Its procuring a Harbour Act in 1780 is typical of many projects of local improvements which increased traffic in and out of the town. Merchants dealing in wares necessary for mining and shipbuilding opened businesses in the town as in others similarly placed.

Spas became very popular in the eighteenth century and attracted visitors to drink their curative waters and to enjoy the social round. Theophilus Evans is credited with having discovered the wells at Llanwrtyd and three springs were also discovered at Builth. By 1740, Llandrindod was proving a considerable attraction and a writer in 1754 described it as ' the only place for diversion in Wales and many genteel visitors frequented the Great House and Long Rooms searching for health and entertainment '. Strolling players performed every evening during Race-Week. Lewis Morris recommended the town in a letter to the Cymmrodorion in 1760 as fit to entertain the best sort of company with diversions for females as well as males. Trefriw became the spa of the North but did not become such a place of resort as the spas of Brecknockshire and Radnorshire. By the 1760s they were losing much of their popularity as the fashion of sea-bathing caught on and led to the rise of the seaside resort.

Sea-bathing was believed to be health-giving and the attraction to the seaside brought the beginning of tourism in Wales. Some parish authorities paid the expenses of invalids to go to the seaside for a cure, Lampeter, for instance, doing so as early as 1779. So great was the concourse at Aberystwyth in the summer season that many visitors had to sleep in their carriages. The development of boarding houses along the sea-front was afoot in several towns by 1800 and town improvements were undertaken and walks and promenades laid out to attract visitors. Swansea, already developing as an industrial town was just as anxious to be regarded as a fashionable resort.

Its houses were described in 1798 as ' chiefly modern, hand-
some and commodious and those along the sea-front were so
designed as to cater for visitors '. The laying of a horse tramroad in 1804 to convey visitors to Mumbles provided the world
with its first passenger railway. Tenby was supposed to attract
the better-class of visitors whilst road improvements brought
scores of Midlands tradespeople to the resorts. Resorts in
north-east Wales were somewhat slower getting under way but
Abergele was described in 1797 as a much-frequented place
though overshadowed by Parkgate in the Wirral. The first
decade of the nineteenth century brought developments along
the north coast as well.

Economic development accounts for the growth of old towns
and also led to the formation of completely new towns. Towns
which were not incorporated were often the centres of various
trades because they were free of guild control. Thus Dolgellau
became a centre for cloth finishing, Bala for the stocking and
hat trade and Wrexham had a variety of small craft workshops
attached to merchants' houses in its main streets. It became a
centre for cloth dealers from Yorkshire as well as a banking
centre for a growing industrial area. The Severn Valley towns
of Welshpool, Newtown and Llanidloes were the only places,
with the exception of the lower Teifi Valley, where a factory-
based industry was successfully established.

It was in the localities of heavy industry that new towns
began to make their appearance. Holywell in the north-east
became an important smelting centre and developed a chemical
industry as well as a textile factory and thereby concentrated
more industry into one location than anywhere else in the
North. The effects of industrial growth on urban development
was more apparent in South Wales, however, and Merthyr
Tydfil was Wales's first industrial town and was soon to become
its largest with a population of 7,700 by 1801. This population
was to increase by a half in every decade between 1801 and
1831. The nucleus of the town was the old village but it was
around the four main ironworks that clusters of workmen's
cottages began to appear mainly as the result of speculative
building. The in-filling process which gave Merthyr the
appearance of a unitary town came somewhat later. The new
community which grew up there showed not only social but

racial complexity that was unknown in Wales previously and that this should have developed without much civic control is all the more remarkable since Merthyr did not have a town council till 1835, the parish vestry still serving as the only unit of local government. The traditional elements in the community were not obscured and farmers still kept their place in the vestry along with ironworks officials, tradesmen and professional men. Even more astonishing is the fact that the smallest of all Nonconformist sects, the Unitarians, had an influence in the civic life of the town far beyond their numbers and were prominent in the Philosophical Society founded in 1807. Conflict between rival interests soon emerged since the interest of the tradesmen who owned much cottage property did not always correspond with that of the ironmasters especially over rating. Developments at Aberdare were comparable to those at Merthyr but at the heads of the Monmouthshire Valleys industrialisation caused more diffuse settlement.

Blaenafon was the largest town in north Monmouthshire but when Archdeacon Coxe visited it in 1798 it was still a community of only a thousand people settled around the ironworks. Settlement around Ebbw Vale was dispersed along the Ebbw Fawr and Ebbw Fach valleys and the town grew out of a collection of industrial villages. Though Pontypool had been a centre of ironworking and tinplate manufacture for some time, settlement was strung out there also in linear fashion along the river. Tredegar was probably the nearest approach to a nucleated town in this area. Coxe noted one unusual development at Nantyglo in the appearance of tenement housing built by ironmasters which is little known outside the Monmouthshire valleys. These buildings were two or more storeys high and overcrowding was common since on average every tenement had 1½ families. The decade between 1801 and 1810 saw a great influx of population, the Welsh-speaking communities gathering at the top of the valleys especially around Beaufort and the English and Irish further down. Racial, language and religious differences as well as geography retarded their coalescence and it is no wonder that these places were the scenes of ' Scotch Cattle ' violence later. The Harfords, local ironmasters, anticipated trouble and forbade the sale of liquor on any of their property—an unusually early example of temperance.

At a time when so little attention was paid to human welfare it is not surprising that so little was given to environmental pollution. This was regarded as inevitable if thought about at all and rivers became open sewers. Though the burgesses of Swansea consigned the activities of Lockwood, Morris and Co. to a village outside the borough this did not minimise the effect of smelting on the landscape of the lower Tawe Valley which is still only too apparent today.

SUGGESTED READING

L. T. Davies and A. Edwards, *Welsh life in the eighteenth century*, London, 1939.

G. N. Evans, *Social life in mid-eighteenth century Anglesey*, Cardiff, 1936.

R. W. Jones, *Bywyd cymdeithasol Cymru yn y ddeunawfed ganrif*, Llundain, 1931.

T. M. Owen, *Welsh folk customs*, Cardiff, 1959.

B. B. Thomas, *The Old Order*, Cardiff, 1945.

H. M. Vaughan, *South Wales Squires*, London, 1926.

Articles:

A. E. Davies, 'Some aspects of the operation of the old Poor Law in Cardiganshire, 1750–1834', *Ceredigion*, VI, 1968.

K. Evans, 'A survey of Caernarvon', *Trans. Caerns. H.S.*, XXXII, 1971.

D. Howell, 'Landed society in Pembrokeshire', *Pembrokeshire Historian*, no. 3, 1971.

D. J. V. Jones, 'The corn riots in Wales, 1793–1801', *W.H.R.*, II, 4, 1964–5.

D. L. B. Jones, 'Notes on the social life of Carmarthenshire during the eighteenth century', *Trans. Cymmr.*, 1963.

E. Inglis-Jones, 'A Pembrokeshire county family in the eighteenth century', *N.L.W.Jnl.*, XVII, 1971.

P. R. Roberts, 'The decline of the Welsh squires in the eighteenth century', *N.L.W.Jnl.*, XIII, 1963–4.

——, 'The Merioneth gentry and local government', *J.Mer.H.* and *R.S.*, V, 1, 1965.

——, 'Social history of the Merioneth gentry', *ibid.*, IV, 3, 1963.

——, 'The gentry and the land in eighteenth century Merioneth', *ibid.*, IV, 4, 1964.

12. The Political Awakening

The American Question

THE dispute between Britain and her American colonists evoked a great deal of interest in Wales on account of the great number of Welshmen who had emigrated to America but still kept in touch with their native land. To many Welshmen in Wales, Pennsylvania and Delaware were a second Wales across the sea, and America was regarded as the apotheosis of freedom, a sentiment constantly reiterated in countless letters to correspondents in Wales. The Nonconformists in particular maintained close contacts with churches in America, some of which had emigrated as whole congregations from Wales. To many Nonconformists the colonists were only so many congregations beyond the sea and Sir Lewis Namier alleges that they were the first to develop a modern view of empire. The spirit of kinship with the colonists in their struggle in turn caused the Dissenters in this country to reject the attitude of acceptance of proscription under which they laboured. This interest and sympathy was felt at the level of '*y werin*' and what started as a sentiment matured into a feeling of common interest and developed political ramifications. Anti-American propagandists roundly accused the Presbyterians, especially the 'seditious writers' among them, of being the authors of the American 'rebellion'. The American question acted as a catalyst in the political development of this country and added political content to elections where none had existed before.

Interest was added to the conflict by the fact that the Americans had many champions in this country. Bishop Jonathan Shipley of St. Asaph was that rare phenomenon—a liberal bishop, and espoused the American cause in the House of Lords. He damned his own chances of preferment when he preached a sermon to the S.P.C.K. in 1773 eulogising the colonists, holding that America was 'the only great nursery of freemen left on the face of the earth', a view echoed by Dr.

Richard Price. His dissemination of such ideas made people more amenable to receive the doctrine of the Rights of Man later on. Dr. Price, a native of Ty'nton, near Bridgend, made a major contribution to the development of political thought in America. He was educated at the Presbyterian academy, then at Chancefield, before proceeding to a Unitarian pastorate in London. He also influenced the minds of sympathisers at home which furthered radical thinking in this country. Through his contacts with Franklin and Dissenters in America, Price was one of the best-informed speakers on the American question. His most important work was *Observation on the Nature of Civil Liberty* which was a justification of the colonial position; it also implied a criticism of a system of government which was not even representative at home let alone abroad. The colonial struggle, he claimed, had as much to do with ' English ' liberties as with their own rights. He raised the argument above constitutional rights and precedents which passed for ' English rights ' urging the colonists to assert the ' Rights of Man ' which were natural and inalienable, thus giving more of a philosophical than a historical justification to their claims. He reiterated Locke's ideas about the popular nature of sovereignty and maintained that self-government was necessary to liberty. These fundamental principles were enshrined in the American Declaration of Independence which was drawn up in the same year as Price's book. Price's work not only inspired the colonists at a critical moment but also re-stimulated the popular cause in this country. The book ran into twelve editions in one year and won popular acclaim but his ideas were retailed mostly at second hand in Wales because no Welsh version was published. The City of London granted Price its freedom and the United States made him an honorary citizen and invited him to settle there. Yale University conferred its doctorate upon him at the same time as it honoured George Washington, the ' father ' of the Union. Thomas Jefferson, who was the principal author of the Declaration of Independence, was proud to acknowledge his Welsh descent and was one of sixteen signatories who were of Welsh stock. In the War of Independence fourteen of the colonial generals were of Welsh descent including the Chief Army Surgeon, Dr. John Morgan.

The War was condemned by Dr. Price in his second work, *Additional Observations* and popular versifiers, too, regarded it as fratricide. The hardship it caused as well as its unpopularity was the theme of ballads, the commonest mouthpiece of protest, alleging that the heavy taxation which accompanied it went to maintain placemen in comfortable sinecures. Thomas Pennant, the literary squire of Downing, warned against the abuse of their power by militia officers in his *Free Thoughts on the Militia Laws* (1781) advising the ordinary people of North Wales about their rights and protesting that taxes to support the militia were heavier than any bar the poor rates. Welsh M.P.s were little in sympathy with popular feeling and never was this as apparent before. Many of them were followers of Grenville, the author of the Stamp Act, and when Lord North came to power in 1770 they switched support to him. North showed them the same kind of attention as Newcastle had done and great was the expectation of reward from his hands. Self-interest activated their political conduct and none more so than those members who held government contracts like Edward Lewis (Radnor boroughs), Capel Hanbury (Monmouthshire), Herbert Mackworth (Glamorgan boroughs) and Anthony Bacon, the Merthyr ironmaster who sat for an English constituency. They backed the policy of coercion to the hilt even when others began to doubt the wisdom of prolonging the War. Reverses to British arms, especially at Saratoga, led many Welsh gentlemen to launch recruiting campaigns in their localities, Thomas Johnes and John Campbell, for instance, raising the 75th (Prince of Wales) Regiment. In 1779 invasion was expected when Britain lost command of the sea and this led to the forming of Volunteer Corps. ' *Y Cartref* ', at Trefeca, contributed a number of recruits who served in America and their letters to their brethren are informative about the life of a British soldier in the conflict. Many American loyalists fled to this country and some found asylum at Cowbridge.

After 1778, failure of success and war-weariness resulted in a fall-off of support for the government. In that same year, North annoyed many of his Welsh supporters by instituting an inquiry into encroachments on Crown land in Wales. Lord Bulkeley was the first to take alarm according to Horace Walpole, publishing ' a warm advertisement ' against ' the tyrannic intentions' of the Administration. He enlisted the support of the young Sir Watkin Williams Wynn and the members for Anglesey and Caernarfon to form what he called ' a little parliamentary phalanx ' against North, calling themselves ' patriots '. This was at a crucial moment when North's ministry, under a barrage of criticism about the conduct of the War, was tottering to its fall and in five critical divisions in 1782 more Welsh M.P.s voted against than for the government. North's fall brought Lord Shelburne, friend of Dr. Price, into office and in carrying through the peace preliminaries he had the support of most of the Welsh Members.

The Reform Movement

The beginnings of the reform movement are to be seen soon after 1760 when the Dissenters, no longer satisfied with their lot, began to agitate for equality of rights with Anglicans. Political disaffection also began to show itself in the sixties from which time reform was in the air. There was no agreement on the extent of the reform that was necessary but by the 1780s the demand could not be ignored. Some regarded the constitution as perfect but thought that it needed an overhaul as many abuses had crept into its operation. Others believed the basis of the constitution to be too narrow and that it needed broadening by the extension of the franchise and the representation. Some of the more doctrinaire reformers went as far as to advocate a republic, especially after the outbreak of revolution in France in 1789. All views are represented in different degrees in the reform movement in Wales.

Dissenters' Grievances

The earliest stirrings are to be seen among the Dissenters. Dissent was given legal recognition by the Toleration Act of 1689 as Lord Mansfield was later to make clear in a famous judgment. It only conferred on Dissenters the right to worship in meeting-houses licensed for the purpose but no equality of civil rights with Anglicans, which branded them as second-class citizens. They learnt to develop an attitude of acceptance being thankful for the protection of the House of Hanover. The Whigs were sensitive to their situation because the Dissenters provided them with electoral support since many of them were freeholders or freemen in towns. After 1763 the Dissenters gradually forsook this passive attitude and became more assertive. Dr. Priestley stated that this post-War period was the most seasonable for the discussion of everything related to civil and religious liberty under the stimulation of events in America which caused Dissenters to identify their own with the colonial cause. The connection between religious and civil reform can be well-authenticated in Wales and the origins of the popular interest in political reform lie in part in the struggle for religious equality. Although the Old Dissenters were agreed on the need for civil rights there was no unanimity as to whom they should comprehend and Roman Catholics were generally regarded as beyond the pale. The Presbyterians, inclining to Arianism in theology, were the most radical politically and were considered an embarrassment by the more orthodox sects. One distinctive feature of Dissent was the rejection of the claim of any human agency to have a right to intervene between a man and his conscience and thereby the right of the State to prescribe any form of religion.

Dafydd Llwyd, the Arminian minister of Llwynrhydowen (Cards.) was one of the earliest voices of protest against religious oppression. A more extreme view was that of Thomas Roberts, Llwynrhudol, who expressed anti-clerical and anti-tithe sentiments and was an advocate of church reform but sought redress by argument, reason and enlightenment of opinion. It is not surprising that Dissenting ministers were in the vanguard since they had a platform in the pulpit and, lacking a press, the sermon was the most effective way of spreading ideas. Sermons were often preached on commemorative occasions and their theme was often political, Dr. Richard Price's sermons, for example, contributing much to the literature of radicalism.

After 1766, there was a concentration of attention on specific grievances, the first being subscription to the Thirtynine Articles of Religion. Welsh Dissenters were averse to dogma especially from the direction of the State. Bishop Watson of Llandaff supported this viewpoint and would abolish subscription if only because uniformity of belief was unattainable. Bishop Shipley of St. Asaph was another prelate who argued the case in the House of Lords but although a measure passed the Commons in 1773 it was repeatedly rejected by the House of Lords. The repeal of the Test and Corporation Acts was another specific issue on which Parliament refused to grant redress between 1787 and 1790. The refusal of the Government to concede their moderate demands led many Dissenters to ponder the need for parliamentary reform and henceforth they were prominent in the struggle.

The Growth of Radicalism

The origins of radicalism in Wales were mainly rural since the urban proletariat did not arrive on the scene till the last quarter of the eighteenth century. There was some upheaval in Glamorgan and Monmouthshire in 1763 whose cause and extent is not known but which was directed against the return of a placeman to Parliament at a Glamorgan by-election of that year. The Association Movement which blossomed during the years 1779-83 brought together reformers of different shades of opinion from those who only wanted the removal of abuses to those who wanted a measure of parliamentary reform and the extension of the franchise. It was organised on a county basis, hence the name County Movement which it is sometimes given. The County Meeting of gentry and freeholders was its platform and its constitutional methods and entirely respectable nature were stressed. Yorkshire was its place of origin but Middlesex became an important centre of activity as M.P.s began to take it over. One arm of the Movement was concerned primarily with economical reform and worked for efficiency and economy in administration and the reform of abuses in Court and government. This was the cause espoused by the Rockingham Whigs with Edmund Burke as their chief spokesman. He was the promoter of the 'Oeconomy Bill' in 1780 which reviewed the administration of the Principality of Wales, the Earldom of Chester and the Duchy of Lancaster which he described as 'nurseries of mismanagement' which needed 'more perfectly uniting to the Crown'. The proposals relating to Wales were dropped by 1782 because 'they did not appear agreeable to the people of Wales'. Supporters of the Association Movement in Wales were particularly opposed to the removal of the separate jurisdiction of the Court of Great Sessions which existed here and which the Westminster courts had sought to abolish since the seventeenth century. The petitioning campaign which the Movement embarked on in 1779 was entirely to the liking of Thomas Roberts, Llwyn-rhudol who advocated this method as a means of acquainting rulers with the feelings of the people.

The Movement spread to Wales probably from the border-land, but there were several persons connected with Wales who were prominent in it. Sir Robert Smyth, who was elected for Cardigan boroughs in 1774, was the chairman of the Essex committee ; Bishop Watson of Llandaff drew up the scheme of association for Cambridge ; Richard Pennant, the owner of the Penrhyn estate was involved in the Lancashire Movement. Dissenters were prominent and the Movement learnt a great deal about organisation from them. There was a literature of Association in England but none has survived if ever published in Welsh. Between February and April 1780 three petitions came out of Wales from Brecknockshire, Flintshire and Den-bighshire and these with a host of others were presented to the House of Commons by John Dunning, friend of Sir William Jones, and were the prelude to his famous motion (1780) which was supported by the majority of Welsh M.P.s, more particu-larly by the county members.

More is known about the Flintshire Association than any other because its activities led to a celebrated lawsuit. The initiative towards forming an Association was taken by Thomas Pennant at a County Meeting in 1779, and he evidently ex-pected to be elected chairman of the committee but was ousted by William Davies Shipley, Dean of St. Asaph. The Flintshire Association was torn from the start by a clash of personalities as well as different objectives and is a microcosm of the Move-ment as a whole. Pennant supported economical reform and the maintenance of the Welsh judicature and accused Shipley of ' levelling principles ' since he wanted to broaden the base of the constitution and would reform the Welsh boroughs. Some counties wanted to bind their M.P.s by ' instructions ' as to their conduct in Parliament but Flintshire rejected this although Pennant did not consider himself bound by it. In 1783, Thomas Fitzmaurice summoned a County Meeting as High Sheriff at which Dean Shipley read a pamphlet published anonymously by his brother-in-law, Sir William Jones, the famous Orientalist who had just left this country to become a judge in India. The pamphlet entitled *Principles of Government in a dialogue between a scholar and a peasant* was approved by the meeting and its translation into Welsh resolved upon. Shipley undertook to publish the pamphlet but a Welsh version was not proceeded with probably because of the controversy it aroused. Its substance was, however, publicised in the form of an ' interlude ' in Welsh, a much more effective way of giving currency to its ideas. Fitzmaurice, who was a supporter of Pennant and an enemy of the Dean tried to institute proceedings against Shipley but the Government would not act. A private indictment was eventually laid by a Wrexham attorney whereby Shipley had to stand trial on a charge of seditious libel. The Society for Promoting Constitutional Information, founded in 1780, was anxious to make this a test case of the rights of a jury in a libel case and employed Erskine, one of the foremost advocates of the day, to defend Shipley. In the course of the trial, Erskine delivered one of the greatest speeches on the law of libel which, in Holdsworth's opinion, made it the most important trial involving seditious libel. The jury found Shipley guilty of publishing only in the same way as the jury in the ' Junius ' case had done in 1770. An appeal was made and the case dragged on in King's Bench for years before Shipley was acquitted and discharged. His homecoming to Llannerch was reminiscent of Dr. Sacheverell's famous progress accompanied by celebrations at Wrexham and at Ruthin. The case which arose from the untimely zeal of Shipley's enemies created a great ferment in North Wales and gave wide publicity to William Jones's ideas. The activities of the County Associations died down in Wales after the election of 1784.

There are indications that the political ferment of 1779-82 effected some change of attitude at elections. ' Independence ' became a common slogan at Welsh elections after 1780 and a pamphlet which circulated during the election of that year refers to the existence of an independent interest at Cardiff and Swansea, two towns which were dominated by borough lords. Independence was interpreted as the constitutional right of electors to choose candidates without pressure from great magnates and the appeal was to burgesses, traders and Dissenters not merely to the gentry, clergy and freeholders. Rising towns like Merthyr and Aberdare had never been subject to a patron's control and radicalism was in evidence amongst the newly-emerging proletariat there very early since there were no established political interests to contend against.

The French Revolution and its sympathisers

The French Revolution affected practically every country in Europe in some degree and though remote from events on the continent it activated minds in Wales to a greater extent than even the American Revolution had done. It contributed much to the political education of the Welsh people but it also bred contention and divisions in society which were to rend the nation in the nineteenth century. For this reason, it was a critical and formative period which disturbed the harmony that had prevailed till then and caused people to take sides for or against the Revolution. The first public pronouncement on the Revolution in this country was made by Dr. Richard Price in a sermon he preached before the Society for the Commemoration of the Revolution of 1688 and the celebration of the centenary of that event naturally caused people to make comparisons ; many sympathised with the French because they were only following our example. Dr. Price's sermon was published under the title *On Love of Country* in which he described the patriot as a man who sought to enlighten his countrymen and to elevate them by virtue. To develop responsibility the citizen must be free to choose according to his own conscience and so he advocated the repeal of the Penal Laws and the removal of inequalities. The civil authorities should be sensitive to popular opinion which, in this country, needed a measure of parliamentary reform to implement it. He held with Locke the doctrine of the popular origin of sovereignty and that the people were the ultimate governors and had a right to cashier misgovernment. Although he favoured republicanism as an ideal Price believed that constitutional monarchy was best suited to this country if the work of the Revolution of 1688 were only completed by a measure of parliamentary reform. He believed that governments elected by the popular will would result in peace and general harmony. The formative influences on his ideas were Locke and the Revolution of 1688 working on his Dissenting background

O

with its inclination towards liberal theology and radical politics. His impact on Wales cannot be assessed since there were no organs of the press for public discussion. It is likely that few Welshmen in Wales read Price at first hand despite the sermon's wide circulation since no translation was made into Welsh. His ideas were propagated indirectly through the many Dissenters who were in touch with Price and his regular visits to South Wales so that we cannot doubt that his ideas were known here. The sermon was greatly approved by the constitutional and political societies and its consequence was an unparalleled crop of polemical literature. The most renowned reply to it was Edmund Burke's *Reflections on the Revolution in France* (1790) which is a classic of conservative doctrine for all time but it hardly did justice to Price's case nor in all instances interpreted him fairly. Price did not reply on his own behalf but many others did including Mary Wollstonecraft, the famous Blue-stocking. What might be called the official reply from Price's friends was made by James Mackintosh and was entitled *Vindiciae Gallicae*. The greatest irritant was Tom Paine's *Rights of Man* (1791) which worried the Establishment for a long time. Price won acclaim in France and was described as a man given to the world and not to one nation ; when he died the National Assembly went into mourning and the citizens of Nantes named part of their town after him.

David Williams of Caerffili was another thinker who reacted to the Revolution and won acclaim outside Wales. He had been educated by Arian teachers at Watford and at Carmarthen and became an Arian and finally a Deist ; he was the author of a new liturgy for public worship which was sufficiently deistic in tone to commend it to Frederick the Great and Voltaire. Rousseau declared himself his disciple and when Robespierre initiated the ' Cult of the Supreme Being ' it bore the impress of many of Williams's ideas. Williams's interest was in the practical working out of ideas, hence his interest in the French attempts at constitution making. He claimed to have laid the basis of political science on account of his writings on political institutions. He regarded himself as a teacher of politics for which purpose he wrote *Lessons to a Young Prince by an Old Statesman*. In 1790, he published *Observa-*

tions on the Constitution which exhibits the influence of John
Locke, but Williams was an avowed republican and considered
the institution of constitutional monarchy in France as a
betrayal. He was made a French citizen in 1792 and associated
himself with the Girondins, and when they were overthrown
by the Jacobins he was cast into prison and narrowly escaped
with his life. He returned to this country on his release bearing
peace overtures from the French Foreign Minister but was not
even accorded a hearing by Government Ministers in Westminster. Although he spent a long time on his *History of
Monmouthshire* there is no evidence that Williams was in close
touch with Welsh life nor that his ideas had any currency here
but he was one of the foremost Welsh thinkers.

Though not in the same rank as Price and Williams, Morgan
John Rhys, another native of the Caerffili district and educated
at Watford and Carmarthen, had more direct influence be-
cause he spent most of his working life in Wales and wrote and
preached in Welsh. He was less concerned with ideas than
Price and with institutions than Williams but sought practical
solutions to problems. For popular enlightenment he founded
Sunday schools whereas Williams wrote an *Essay on Education*.
Convinced that the cause of all the trouble in France was its
thraldom to Popery, he founded a Bible Society for distributing
Bibles in Paris. To him, the Revolution was a judgment of
God and the overthrow of tyrannical power a just retribution.
Rhys believed that it was the Word of God that set men free
and acted accordingly. His interpretation of the problem was
too narrow and he was to be disappointed with the turn of
events ; he returned to his first love—America, and emigrated
there in 1794. One thing Price, Williams and Rhys had in
common was their Dissenting background and their education
at the hands of Arian teachers. Rhys however, did not forsake
Calvinism and that is why he was more acceptable to his
fellow-Dissenters in Wales.

Though they attracted no attention outside Wales some of
the lesser leaders of thought had more influence at home
because they were closer to '*y werin.*' Iolo Morganwg (Edward
Williams), self-styled ' Bard of Liberty ', was as eager to
welcome the Revolution as he was to disembarrass himself of
it some years later. His *Poems, Lyrical and Pastoral* had marked

political undertones and though dedicated to the Prince of Wales some of the poems attacked King and clergy, but with apologetic footnotes. His *Gorsedd* ceremonies in Glamorgan were stopped by the authorities on suspicion of being a cover for ' democratic principles '. Under the impact of War and Terror, Iolo forsook his Jacobinism and before long we find him penning loyalist songs. David Davis, Castellhywel, a popular poet and Arian schoolmaster, retained his revolution- ary sympathies at least to the end of the century. Tomos Glyn Cothi(Thomas Evans) was an amateur journalist and also wrote popular verse in praise of freedom and condemning tyranny and wars ; in 1801 he was imprisoned for two years for singing seditious songs at Carmarthen. One of the doughtiest of Welsh radicals was William Jones, Llangadfan (Monts.), sometimes referred to as ' the rural Voltaire '. He wrote an ode on *Liberty and Oppression* and was a constant agitator against landlordism urging people to emigrate. He was denounced by both Anglicans and Methodists as ' a rank republican and leveller ' and for a time was under constant surveillance and his letters were opened. The ballads were full of references to the condition of the times and in default of a developed press are one of our main sources of evidence about how the common people felt. Most of them relate to conditions in North Wales since the practice of poesy was not as vigorous in the South by this time.

The Press

The growth of political interest contributed to the develop- ment of the press as an organ of opinion to fill a much-felt need in Wales. *Yr Eurgrawn* ('The Treasury') of 1770 was the earliest known attempt to launch a journal and it had backing from the Dissenters ; its character was, however, more literary than political. The 1780 election in Glamorgan produced at least one political pamphlet and this was also a novelty. The first serious effort at journalism was Morgan John Rhys's *Cylchgrawn Cynmraeg* ('Welsh Journal') of which five numbers appeared in 1793 under the patronage of the Gwyneddigion. Rhys was undoubtedly the first to realise the importance of a free press for informing opinion in Wales. His journal was intended to be a platform for discussion of a variety of topics including parliamentary reform, disestablishment, the French Revolution, the slave trade, missions and education, but it drew attention to itself and invited the suspicion of the authorities on account of its radical views and politics. It cost six pence and Rhys experienced much difficulty with its distribution which limited its circulation to a thousand. It was an important pioneering venture and although periodicals were to appear only sporadically for some time a future was assured for them as political discussion matured. Thomas Evans's (Glyn Cothi) *Trysorfa Gymmysgedig* ('Miscellaneous Treasury') (1795) was the mouthpiece for Priestley's ideas but it also showed some perspicacity in linking the French with the American Revolution and in detecting the influence of the *philosophes* upon the trend of events in France. It also gave a great deal of publicity to the treason trials which started in 1794. It succumbed after three numbers. Its successor was David Davies's (Holywell) *Geirgrawn* (1796) whose sub-title was *Trysorfa Gwybodaeth* ('Treasury of Knowledge') which ran to nine numbers and in which a protracted debate took place on the merits of John Jones's (Jac Glan y Gors) pamphlet *Seren Tan Gwmwl* ('Star under a Cloud'). This journal was also supported by the Gwyneddigion and was intended to revive the cause of reform after the treason trials.

The *Seren* was a rendering into Welsh of Tom Paine's ideas but cleverly adapted to the situation in Wales and written in a style which was intelligible to the common people. It aired grievances and criticised indolent M.P.s but it condemned the violence which had occurred in some parts of Wales against magistrates. The book certainly found an audience and the Methodists did their utmost to counteract its influence. It also attracted the attention of the authorities and Jac had to hide at his native Cerrig y Drudion for a time. In 1797 he published a sequel *Toriad y Dydd* ('Day Break') which was less effective and less influential. One of the most effective journalists at a time when few had experience of the craft was David Jones Llandovery, writing as 'Welsh Freeholder'. He was a disciple of Dr. Richard Price and taught at the Hackney Academy and succeeded Dr. Priestley as Unitarian minister at Birmingham. He expounded the Dissenters' demands as a reform of the constitution, a parliament free of corruption and

the freeing of religion from State control and interference.
He justified the Dissenters' support of the French Revolution
on the grounds that the spread of liberty to other countries
gave them a just expectation of peace, but they were dis-
illusioned. The Methodist journal *Y Drysorfa Ysbrydol* ('The
Spiritual Treasury') (1799), was in marked contrast to its
predecessors and utterly conservative in its views. It condemned the French Revolution and asserted that to overthrow
the existing system would be admitting French methods. The
appearance of *The Cambrian* at Swansea, in 1804, provided
Wales with its first weekly newspaper and although it purported to eschew politics it was really a conservative organ. It
was not until 1814 that political discussion was revived with the
appearance of *Seren Gomer* from the Baptists, edited by Joseph
Harris and this was the fore-runner of a crop of journals which
appeared with more regularity from then on.

Political Clubs
     Political clubs were not as evident in Wales before 1815 as
after but they did exist from 1780 on and contributed somewhat to the political education of at least part of the nation.
David Williams (Caerffili) was active in founding political
clubs in London as was a little-known Welshman, John Gale
Jones. Dr. Richard Price and Dr. Abraham Rees were prominent in the Society for the Commemoration of the Revolution
of 1688 which Burke described as a Dissenters' club. The Society for Promoting Constitutional Information was particularly
active in North Wales during Dean Shipley's trial and was
responsible for the original publication of Sir William Jones's
pamphlet. Morgan John Rhys, who founded a society for
distributing Bibles in France in 1791, was also active on behalf
of political clubs in Wales. He particularly commended 'The
Friends of the People', a Whiggish club founded in 1792, to
readers of *Y Cylchgrawn Cynmraeg*, and went around lecturing
on its behalf. He also formed branches of the London Corresponding Society and the Society for Promoting Constitutional
Information which he addressed on subjects like parliamentary
reform, the abolition of class privileges and the reduction of
taxes by retrenchment on corrupt practices. An offshoot of the
London Corresponding Society existed at Cardiff and itinerant

lecturers came down to South Wales from London. A vigorous Jacobin club was said to exist at Brecon and even Bala boasted some Jacobins. These were offshoots of English clubs and it is not known that any made an appeal through the medium of Welsh.

The London Welsh societies were not political clubs but, coming into existence at the time they did, they could hardly have avoided political discussion and it is fairly certain that they were the source of many Welsh radical ideas. The Gwyneddigion was the most democratic and influential of them and had taken as its motto ' Liberty in Church and State '. Debates were a normal part of its activities and it also sponsored political journals like Rhys's *Cylchgrawn* and David Davies's *Geirgrawn*. It was also the patron of the revived Eisteddfod and though literary subjects were set for competition which invited political comment very little of note was produced. Even the old Welsh poetry that the Society published was suspected of being a cover for the propagation of radical ideas. Politics brought the Caradogion Society into trouble since its papers were impounded by constables which behoved it to exercise great caution after 1795. Little is known about the Cymreigyddion founded by the two radicals Jac Glan y Gors and Thomas Roberts, Llwynrhudol, but their association with it suggests that it had a strong political bias. When its constitution was revised in 1827 political discussion was forbidden which again suggests that it had led it into tribulation in the past.

The Counter Revolution

Anti-Revolution propaganda stemmed from the gentry and the clergy, the latter mainly. They used both pulpit and press since they could better afford the cost of publishing pamphlets. Their theme was that the Church of England was the only bulwark against atheism and revolution and quite typical was the sermon preached by the Rev. Edward Parry of Llanferres at Mold parish church indicting the French as atheists and blasphemers who were sinking into depravity. Their method of attack was to heap every calumny they could upon their opponents and, as often as not, with little regard to truth. Arminianism, Arianism and Socinianism were equated with French atheism and people of that way of thought were alleged to be the source of revolutionary principles in this country. Bishop Horsley of St. David's wanted churchmen to extend hospitality to French Catholic clergy, holding that they had more in common with them than with the Dissenters. Not all clergy were uncritical ; Dr. Charles Symmons of Llanstinan (Pembs.) writing under the pen-name ' Curate of Snowdon ', addressed a pamphlet to the Archbishop of Canterbury and called it *Religion in Danger* but the danger as he saw it came from within rather than from outside; he hinted that the Pope was already in danger and that the Church of England had better take heed. Bishop Watson in his ' charge ' to his clergy in 1791 approved of the Revolution and it was translated into Welsh probably by David Davis, Castellhywel, as *Meddyliau'r Esgob Watson* (' Bishop Watson's Thoughts '). It had considerable circulation in Wales and was warmly received by Dissenters whose civil rights he also championed. By 1798 Watson was much more cautious ; hearing that there were seditious tendencies in his own diocese he delivered another charge to his clergy in which he warned against misconceptions of liberty. This was more to the taste of the temporal authorities and the Quarter Sessions of Monmouthshire asked him to publish it so that the magistrates could distribute it. The prejudice stirred by Anglicans was responsible for the sacking of Dr. Priestley's house and laboratory in Birmingham which evoked a message of sympathy from his co-religionists in assembly at Llechryd (Cards.). Similar prejudice was exhibited at Wrexham and the butt of it there was John Wilkinson the ironmaster, Priestley's brother-in-law. He used tokens to pay his workmen and these were misrepresented as French '*assignats*' which were exchangeable at shops kept by local Presbyterians ' thereby corrupting the principles of all manner of men ', it was alleged. Wilkinson was even accused of helping the French since at one time he had holdings in the French iron industry. In the poisoned atmosphere created by irresponsible accusations reason could not prevail.

The French Revolutionary War in which Britain became involved in 1793 greatly altered the situation since its outbreak was contrary to all that the friends of the Revolution had expected. Religious and political issues had to be shelved and religious prejudice was exploited at elections especially against

candidates who favoured Catholic Emancipation. The hostility
that was shown towards Catholics in the eighties was turned on
Dissenters in the nineties. Dissenters had to be on their guard
and in meetings of the three denominations assertions of loyalty
to the constitution submerged demands for reform. At a
meeting held at the Pen-y-bont Tavern, Newcastle Emlyn, to
which representatives of the three denominations in the south-
west came, resolutions asserting their loyalty and respect for
the constitution were passed and reports were sent to the
London, Bristol and Hereford papers and currency was given
to them in Wales by the balladmongers. The most that the
Independents in their meeting at Bala in 1793 could hope for
was that reasonableness would prevail and though reform was
still argued in moderate terms many Dissenters felt it was a
forlorn hope. Loyalist associations grew up all over Britain
on the model of the one founded at the Crown and Anchor
Tavern in London, and branches were not hard to come by in
Welsh towns. Flintshire formed an ' Association for the Defence
of our Religion, Constitution and Property ' in 1792 which
pledged its loyalty to King and Constitution and to be vigilant
against tumults, seditious meetings and publications. Its
resolutions were translated into Welsh and signed by an
' incredible number of persons ' including Dean Shipley and
Thomas Pennant.

The loyalist associations spread anti-revolutionary propaganda through pamphleteering and realised the need to do so
in Welsh. Hannah More's *Village Politics* was translated and
set in the form of a dialogue between a blacksmith and a
mason. *Ashurst's Charge* was a popular pamphlet which was
done into Welsh and distributed by the Carmarthen and the
Holywell Associations. *Cinagwerth o Wirionedd* ('Pennyworth of
Truth') appears to have been written in Welsh in the form of a
letter praising our form of government and pointing to the folly
of the French in starting a revolution which showed no signs
of ending. The loyalist associations were also behind the
demonstrations against Tom Paine in various places. His
Rights of Man was reputed to be circulating freely in the
mountains of Wales, in Jac Glan y Gors's version, most likely.
His books were sought and burnt by government spies. Paine's
effigy was burnt in Cardiff, the Corporation promising to pay

the cost which it later declined to fulfil. A popular song with the refrain ' They hanged and burnt poor Tommy Paine, In 1792 ', was composed for the occasion. His effigy was burnt at Carmarthen and Llandovery too and loyalist workmen in Merthyr execrated his name by setting their hob-nails in the pattern of the initials T P which they trod under foot. Needless to say, the balladmongers joined in the popular execration, sometimes at the instigation of the gentry.

The execution of Louis XVI and the institution of the Terror had a traumatic effect on many erstwhile sympathisers. Dr. William Richards rightly saw it as the outcome of the Allies' attitude towards the Revolution. When an attack was made on the King's coach on his way to Parliament in 1795 County Meetings in Cardiganshire and Merioneth sent him congratulatory messages on his escape. ' *Y werin* ' were more concerned with the hardship of the times, one consequence of which was the re-starting of emigration on a large scale. The Government and the landlords countered with anti-American propaganda and the correspondence of emigrants exhibits a doctrinal hostility to Government and an irritation at the flood of anti-American propaganda poured from Anglican pulpits and the press. Dissenting leaders on the other hand were urging people to emigrate and there was some talk of the Independents in North Wales going *en masse*. The ballads are eloquent on the question of hardship and if the voice of reform had been stilled the voice of protest against the plight of the poor had not. Thomas Roberts enumerates the anomalies like tithes which oppressed the Welsh people in his *Cwyn yn erbyn Gorthrymder* ('Plaint against Oppression') (1798). In the verse of Hugh Jones, Maesglasau, there is talk of rents being doubled, rates rising and a trail of debts to shopkeepers. David Davies, the Welsh rector of Barkham, was more specific and scientific. In his *The Case of Labourers in Husbandry* he published a number of family budgets including some from North Wales which showed that a labourer's wage went almost entirely on food because of high prices and he was rarely able to make ends meet without resort to outside assistance.[1]

Riots were common occurrences in 1794-5 ; there were out-breaks at Swansea in 1794 because of corn duties and an

[1] See page 191

abusive paper circulated in the town entitled *Resolutions of all the Poor* in which the rioters reminded their masters of what had happened in France. In 1795, miners attacked Aberystwyth by night ; the colliers of Hook (Pembs.) marched on Haverfordwest to seize a sloop laden with butter for Bristol. Fighting occurred in the streets and the Riot Act was read ; the Fishguard Fencibles occupied the town for a week. Twm o'r Nant described the disturbances at Denbigh in 1795 as a conflict between ' *bonedd a'r cyffredin* ' (' the gentry and common people') and the gentry called in the cavalry which aggravated the situation by consuming scarce food and fodder. Bala, Wrexham and Oswestry were other centres of violence and the complaint on everyone's lips was ' *drudaniaeth* ' ('dearness'). The situation in Pembrokeshire was alleviated by the gentry coming together to bring in cheaper corn despite the preference of John Campbell of Stackpole for bringing in the yeomanry. From 1795 till the end of the century the common plea was ' Bread and Peace '. Protests against landlords for rackrenting became common and they were often pilloried in the ballads. The activities of the press gang added to the general anxiety and Elis y Cowper had much to say about their conduct in Anglesey and Caernarfonshire.

In 1794, the Government launched the Volunteer Movement as a national conservative coalition with a view to discrediting the opposition and to initiating judicial persecution against radicals. Men of property were prominent in it which made it a useful police force and it kept a watchful eye on radicals, protestors against high prices and malcontents. The Volunteers were armed and recruits came forward readily because it exempted men from militia service. Poor Volunteers were paid for wages lost while training and the Tivyside Volunteers took less wages from their employers because they lost up to two days a week in training. Some groups even launched insurance schemes against sickness and acted like mutual benefit societies ; this also made members more submissive. Iolo Morganwg who had by now changed his tune, composed warlike songs for the Cowbridge Volunteers and for those of Neath and Glamorgan. A corps existed at Merthyr and several in Pembrokeshire and their activities were a popular subject for the balladmongers. At a time of invasion scare they gave people some reassurance especially when events in Ireland caused panic in 1796-7.

The French landing in Pembrokeshire in 1797 showed how unprotected the Welsh coast was and the County was thrown entirely on its own resources. The French force was composed of the scourings of prisons commanded by a renegade American general named Tate. They were transported to the Pembrokeshire coast by a naval force under Hoche who withdrew after landing them at Carreg Wastad, near Fishguard. The plan was to march cross-country to take Chester and Liverpool. Tate had no control over his undisciplined, mutinous rabble especially when their forays brought to light stores of liquor which the country people had laid in when a ship carrying wine had been wrecked on the coast. Lord Cawdor was given local command and gathering what militia groups that were available marched on Fishguard. He bluffed Tate into believing that he was outnumbered and tradition has it that it was a never-ending column of women marching in their red shawls around Pen-caer that fooled him. One woman, Jemima Nicholas won fame by capturing twelve Frenchmen single-handed armed only with a pitch-fork for which the Government awarded her a life pension. The French capitulated on Goodwick Sands and were dispersed over the County as prisoners of war and there followed a long altercation between the County authorities and the Government before they were relieved of this responsibility. The whole affair was a fiasco but it left a trail of consequences. The Bank of England suspended cash payments to stop the run on specie which the panic had started. The assumption behind the landing must have been that the Welsh would rise spontaneously although no previous contacts were made by the French as they did in Ireland. Nevertheless, suspicion rested on the locality which had its sequel in local men being charged with treason. Eight were imprisoned but only two stood trial, Thomas John, a local Baptist deacon and the Rev. Samuel Griffiths, a Presbyterian minister, and the evidence against them was procured from French prisoners by bribery. The case collapsed when this perjured evidence was withdrawn but by this time the accused had been in prison for six months. Dr. William Richards set the trial on record in *Cwyn y Cystuddiedig* (' Complaint of the

Afflicted ') (1798) in which he asserts that it was a plot laid by the gentry and clergy against Dissenters.

The effect upon the nation as a whole was one of shock which caused many sympathisers with the Revolution to change their minds. Recruitment for volunteer organisations was stepped up and more and more were formed. Hostility against Dissenters was unremitting and the Methodists suffered by association. A Methodist ' plot ' was alleged and when it was known that John Elias and Richard Lloyd, Beaumaris, were visiting Ireland to preach to Welsh militia groups stationed there this seemed to be sufficient justification for the allegations. John Elias was described as a Jacobin ' fierce and ignorant ' and the Sunday schools ' a nursery of revolutionary principles '. Nothing could be further from the truth of course since the Methodists had little sympathy with the Dissenters and did everything possible to assert their loyalty, even making collections for internal defence and holding thanksgiving meetings for the repulse of the French at Fishguard. But Anglicans did not want to be convinced and continued to assert that ' the shoal of schism was very close to the rock of revolution '.

It was probably the growing strength and organisation of the Methodists that was causing alarm and especially the proliferation of their societies and Sunday schools and the Anglicans resorted to harassment to try to stem the tide ; despite the false accusations and calumny more and more joined their ranks from the Established Church. Nevertheless, they had to defend themselves vigorously. Thomas Jones, Denbigh, published *Gair yn ei Amser* (' Word in Season ') (1798) to counteract the influence of Jac Glan y Gors and its general tenor was loyalty and obedience to authority. Thomas Charles replied to two Anglican pamphlets by the Rev. T. E. Owen entitled *Hints to heads of families* and *Methodism Unmasked* with *The Welsh Methodists Vindicated* refuting ' these dark surmises, assumed data, malignant hints, false deductions and irrelevant conclusions'. This sums up fairly well the nature of the verbal warfare that had dragged on for years. The persecution of the Methodists took a more active turn in some areas, notably in Merioneth. Edward Corbet, a Tywyn magistrate, indicted the local Methodists for worshipping in an unlicensed meeting-house and on his own authority had their meeting-house at Corris demolished. Unlicensed preachers were brought before Quarter Sessions and the Bala magistrates imprisoned one for preaching at Llanrwst. In self-defence, the Methodists were forced to take a step which they had so long avoided—licensing their meeting-houses and their preachers which technically branded them as Dissenters. This was an important milestone on the road to complete secession from the Church.

The Unitarians remained more assertive and in some areas like Merthyr and Aberdare were very prominent in local affairs and formed the backbone of the Cyfarthfa Philosophical Society formed in 1807 and nourished on a diet of Tom Paine and Voltaire. Thomas Evans (Glyn Cothi), the minister of Hen Dy Cwrdd,[1] Aberdare, held clandestine meetings on the mountain between Aberdare and Merthyr at which Priestley's ideas were retailed. Dissenters otherwise sought to avoid trouble and down to 1807 at least were more concerned with vindicating their good name than in issuing political manifestos. In 1811 the Protestant Society for the Protection of Religious Liberty was formed to which Thomas Charles of Bala was co-opted and this was the first organisation to draw attention to the special circumstances of Wales. Charles was also one of a deputation to protest against Sidmouth's Bill in 1811 which could have restricted the licensing of Dissenting ministers and which would have been fatal to Methodism at a critical time in its history.

The Peace of Amiens brought welcome relief for all too brief a period and the resumption of war in 1803, although it brought Pitt back to power, was unpopular. Praise of the constitution continued to stifle demands for reform at least till 1806. Victories, especially Trafalgar, were still applauded by the ballad writers although they otherwise complained of the hardship of the times. There is no mistaking the depression of living conditions and the brutalisation of the working class especially in the rapidly growing industrial towns of the south-east. In 1800, Merthyr ironworkers went on strike and two of their leaders were hanged which deterred workmen from giving vent to their indignation till 1815 but thereafter there followed a wave of disturbances. It is no wonder that the

[1] The Old Meeting House.

new towns became centres of reform agitation and in this case its origin was secular not religious. The climate was ripe for the resumption of political activity in 1815 and Cartwright, the founder of the Hampden Clubs (1812), was quick to seize the opportunity by sending his assistant Cleary to Wales to contact leaders, organise petitions and to instruct people in the use of the press. Welsh artisans who went to England, like John Frost, came back under the influence of political agitators. Rural discontent was scarcely less and complaints against taxation on the necessities of life and the practice of agriculture were common and criticism of the government for its economic policy became increasingly vocal by 1815.

The opposition of Welsh M.P.s to reform began to relax and some became openly critical of the workings of government and supported moves to cashier ministers for corruption and ineptitude ; when the catastrophic Scheldt expedition was debated they were equally divided for and against the government. After 1806, parliamentary reform revived and interest in it spread down to the counties as was evident in West Wales. By 1810, half a dozen Welsh M.P.s were prepared to support Brand's reform measure. The imprisonment of Sir Francis Burdett, the reform leader, in 1810 caused considerable reaction in Wales. Sir Robert Salisbury of Llanwern who moved his committal incurred great unpopularity in Monmouthshire and the radicals organised a run on his banks whilst a town meeting at Carmarthen protested against Burdett's imprisonment. Greater note was taken of the conduct of individual members and government lackeys like Lord Robert Seymour and Col. Wood were asked to explain their conduct for voting against the interests of their constituents. This was made easier by the development of the press ; in 1804, *The Cambrian* appeared at Swansea ; in 1808, the *North-Wales Gazette*, and although they affected to eschew politics they really reflected the conservatism of the times. The *Carmarthen Journal* (1810) was somewhat more liberal in outlook.

Certain trends were already becoming apparent ; one was a growing divergence between M.P.s and the people they represented. The estrangement of the Church from the outlook of the common people was another. The Church and its clergy had done their utmost to exploit the crisis of the times to harass the Dissenters, an indication that a century of toleration had done little to change its attitude. It is no wonder that it emerged into the nineteenth century an un-loved and alien institution increasingly deserted by the mass of Welsh people and with which the Methodists officially severed connections in 1811.

SUGGESTED READING

The titles at the end of Chapter 1 are relevant.

D. Davies, *The Influence of the French Revolution on Welsh life and literature*, Carmarthen, 1926.

J. J. Evans, *Dylanwad y Chwildro Ffrengig ar lenyddiaeth Cymru*, Lerpwl, 1928.

——, *Morgan John Rhys a'i Amserau*, Caerdydd, 1935.

——, *Cymry enwog y ddeunawfed ganrif*, Aberystwyth, 1937.

T. Evans, *The background of modern Welsh politics*, 1789–1846, Cardiff, 1936.

D. Jones, *Before Rebecca*, London, 1973.

E. H. Stuart Jones, *The last invasion of Britain*, Cardiff, 1950.

R. Thomas, *Richard Price*, Oxford, 1924.

G. Williams (ed.), *Merthyr politics*, Cardiff, 1966.

Articles:

W. Ll. Davies, 'The riot at Denbigh in 1795', *B.B.C.S.*, IV, 1927.

R. T. Jenkins, 'Political propaganda in West Wales in 1793', *B.B.C.S.*, VI, 1932.

E. D. Jones, 'The Dolgellau Military Association', *J. Mer. H. and R.S.*, III, 3, 1959.

R. D. Rees, 'South Wales and Monmouthshire newspapers under the Stamp Acts', *W.H.R.*, I, 3, 1962.

——, 'Electioneering ideals current in South Wales, 1790–1832', *W.H.R.*, II, 3, 1964.

D. O. Thomas, 'Richard Price', *Trans. Cymmr.*, 1971.

G. A. Williams, 'The making of radical Merthyr, 1800–36', *W.H.R.*, I, 2, 1961.

——, 'Morgan John Rhys and Volney's *Ruin of Empires*', *B.B.C.S.*, XX, 1962.

——, 'Morgan John Rhees and his Beula', *W.H.R.*, III, 4, 1967.

13. The Cultural Background

The Welsh Language

The Welsh language still held sway in all parts of the country including Monmouthshire down to 1815 excepting the long-established anglicised areas of Gower and south Pembrokeshire. Though a Monmouthshire clergyman might lament in 1651 that no nation was more hostile to its own language than the Welsh, the Rev. John Thomas of Llangibby was still translating pious literature into Welsh for his parishioners many years later. Some Brecknockshire people complained that Welsh was too much used in Griffith Jones's schools than was good for the children. By 1700, the erosion of the language in the parishes of the Vale of Glamorgan in trading contact with the West Country was noted by Edward Lhuyd, but this was as yet exceptional.

There were indications of a decline in the standard of speech and the expression '*heneiddiodd yr iaith*' (the language has aged) suggested that it was becoming decrepit with age. It had ceased to be the language of high society by the eighteenth century and the gentry had lost any facility in it. William Vaughan of Corsygedol, first President of the Cymmrodorion Society who could still write and adjudge *cynghanedd*, was truly singular amongst his class. For most of the gentry the greatest justification for the survival of the language was that it insulated ordinary Welshmen against the insidious propaganda of English radicals. Till the 1790s, there was no alternative leadership to them, but the new leaders when they emerged were Welsh-speaking. By the end of the seventeenth century the written language was also debased and even such a redoubtable champion as Stephen Hughes was apologetic for his shortcomings. In the course of the eighteenth century the spoken word became much more important than the written under the influence of the pulpit which did so much to revive the language.

The contribution of the Church of England to the native language and culture was a declining one. In the first decade of the century Bishop Humphreys of Bangor was addressing his Episcopal Queries in it and urging its use for official as well as ministerial purposes. Dean John Jones of Bangor had also been a firm advocate of its use in schools in the diocese. The decline after 1716 was conspicuous and was attributed by the Rev. Evan Evans (Ieuan Fardd) to *yr Esgyb Eingl* (English bishops) who were without exception preferred to Welsh sees. English sermons were often preached in Welsh parishes and English incumbents appointed to Welsh livings. The Church, which had some claim to being national in Queen Anne's reign, ceased to be so and an ever-increasing part of the nation dissociated itself from it. Against this tide the efforts of some exceptional clergy like Griffith Jones were unavailing in the end.

The language was probably more in use in the law courts than is now known. Lewis Morris had interrogatories translated for the benefit of Cardiganshire witnesses in a lawsuit whilst the retention of the Court of Great Sessions in Wales was justified by Thomas Wood, M.P. for Brecknockshire in the 1820s until at least such time as the language became extinct.

Even among the intelligentsia like the Morris Circle English was considered to be the more proper form of address and Welsh was seldom used except for familiarities. Ieuan Fardd still resorted to Latin for his treatise on the history of Welsh literature. The Cymmrodorion Society which affected to patronise Welsh learning became increasingly anglicised as more and more of the gentry were admitted as members and even among humbler London Welshmen ' Dic Siôn Dafydd '— the Welshman who had precipitately lost his Welsh—was a common taunt.

In the circumstances which prevailed the survival of the language was regarded as improbable, its revival as nothing short of miraculous. There was no political capital to bring national life into a focus and the lack of national institutions like a University meant the absence of cultural centres. There was no establishment of any sort to provide patronage and no towns of any size to foster a civic tradition and to encourage the arts. Lack of communication between North and South was culturally as well as socially divisive. In these circumstances, London was the only possible centre for Welsh activities and it was from there that the vision, the aspirations and the organisations were supplied which were to infuse some new life in and respect for the language.

The Press

Until the beginning of the eighteenth century London was the most important centre for Welsh publishing inasmuch as the Bible was printed there, Charles II having appointed a ' King's Printer for the British language ' in 1676. Shrewsbury developed as a rival centre after 1696 when Thomas Jones of Corwen moved there from London having received a grant under letters patent to publish almanacks ' in the British tongue ' ; he had agents selling books and almanacks in several towns in Wales and the borderland. He has been called ' the father of Welsh journalism ' since he intended to publish a newspaper in Welsh but through lack of co-operation this did not get beyond the initial number which appeared in 1705.

Carmarthen became a publishing centre when Nicholas Thomas moved there from Shrewsbury and John Ross from London and in 1725 Isaac Carter, who had set up the first Welsh press at Trefhedyn, near Newcastle Emlyn in 1718, also settled in the town. It was prominent in the publication of religious books since it was near the centres of the religious revival and of the charity school movements. By 1800, presses had been established at Brecon, Machynlleth, Dolgellau and Trefriw. There were also private presses ; Lewis Morris set one up to print MSS. and Thomas Johnes brought a Scots printer to Hafod to print his translations of the French chronicles. The press established at ' *Y Cartref* ', Trefeca, printed at least one number of Morgan John Rhys's *Cylchgrawn Cynmraeg*.

The growth of the press was a response to the growth of a reading public, itself the result of the spread of literacy. The desire for self-improvement permeated lower down the social structure and more people came to own books. Four times as many books were published in 1790 as in 1710, mainly on religious and moral themes. They had to be cheap and so were sold unbound, editions rarely exceeding 1,000 copies. When book production was limited, costs were usually borne by patrons but the increase in publication obliged authors to look to subscribers to finance their work. Lists of subscribers were printed in the book and represent a cross-section of the community down to the level of artisans.

The products of the English press circulated amongst the gentry in Wales and the Chester, Shrewsbury and Gloucester papers carried much Welsh news and correspondence. Political pamphlets also had much currency among them and during the French Revolutionary period the gentry and clergy had some of the anti-Revolution propaganda done into Welsh. Attempts at journalism in Welsh in the eighteenth century were, however, abortive. Lewis Morris sought to emulate the English literary journals and to exploit the current interest in antiquarianism in publishing *Tlysau yr Hen Oesoedd* ('Gems of the Old Ages') in 1735 which must be the first Welsh literary journal though shortlived. Josiah Rees, a Unitarian minister, had a longer run of 14 numbers with his *Trysorfa Gwybodaeth* ('Treasury of Knowledge') in 1770. The failure of M. J. Rhys and others in the nineties indicated that the period of the French Wars was an inauspicious time for journalistic ventures.[1] ' To investigate the vast treasure . . . contained in the Welsh language in MSS. and the oral traditions of the people' was the purpose of *The Cambrian Register* edited by Dr. William Owen Pughe but only three numbers appeared in 1795-6 and 1818.

An English-language weekly like the Swansea *Cambrian* (1804) attracted the backing of businessmen to foster ' the spirit of Improvement' and commercial enterprise. The *Carmarthen Journal*, somewhat more liberal in its views, followed in 1810 also as a weekly. The attempt to print a Welsh newspaper at Swansea, *Seren Gomer*, was, however, abortive in 1814 because, unlike *The Cambrian*, it failed to attract advertisers. It was a missionary rather than a business effort with the aim of spreading knowledge, improving manners and helping to correct and purify the language. These pioneer efforts were to blaze the trail for the great effusion from the Welsh press in the nineteenth century.[2]

[1] See pp. 218 ff.
[2] ibid.

The Literary Revival. Poetry

There was some justification for the oft-expressed belief that the poetic art was in decline and had become formalised and lacking in vigour. Bardic learning, handed down by oral tradition, was waning but far from extinct and it was possible in the second half of the eighteenth century for Iolo Morganwg to learn his poetic art and acquire a wealth of literary tradition from country poets who lived in Glamorgan. The state of bardic education evidently differed as between one part of the country and another.

Poetry had ceased to have a social function and the Phylip family which had served as family bards to the Vaughans of Nannau and Corsygedol were about the last of their kind. The future lay with the amateurs and one of the foremost poets of the end of the seventeenth century was Edward Morris, a cattle dealer. He abandoned the strict metres with their intricate pattern of '*cynghanedd*' for '*canu rhydd*' ('free verse') which was not, however, unmetrical but allowed more scope for experiment. The poems of Huw Morus of Glynceiriog gained great popularity and were sung to popular tunes.

Two of Wales's most illustrious poets were born in the eighteenth century, Goronwy Owen and William Williams (Pantycelyn). Although Owen represented the old literary tradition and used the traditional '*cywydd*' form, his verse shows the influence of the Age of Reason with the emphasis on form and accuracy of expression as in contemporary English poetry. This demanded a mastery of poetic art which had to be acquired and Goronwy Owen's self-criticism had a profound effect on the critical standards of his age. William Williams cut new ground and was bold in experiment with metric forms. He owed nothing to literary tradition except to the language of the Bible but the tradition of free verse in South Wales went back through Vicar Prichard, Llandovery, to the writers of the religious verses known as '*Cwndidau*' and other free verse of the sixteenth century. The lyrical touch which comes through even in his numerous hymns marks him as a herald of the romantic movement. He achieved something that eluded Goronwy Owen and earlier poets—the writing of two epic poems, *Theomemphus* and *Golwg ar Deyrnas Crist* (' View of the Kingdom of Christ '), which relate the spiritual pilgrimage of a

P*

soul in the style of Bunyan. It is the work of these two poets that marks the genesis of modern Welsh poetry.

The Morris Circle was often consulted as literary pundits by aspiring poets and Lewis Morris who was no mean poet himself was generous with help and advice to the rising generation. Though they all were sons of '*y werin*' they were professional men and their tastes were aristocratic and their standards academic. The Circle included Goronwy Owen and Evan Evans (Ieuan Fardd) who were both masters of the traditional bardic craft as well as Edward Richard, at whose feet Evans had acquired his classical education and who was the first to write Welsh pastorals in the classical style. Thus the Circle was an amalgam of two literary traditions—the old Welsh bardic tradition and the classical. In Evans the two blended very happily and he influenced and was influenced by Thomas Gray who was greatly interested in Celtic antiquities. There was a good deal of cross-fertilisation between English and Welsh literature at this period and several of the English romanticists found inspiration in Celtic legends and mythology.

Much popular verse was produced in the form of '*penillion telyn*' (literally, ' harp verses ') which were short, epigrammatic and often lyrical. It was Lewis Morris who first set store by them and began their collection. Carols were written for religious and moral purposes and set to popular songs, usually English. The ballads which poured from the presses are a mirror of the age, dealing with matters of popular interest and often speak of poverty and hardship.

The revived interest in our poetic tradition, the desire to experiment with new forms and to write on new subjects are unmistakable signs of a poetic revival which led the way to the great literary output of the nineteenth century.

Prose

The prose works of the period were mainly religious and moral in tone but designed for religious uplift rather than social betterment. Thus prose was not cultivated for its own sake but for the purpose of exhortation. Most of the products were translations from English which discouraged creativeness and frustrated the development of Welsh prose. Roman Catholics issued tracts to nourish their faith and Puritans produced counter-tracts to discount their influence. Stephen Hughes enlisted the support of scholars like Moses Williams to carry through the programme of the Welsh Trust but apart from Charles Edwards's *Y Ffydd Ddiffuant* ('Sincere Faith') the movement hardly produced any original work.

The greatest original prose work of the period was Ellis Wynne's *Gweledigaetheu y Bardd Cwsc* ('Visions of the Sleeping Bard') which although indebted for its form to the Spaniard Quevedo, was an original literary classic ; though it displayed a typically Anglican social outlook it was in harmony with the modern viewpoint and had a satirical vein in the manner of Swift. Wynne turned the language of everyday use into a medium for literary creation and thus made a significant contribution to the development of Welsh prose. William Williams, Pantycelyn, was as much an innovator in prose as in verse and adapted the language to discuss unusual topics and must be considered a major prose writer of the period. Theophilus Evans's *Drych y Prif Oesoedd* ('Mirror of the Primitive Ages') was very spurious history but a very popular classic which ran into thirty editions.

Polemical writing on religious topics was not uncommon but was more novel in political discussion. The writings of Dr. Richard Price and David Williams were a significant contribution to English political theory and political science and contemporary political ideas were retailed in Welsh in the works of Jac Glan y Gors and Thomas Roberts. With their pamphlets we see Welsh prose being put to a secular purpose in contrast with earlier practice.

The improvement in travel facilities and the growing romanticism of the age made travel in Wales very popular and most travellers capped their journey with a 'Tour', being an account of their journey invariably in English. Few are original since they copied from each other and their value is mainly topographical. The best was produced by a native, Thomas Pennant of Downing, because he was better-informed and was an expert in Natural History ; he took a Welsh-speaking friend around to inquire into the antiquities and traditions of the places they visited. It was illustrated by Moses Griffith, a self-taught artist from Llŷn.

Few diaries have survived from this period. Those of Howell

Harris are invaluable for the early history of Methodism but for little else. The diaries of William Bulkeley of Brynddu by contrast are a valuable social record of the mid-century. David Samwell, a naval surgeon and literary man left a good picture of life at sea in his journals especially of Captain Cook's last voyage and death.

The eighteenth century was not a great age for prose with the single exception of Ellis Wynne's work. The absence of such literary forms as the essay, the novel and *belles lettres* is in itself indicative that Welsh prose was as yet little used for secular purposes although the beginning of political journalism was a move towards diversity.

Antiquarian Interest

A growing awareness of a country's historic past has in more than one instance led to a regeneration in national life. Such was the case in eighteenth century Wales and the developing national consciousness of the nineteenth century was the outcome of it. It stemmed in part from the great interest in antiquarianism which was common to both England and Wales from mid-eighteenth century on when English scholars as well as Welsh began to take an interest in the Celtic past of these islands. The publication in 1765 of Bishop Percy's *Reliques of Ancient English Poetry* was an event which led to links being forged with Welsh scholars like Evan Evans in whose researches Percy and Thomas Gray showed great interest. It was to Gray that Evans submitted his *De Bardis Dissertatio* for criticism and Gray's poem *The Bard* was inspired by the Welsh legend about the alleged slaughter of the bards by Edward I. Blake and Southey also found themes to exploit in Welsh legend and history. The English scholar Sharon Turner was sufficiently curious about the Welsh romances to learn Welsh better to evaluate their authenticity. This was understandable when the controversy over Geoffrey of Monmouth's twelfth century *Historia Regum Britanniae* was still raging. His spurious attribution of the origin of the Britons to Brutus, grandson of Aeneas, and origin of the Welsh tongue to the Tower of Babel and the romantic stories about Arthur had only recently been given further currency in Theophilus Evans's *Drych y Prif Oesoedd* (1716). The interest in Druidism even ante-dates Iolo

Morganwg who raised it into an institution, having much stimulus from the search for archaeological remains which brought to light chambered tombs and stone circles which confirmed the antiquity of our nation. It also gave us our first county history in Henry Rowland's *Mona Antiqua* which was for a long time the antiquary's bible. This interest in early history also had the effect of conferring on the Welsh language an aura of romanticism.

Collectors and Libraries

The tide of Renaissance scholarship ebbed in the latter half of the seventeenth century which saw the last of scholarly squires like Robert Vaughan of Hengwrt (Mer.) who was a pillar of learning and outstanding collector of manuscripts. His intention of writing a history of Wales was not realised but his genealogical and historical collections were to be a quarry for generations of Welsh scholars. He corresponded with English scholars like John Selden, Sir Simonds d'Ewes and James Ussher and was their point of reference on anything relating to the Celtic countries. After his day, the tradition of collection and copying of MSS. found most succour in north-east Wales among lesser gentry like William Maurice of Llansilin (Denbs.), who compiled a useful record of Welsh MSS. and their location. Many Welsh MSS. gradually drifted into this area which a generation later produced Edward Lhuyd who inherited many of his scholarly interests from Maurice. The gentry who had done so much to preserve our literary heritage were, however, no longer able to appreciate their collections for their intrinsic worth and now prized them more for their commercial value. It was for this class that professional copyists like the school which survived in south Cardiganshire into the early eighteenth century had worked. But scholars now began to think of publishing the contents of MSS. thereby reaching a wider audience than the copyists catered for. Edward Lhuyd had formulated a plan of research and publication and Ieuan Fardd and Iolo Morganwg were intent on making the Welsh literary heritage known to the world. Lhuyd had succeeded in creating tremendous enthusiasm amongst the gentry and clergy by involving them in his work but as the century wore on it became more difficult to persuade them to open the contents of their libraries for fear that publication would depreciate the value of their collections. Nevertheless, the libraries of Hengwrt, Hafod, Wynnstay and Plas Gwyn among others extended hospitality to a succession of scholars like Ieuan Fardd and Iolo Morganwg fortunately, since some of the collections were later to be lost in disastrous fires.

Scholarship

Eighteenth century scholarship dates from Edward Lhuyd who was himself of the gentry class. His interests included heraldry, botany, geology and antiquity and after a period at Oxford he became an assistant to Dr. Plot whom he succeeded as Keeper of the Ashmolean Museum. Lhuyd's work brought him to the notice of Sir Hans Sloane who rated him as the best naturalist in Europe. He contributed the section on Wales to Gibson's edition of Camden's *Britannia* and this turned his mind to the idea of a series of volumes on Wales and the Celtic countries. Lhuyd's interest in manuscripts caused him to study philology in order to interpret them the better. In the process he laid the foundations of the study of Celtic philology but the significance of his work was not realised at the time and it was not pursued. He published in 1695 his *Design* for an *Encyclopaedia Britannica* but only one volume, mainly philological, appeared. He travelled Wales and the Celtic countries recording archaeological remains, traditions and even dialects and addressed *Parochial Queries* to the gentry and clergy of Wales and Cornwall. Lhuyd did not live long enough to bring any of his ambitious plans to fruition but he pointed the way that it was necessary for Welsh scholarship to take and he securely laid the foundations. He trained some of his students to carry on his work but only Moses Williams came up to expectation. He edited some Welsh texts including the Laws of Hywel Dda which was an important start to the programme of publishing Welsh records and manuscripts.

The Cymmrodorion Society, founded in 1751, kept alive Lhuyd's proposals and it made known its plans in the published *Gosodedigaethau* ('Proposals') which bear the imprint of Lewis Morris's hand and included the publication of Welsh MSS. .

Despite their laudable intentions the Cymmrodorion achieved very little.

The Morris Circle were the heirs of Edward Lhuyd and supplied the new cultural leadership. Lewis Morris's interests were probably as wide as Lhuyd's and he might have accomplished some of Lhuyd's proposals especially in the field of Natural History but he lacked his scholarly authority. Morris's proposed *Celtic Remains* did not see the light of day but he left his MSS. to the Cymmrodorion library and these were to be later useful to Dr. Owen-Pughe. It was another member of the Morris Circle, Evan Evans, who tried to carry out Lhuyd's intention of publishing the gems of Welsh literature, fired by the desire to extol the greatness of Wales's literary past and goaded by the scepticism of contemporary English scholars. Evans went around the libraries of the gentry copying their MSS. but lacked a settled Church living to be able to carry out an extended programme of work. His knowledge of the content of Welsh MSS. was incomparable and his treatise *De Bardis Dissertatio* was the first systematic attempt to explain ancient poetry. The publication in 1764 of *Some Specimens of the Antient Welsh Bards* included the work of the earliest Welsh poets with translations and was intended as a foretaste to stimulate some patrons to support a more ambitious scheme. This did not happen to Evans and he had to sell his manuscript collection to Paul Panton of Plas Gwyn but like Lewis Morris's collection, it was made available to Dr. Owen-Pughe for his work. Evans was probably held in greater esteem by English scholars like Thomas Gray and even Dr. Johnson, who tried to influence the Welsh bishops on his behalf so that he could carry on his work in Wales.

By 1787, the Cymmrodorion Society was defunct and its mantle fell upon the Gwyneddigion. It was not the Society as such but two of its members, Owain Myfyr (Owain Jones) and Dr. William Owen-Pughe, who were responsible for bringing to fruition schemes which had been mulling since Edward Lhuyd's time. Owain Myfyr had made a fortune in London as a skinner and no better instance can be found of private munificence being put to more practical and enduring use. He had no scholarly pretensions himself but gave financial support to Dr. Owen-Pughe who was the greatest Welsh

scholar of the end of the century and paid for the publication
of his work.   The first of the edited texts, that of the work of
Dafydd ap Gwilym, appeared in 1789.   In 1793, his Dictionary
began to appear and though it confused Welsh orthography for
a century it was still a valuable adjunct to literary scholarship.
His most valuable contribution was the publication of *The
Myvyrian Archaiology* in three volumes which was named after
his bountiful patron.   At last the intention of publishing Welsh
MSS. which Lhuyd and Evan Evans had dreamed of was
realised and it included much of Lewis Morris's and Evan
Evans's work.   Iolo Morganwg also collaborated, mainly as a
copyist, but he managed to interpolate some of his own work
which he passed off as the work of medieval Glamorgan bards
in his zeal for the poetic tradition of his native province.

Welshmen made significant contributions to scholarship
outside Wales as well.   Sir William Jones laid the foundations
of Oriental scholarship and contributed to the study of Indian
jurisprudence.   His father was a leading mathematician from
Anglesey and was responsible for editing the works of Sir
Isaac Newton.   Both Robert Owen and David Williams
contributed to educational theory, the former being one of the
first to emphasize the influence of environment on upbringing.
In an age when the diffusion of knowledge led to the writing
of encyclopaedias, Dr. Abraham Rees from Llanbryn-mair
made a voluminous contribution.   Dr. Richard Price enriched
the literature of economics as much as he did that of politics ;
he put before Pitt schemes for liquidating the National Debt
and also laid the foundations of modern insurance business.
For his scholarly contribution in his own field Thomas Pennant
was elected Fellow of the Linnaean Society as well as of the
Royal Society.   When one remembers the poverty of their
background and the lack of educational facilities notably of a
University, Welsh contribution to scholarship was truly remarkable.

The Arts

Outside the field of literature Wales's contribution to the
Arts was meagre.   This cultural barrenness can be attributed to
economic poverty on the one hand and the lack of patronage
on the other.   The Welsh upper-class found its pleasures

elsewhere and there was not as yet a sufficiently strong middle class to fill this social void. Until the end of the eighteenth century urban growth had been retarded and a sense of civic tradition was slow to emerge. The lack of suitable facilities frustrated the growth of theatre and opera and denied an opportunity for native talent. Literature remained the dominant means of expression as it had traditionally been but it changed from being a Court art to a folk activity.

There was a traditional fondness for singing but this stimulated little original composition nor cultivated musical taste other than for folk music. The music of Handel was hardly heard in Wales before 1800 because of a lack of assembly halls but by 1785 we hear of the existence of a musical society at Wrexham. There was a strong folk tradition in songs, carols and ballads but there was also an extensive borrowing of English tunes. Tourists often remarked on the popularity of the harp and the art of *penillion* singing was cultivated in North Wales. Few gentry families employed the services of a harpist any more and the most enterprising harpists went to seek fame and fortune in London where they were noticed by both Pepys and Evelyn. John Parry, the blind harpist of Ruabon and protégé of Sir W. W. Wynn, was the rage of Ranelagh in 1746. The eighteenth century interest in antiquarianism stimulated interest in folk music and one of the aims of the Gwyneddigion Society was to revive *penillion* singing. Several collections of Welsh airs were made after 1742 and Edward Jones, '*Bardd y Brenin*' ('King's bard') added an account of Welsh music to one of them.

The development of the theatre had to await the nineteenth century when towns began to grow in size and wealth. The art of the theatre was introduced from England and was not a development of native forms although we hear of miracle plays in the sixteenth century and *chwaraeon* (plays) in the seventeenth century but none of them have survived. The *anterliwt* (interlude) was a popular form of stage-play in North Wales in the eighteenth century and was written in verse on popular metres. The ' prince of *anterliwt* writers ' was Twm o'r Nant (Thomas Edwards) who was also both producer and actor. With him it reached its maturity of development and after his day declined to the point that it failed to survive the eighteenth century.

The strolling players were not professionals and persons who had a natural talent for acting often found it a profitable venture. The *anterliwt* was decried by Ellis Wynne, belittled by the Morris brothers and considered a nuisance by William Bulkeley, the Anglesey squire, who thought it unsettled people. The cast only needed two or three actors who turned a farm wagon into a make-shift stage, the audience standing out in front. Some of the plays were bawdy and pandered to the lowest taste but others were moralistic and contained a good deal of social comment and exhortation. Despite this, the Methodists had no truck with them and their growing influence undoubtedly helped to kill them.

By 1800, the *anterliwt* players also suffered from the growing popularity of the English theatre in towns like Denbigh and Wrexham where English troupes passing between London and Dublin stopped to give performances. They were patronised by the local gentry who often bespoke plays and by the middle class—a following that had never graced Twm o'r Nant's productions. During the off-season at Bath and Bristol, companies went on tour and visited towns like Cardiff and Swansea and smaller towns *en route*. The growth of spas and seaside resorts attracted players for the summer season. At Swansea the season might last from six to eight weeks and a vigorous theatre developed there despite the opposition of the Duke of Beaufort's steward. By 1815 at least seven towns had theatres and some of the clsssics like the works of Goethe in translation had been produced in Wales. Plays with a Welsh flavour had a distinct appeal and performances were well-larded with songs, many composed for the occasion giving them more the appearance of music-hall shows than straight theatre. The gentry not only frequented the theatre but also took part in amateur dramatics and plays were part of a great house's entertainment especially at Christmastide. Sir W. W. Wynn built a theatre at Wynnstay in 1782 to which London actors, including Garrick, came to play. It is evident that cultural patterns were beginning to change. The growth of urban economy stimulated civic tastes but it was unfortunate that the new forms of expression forsook the native language.

There was no Welsh school or tradition of Art and Welsh artists did not begin to make their appearance till the eighteenth century, brought on, no doubt, by the English artistic renaissance which gave rise to the Royal Academy. Wales lacked a centre for Art education and the necessity to go to London for it kept the number of professional artists very small. Would-be artists either had to have means of their own or have a wealthy patron to pay for their education ; not surprisingly, several sons of gentry families are to be found among them. Since the sixteenth century the gentry had followed the fashion of having their portraits done in oils. The number of paintings in private collections that cannot be attributed to any known artist rather suggests the work of travelling artists or painters of local renown who were probably self-taught and who cashed in on the lucrative trade in portrait painting. By 1700 many gentlemen owned collections of pictures which contained works of the masters as well as family portraits, rather more having survived in North than in South Wales.

Interest in landscape was stimulated by the romanticists, first, as background to portraits or groups but after 1750, increasingly for its own sake. Several artists turned to Wales for their subjects though some interpreted what they saw with an Italian rather than a native eye. Richard Wilson (1713-82) born at Penegoes (Monts.) won sufficient recognition to become one of the founder members of the Royal Academy. His education at London and subsequently in Italy was financed by a wealthy kinsman, Sir George Wynne of Leeswood. His interests had early turned to landscape and Welsh scenes are the subjects of much of his early work. His sojourn in Italy influenced his style and on his return his landscapes bore an unmistakable Italian imprint which displeased George III who had commissioned him to paint a view of Kew Gardens. Wilson lost Court favour and public acclaim and though his declining years were spent in Wales, Welsh themes are few among his later works. His pupil, Thomas Jones of Pencerrig, the son of a Radnorshire country squire, copied his style but did not achieve Wilson's status. The tourists sometimes called on the services of illustrators for their ' Tours ' amongst the best being Moses Griffith, ' an untaught genius ' who accompanied Thomas Pennant and who illustrated his botanical works as well as his *Tours in Wales*. Though not Welshmen, the names of ' Warwick ' Smith and J. C. Ibbetson should be mentioned for their contribution to our knowledge of Welsh topography at the end of our period.

Few Welsh gentlemen had the wealth and the inclination to commission works of sculpture. Thomas Johnes of Hafod was an exception here as in so many other things and engaged both Thomas Banks and Chantrey to execute works for him in which his family figured. Craftsmanship in wrought-iron is seen at its best in north-east Wales where the Davies family of Croes-foel, probably influenced by the Frenchman, Tijou, executed work for the local gentry at Emral, Erddig, Leeswood and at Eaton Hall, near Chester. A novel product of the industrial age was the 'japanned ware' of Pontypool, using sheets of tinplate as a base varnished over to give a finish like Japanese lacquer. Though not as successful as a financial enterprise as Wedgwood's Etruria, the pottery at Swansea which produced china and earthenware and that at Nantgarw which produced porcelain were brought under single control in 1801 and entered upon their finest period of production which has made their product collectors' pieces.

Societies

The eighteenth century was a gregarious age when societies were formed for various purposes and to promote different causes. The habit spread outwards from London and was expressed in Wales in the form of county agricultural societies on the one hand and a plethora of religious societies on the other. Welshmen were prominent in London societies and took to forming their own which were mainly cultural though often touching on other subjects. Richard Morris, brother of Lewis, was at the centre of this activity and his mantle fell on Owain Jones (Owain Myfyr) ; between them they span the golden age of London Welsh organised societies.

The pioneer society was The Honourable and Loyal Society of Antient Britons, formed in 1715,[1] consisting mainly of gentry and clergy. Though its aims were mainly political, it met to celebrate St. David's day with a sermon followed by a dinner but there was little Welsh flavour to the proceedings and some Welsh bishops exploited the opportunity to decry the Welsh language. Its only practical achievement was to found a Welsh

[1] See p. 59

charity school at Clerkenwell but its cultural contribution to Wales was negligible.

In 1751, the Cymmrodorion Society[1] was formed, again patronised by gentry and clergy but it attracted many humbler members as well. It became more aristocratic as time went on but though great personages acted more as patrons than as active members, the Society did stimulate their interest in Welsh culture. There was a whiff of social snobbery about it— Lewis Morris, for instance, complaining that the trades of artisans were published in the members' lists. The Cymmrodorion was intended to be a learned society not a social club and its importance lies in the fact that it was the forerunner of societies which patronised Welsh language and culture. In a more practical way it sought to encourage the arts of farming and manufacture and emulated the Royal Society in awarding medals and bounties for improvements in agriculture, forestry, manufactures and commerce, possibly, from motives of self-interest. Its aristocratic inclinations caused the humbler members who were more Welsh in nature to leave to join more congenial and democratic societies and the Cymmrodorion itself became defunct in 1787.

The mantle of the Cymmrodorion fell on the Gwynedd-igion[2]; originally a society of North Walians, it later opened its doors to all Welshmen. It was a social and convivial club meeting at The Bull, Walbrook, usually referred to as *Y Crindy*. It was interested in singing and particularly in fostering *penillion* singing which the more sedate Cymmrodorion forbade. It was thoroughly Welsh and democratic and after 1789 exhibited a great deal of interest in politics. Its main concern was, however, with literature and literary criticism and several poets submitted their work for consideration by the Society. It was this interest which led it to accept the sponsorship of the revived *eisteddfod*[3] in 1789 which came to be known as the 'Gwyneddigion *Eisteddfod*'.

Two lesser known societies were the Caradogion and Cymreig-yddion which were contemporary with the Gwyneddigion. The aim of the Caradogion was to teach English to the many monoglot Welshmen who settled in London but it was short-

[1] See pp. 72, 240
[2] See p. 221
[3] See infra p. 249

lived. It exhibited a great deal of interest in the alleged existence of a Welsh Indian tribe, the Madogwys, a subject given
much currency by John Evans's journey up the Missouri to
find them in 1792.[1] The Cymreigyddion survived longer in
London and its offshoots were flourishing in Wales well into
the nineteenth century. Of the twelve founder members, six
were Gwyneddigion. Its aim was ' to promote national and
brotherly feeling and to succour the language ', in marked
contrast to the Caradogion. Its members came mainly from
North Wales, Dissenters being very prominent ; from the
Society's minutes it appears that even its officials were ill-
educated which suggests a low social class which is confirmed
by the low subscription fee. This probably also explains the
greater fervour for the language and one of its practical
services was to lend books to members. Though it was much
given to debating it professed to eschew politics.

More is known about London societies than any other
because their records are more complete, but little is known
about societies in different parts of Wales. A literary society
is known to have existed in Cardiff in 1773 to which Iolo
Morganwg was a visitor. It is known that there was an intention
to establish a literary society at Llantrisant in 1771 for the
purpose of fostering literature. It was to be ' a society of
gentlemen and others ' for perpetuating the language ' once
in so much respect, now ignored '. It coincided with the burst
of activity among Glamorgan men of letters and grammarians
and the *eisteddfodau* which were held at Llantrisant. Even in
Merioneth, despite difficulties of travel, a literary society, *Y
Gymdeithas Loerig* (' The Lunar Society ') met at Drws y Nant
drawing its members from a wide area. It was at the neighbouring towns of Bala and Corwen that the Gwyneddigion
Eisteddfod was to be held after 1789. Rather different were the
societies which existed in a social centre like Wrexham which
had its Assembly, Beef-steak Club and Musical Society about
which little is known apart from their patronage of strolling
players who visited the town.

The Eisteddfod

The *eisteddfod* has its origins in the Middle Ages but the

[1] See infra p. 258

modern institution stems from 1789. Bards commonly met for sessions in taverns in the seventeenth and eighteenth centuries —hence the name '*eisteddfod y dafarn*' ('tavern eisteddfod'), but as they were solely poetical sessions they did not command a popular following. William Price of Rhiwlas (Mer.) describes it as ' a custom long kept up chiefly amongst ye most mountainous parts ' and certainly it was more in evidence in the counties of Denbigh, Merioneth, Montgomery and Cardigan than elsewhere. The *eisteddfod* was already considered an old institution and Iolo Morganwg had some justification in insisting on the continuity of literary tradition and bardic education even though in a debased form in parts of Glamorgan. The poetical output was, however, of low literary merit and much of it was printed in contemporary almanacks whose publishers were often the sponsors of these *eisteddfodau*. There was some attempt at reform at the Bala *eisteddfod* of 1760 which sought to emulate the Caerwys *eisteddfod* of 1568 by imposing some rules recently published in Siôn Rhydderch's Grammar (1728) as a standard and thus to restore the language to some status and regard.

The reformed *eisteddfod* which dates from 1789 was initiated by Jonathan Hughes at Llangollen and he was soon joined by Thomas Jones ' the exciseman '. The patronage of the London societies was sought and the Gwyneddigion responded. Thomas Jones organised most of the ' Gwyneddigion *eisteddfodau* ' till his removal to Bristol in 1795, and most of them were held in the vicinity of the Denbighshire-Merionethshire border. Unlike the earlier *eisteddfod*, musical competitions were admitted and so it became a competitive meeting in both literature and music which attracted a wider audience. It appeared to be very much a North Wales affair ; not to be outdone, Iolo Morganwg, who was so jealous of the reputation of his native Glamorgan, established the *Gorsedd* of Bards claiming it to be a Druidic survival in Glamorgan but it was entirely the figment of Iolo's fertile imagination. It was inaugurated on Primrose Hill in London and got Gwyneddigion support ; in 1819 it was incorporated into the *eisteddfod* proceedings at Carmarthen. The *eisteddfod* stimulated an interest in the arts albeit on a narrow front and gave the opportunity for literary composition to reach a wider audience than a local one. Until the time when literary journals were founded literary men were dependent upon it and it certainly raised the Muse from the slough of the ' tavern ' and ' almanack ' *eisteddfod.*

SUGGESTED READING

L. T. Davies and A. Edwards, *Welsh life in the eighteenth century,* London, 1939.

W. J. Gruffydd, *Y Morysiaid, The Morris Brothers,* bilingual, Cardiff, 1939.

W. J. Hughes, *Wales and the Welsh in English literature,* Wrexham, 1924.

R. T. Jenkins and H. Ramage, *A history of the Honourable Society of Cymmrodorion, Y Cymmrodor,* I, 1951.

S. Lewis, *A School of Welsh Augustans,* Wrexham, 1924.

D. Morgan (gol.), *Gwŷr llên y ddeunawfed ganrif,* Llandybie, 1966.

T. Parry, *Hanes llenyddiaeth Gymraeg hyd* 1900, Caerdydd, 1964. In translation, H. I. Bell, *A history of Welsh literature,* Oxford, 1955.

C. Price, *The English theatre in Wales,* Cardiff, 1948.

G. J. Williams, *Traddodiad llenyddol Morgannwg,* Caerdydd, 1948.

Articles:

G. Daniel, 'Edward Lhwyd', *W.H.R.,* III, 4, 1967.

W. Ll. Davies, 'David Samwell', *Trans. Cymmr.,* 1926–7.

F. V. Emery, 'Edward Lhuyd', *Trans. Cymmr.,* 1969.

B. L. Jones, 'Goronwy Owen', *Trans. Cymmr.,* 1971.

E. Rees, 'An introductory survey of eighteenth century Welsh libraries', *J. Welsh Bibl. Soc.,* X, 1971.

14. Welshmen Overseas

America

The poverty of Wales caused many enterprising Welshmen to seek opportunities elsewhere, notably in England, and from the accession of the Tudors many were attracted to careers at Court, in government and in the professions. Welsh farmers who engaged in the cattle trade established themselves as graziers in the counties of Leicester and Northampton and many who followed the drovers to London set up in business there. The growth of maritime trade in our period took our sailors ever further afield and others for various reasons made their permanent settlement abroad.

A. H. Dodd attributes Welsh interest in emigration after 1660 to disappointment at the failure of the Propagation experiment of 1650.[1] The hope of bringing Wales under ' Gospel order ' vanished with the return of the ' merry monarch ' in 1660 but the vision was not extinguished. The Penal Laws also instituted sporadic persecution and though the Quakers who were quietists adopted an attitude of forbearance they recognised that their vision could not grow in such an uncongenial atmosphere.

The initiative was taken by the Baptists. The congregation which met at Ilston in Gower left *en bloc* in 1663 under its pastor, John Miles and successfully planted the first group settlement by Welshmen in Massachusetts, naming it ' Swanzey ' as a permanent reminder of home. Religious intolerance was rampant in Massachusetts and subsequent Baptist migrations turned elsewhere. By 1679, the interest of Welsh Quakers was roused in William Penn's ' Holy Experiment ' to found a colony in America based on religious toleration. In 1681, twelve persons from North Wales went to London to see Penn and negotiated the purchase for £600 of 30,000 acres of land over which he had obtained charter rights from the Crown.

[1] See Vol. I, p. 218

Seven companies were formed to provide the capital and to re-sell the land later to individuals. The first Quakers left in 1682, the vanguard of a movement which denuded Merionethshire and Montgomeryshire of most of their Quakers. They were admirable pioneering material and they soon established a settled way of life which was largely self-governing, their quarterly meeting forming a kind of moot or assembly where things were decided in common. The three initial settlements were called Merion, Radnor and Haverford reflecting the parts of Wales whence the settlers came. Gwynedd was added in 1698 as the area of occupation steadily grew over the years. Their expectation of being allowed to establish a ' separate barony ' where ' we might live together as a Civil Society to endeavour to decide all controversies and debates among ourselves in a Gospell order, and not to entangle ourselves with Laws in an Unknown Tongue ' was not fulfilled. A long dispute with Penn ensued in which the Merion settlers were prominent because European settlers, notably German, were allowed to settle among the Welsh communities. They vigorously asserted their right to use their own language in legal proceedings as they claimed to have done in the old country. But the dream of having ' their bounds and limits to themselves' had to be foresaken as the settlements began to change their character, Merion being the only settlement from the start which was almost totally Welsh in speech. The Welsh Tract, as it came to be known, lost some of its cohesion when it was divided between Pennsylvania and Delaware. The Welsh Quakers' isolationism gradually gave way as more of them became involved in politics and government since it was important for them to have some say in the affairs of the State where they had cast their lot. Thomas Lloyd (Dolobran) acted as Penn's deputy when the proprietor was away in England. Rowland Ellis (Dolgellau) who emigrated in 1686 was by 1700 elected to the State Assembly. Both at county and state levels Welshmen were to play a significant part in proportion to their numbers.

It was to Pennsylvania that the second group of Baptists who hailed from Radnorshire migrated to settle an area they called Radnor. This settlement had a substantial English-speaking element and the Welsh language did not long survive in their church records. They founded the historic Pennepek Church and the missionary efforts of their ministers established seven early Baptist causes in Pennsylvania and five in New Jersey and the Welsh Baptists made a significant contribution to the Baptist cause from Virginia to New York. In 1701, they were joined by sixteen Baptists from Rhydwilym in West Wales who were already constituted into a church before they left. Differences of religious observances and probably of language caused them to move on to Delaware to settle on what was known as *The* Welsh Tract, there being several so-called. They kept their church records in Welsh and sermons were regularly preached in the language so that it retained its hold longer here than in any settlement.

Between 1682 and 1700, the Welsh were the most numerous body to settle in Pennsylvania running to at least 300 families without counting individuals. The fact that the level of migration continued as high between 1689 and 1700 as it had done between 1682 and 1689 shows that religious persecution was not the only or the major cause. Nor was poverty more than one contributory cause since many of the migrants came from the relatively prosperous parts of Montgomeryshire and Pembrokeshire. By 1689, many Welshmen had relatives or friends in the New World whose letters home kept their correspondents in a continuous state of uneasiness. Conditions at home acted as a goad but the prospect of land in plenty and a good living were powerful attractions also to the most venturesome.

The migrants represented a wide social spectrum. Quakers were largely drawn from the lesser country gentry like Robert Owen, Dolserau (Mer.) who took five servants with him. Thomas Lloyd of Dolobran had received a University education. But the economic fortunes of this class as a whole were in decline after 1660 and this must have been a determinant in their case. Many of the smaller people who bought land from the companies were of yeoman stock. An analysis of 300 families made by T. A. Glenn reveals that 28% of them were of gentry stock ; 40% were yeomen ; 11% were artisans with 5% as shopkeepers and professional men. The 6% Glenn includes for servants or labourers is probably an underestimate since, apart from servants accompanying their masters, many crossed the Atlantic as indentured labourers as the records of ports like Bristol and Liverpool testify. These were servants who bound themselves to masters for a term of years, usually seven, in return for the cost of their passage outwards. Some took advantage of the ' head-right ' provision whereby a person who defrayed the cost of transporting an able-bodied immigrant received 50 acres of land as a gift. The background of the migrants at this period was almost universally rural with Radnorshire providing most of the artisan element. Another limitation of Glenn's figures is that he only accounts for Quaker families whilst it is known that many Anglicans amongst others emigrated in the last two decades of the seventeenth century who were not fleeing from persecution. They were usually of a lower social origin than the Quakers being mostly yeomen, husbandmen and artisans to whom the prospect of their own land or remunerative work was the attraction. There must have been many like the tenant farmer from Bala who had a numerous family and little prospect who felt ' an inclination ' to move to Pennsylvania where his land-hunger could be assuaged. Whilst Merion was almost entirely Quaker the Anglican presence was much more pronounced in Haverford and Radnor counties. The strong Dissenting element of Quakers and Baptists ensured that education had due recognition from the start. Rowland Ellis's home at Brynmawr became the seat of one of the most famous women's colleges in America which still proudly bears the name. Even the smallest of Welsh Dissenting sects, the Presbyterians, made a significant contribution to education in the Welsh Tract as they did at home with the founding of a Presbyterian academy at Pencader (Delaware).

Though organised emigration, especially by churches, declined after 1700, it did not entirely cease and individuals and small groups continued to emigrate. For the Welsh settlers in America it was a period of consolidation when they were hard at work realising the full potential of their concessions. Their hold on the old way of life and culture began to slacken as they came more into contact with European settlers and some of the ideals which they had long nurtured began to pall. This was a natural process of erosion over generations although deliberate efforts were made to preserve their way of life and institutions in which religious leaders played an important

part. The Anglican Church, so often accused of being moribund at home, was very active and sensitive to its call in the
American colonies acting through its agency, the Society for
the Propagation of the Gospel (S.P.G.) founded in 1699. The
Society maintained resident missionaries in Pennsylvania, one
of the first being Henry Nicholls, a native of Cowbridge. Many
Welsh clergy were amongst those licensed to the colonies and
they worked among their fellow-nationals irrespective of sect.
The Society also sent out schoolmasters and of nine who served
between 1704 and 1731 at least three were Welsh-speaking.
The Anglicans continually petitioned the Bishop of London to
send out Welsh-speaking clergy since in Merion as late as 1734,
74% of its tax-payers were Welsh-speaking ; a supply of pious
literature in Welsh was also sought to forestall the growth of
Dissent. The tide flowed both ways, many Anglicans becoming
Quakers but Quakers were also rehabilitated into the Church
of their fathers especially in the Welsh Tract. This was due
to the regular provision for worship which the Anglican
Church made and the calibre of the clergy it sent out to serve
the mission field.

As a result of a petition to the Bishop of London in 1715,
St. David's Church in Radnor county was built. It was
served by a succession of Welsh incumbents and provided
regular sermons in Welsh as well as in English. The Anglican
Church certainly took into account the national consciousness
of the Welsh and did a great deal to foster it. The Radnor
Anglicans named their church after the patron saint and the
Philadelphia Anglicans were the first to commemorate him
with the foundation of a St. David's Society which was in
existence by 1729. Christchurch, Philadelphia, was an important centre of Welsh activities, the church having a strong
Welsh membership though not designated as a Welsh church.
During the incumbency of its second rector, the Rev. Evan
Evans, a native of Carno (Monts.), missions sent to the countryside around resulted in the establishment of several new
churches. When he died in 1721, he was recognised as an
outstanding leader of the colonial church. One American
authority writes of this period : ' An inclination to consider
the Episcopal Church in colonial Pennsylvania and Delaware
as ' English ' is soon corrected by the documents which reveal

Q

that to a large extent it was Welsh '. Griffith Hughes, F.R.S., a native of Tywyn (Mer.), was an S.P.G. missionary at Radnor from 1732 to 1736 and he not only distributed Welsh literature from the Society free among his scattered flock, but also supplemented it by printing Welsh pamphlets on his own accord.

Contacts between church congregations and individuals on both sides of the Atlantic were close and the attachment to religion was important in a social as well as spiritual context as many of the Welsh settlements were not new communities as much as old ones renewing themselves. A community of interest developed on each side which, at the time of the quarrel between the colonists and the mother country ensured that the colonial cause received a powerful advocacy especially from the Dissenters. The flow of Dissenting ministers to the colonies, however, was drying up in the second half of the eighteenth century and it was to meet this need that the college at Providence, Rhode Island, was founded. Funds for it were raised on a visit to this country by Morgan Edwards, a Baptist minister, and William Richards of Lynn, a prominent Welsh Baptist leader, bequeathed his library to it. The College, which later became Brown University, conferred its doctorate on him. Likewise, Elihu Yale became a benefactor of the College at New Haven which became Yale University. Thus Welsh attachment to education helped to lay the foundations of the premier seats of learning of the new republic.

The seventeenth century emigrants had settled in communities which were often isolated and independent. In the eighteenth century after the settlers had become acclimatised there was a more noticeable trend towards dispersion as the tidewater areas were filling up and individual families looked to the interior to assuage their land hunger. The mass migration in 1735 from the Welsh Tract to the Pedee River in South Carolina which came to be known as Welsh Neck became more and more untypical. Here they still aspired to an exclusive Welsh settlement to which the State government was prepared to agree. Here they also came into contact with the institution of slavery but it is not known, individual settlements apart, that any Welsh communities other than that of Welsh Neck were slave-owning. The Welsh were well to the fore in opening up the Ohio Valley after independence was won. By the end of the century, the new arrivals were passing by the old settlements on their way to the interior especially to the area which lies between the Ohio and the Great Lakes. John Rice Jones, who emigrated from Merionethshire in 1784 became a prominent figure in the opening up of new states even beyond the Ohio. Alleged to be the first lawyer to practise west of that river he became the first Attorney-General of Indiana and drew up its first code of laws. He later became one of the commissioners to draw up the constitution of Missouri ending his days as a judge of the Supreme Court of that state.

The early settlers had been mainly farmers and artisans but by 1776 more and more immigrants were being attracted to industrial jobs as an increasing variety of prospects opened up. General Lynch had to be sent to treat with some rebellious Welsh lead miners in Virginia during the War of Independence when the mines were taken over by the State. Two Caernarfonshire quarrymen established a successful slate business catering for the needs of New York State. Many Welsh labourers found work as 'navvies' when the early canals were being cut.

The second great wave of emigration to America occurred in the 1790s and continued into the nineteenth century. It was similar in its idealism to the Puritan emigration but it was no longer activated by religious persecution though the attachment to founding churches remained a characteristic. The emigration cannot be satisfactorily explained by the negative reasons of economic hardship and social and political deprivation. A great deal of propaganda from America kept the cause of emigration before the public eye and many enterprising Welshmen responded to it rather than endure the pessimism of life at home. The opportunities mentioned by numerous correspondents were not merely economic ones since many Welsh settlers had also tasted the excitement of public life and political power for the first time. One subtle form of propaganda was the revival of the Madog legend which claimed the discovery of America by Madog ab Owain Gwynedd c. 1170. Unauthenticated reports alleged the existence of an Indian tribe in the vicinity of the Missouri River which was Welsh-speaking and to whom the name *Madogwys* was given. The appearance of a book by Dr. John Williams, Sydenham, in 1791, in support of the legend aroused a great deal of discussion in the London-Welsh societies which was parodied by David Samwell in a long poem entitled *The Padouca Hunt*. The outcome was the expedition by John Evans of Waunfawr (Caerns.) to find them in 1792 which led to the exploration of the headwaters of the Missouri River for the first time. A map which he produced passed into the hands of Thomas Jefferson who, as President of the U.S.A., sponsored an expedition in 1804 led by Lewis and Clarke who used Evans's map to explore the area which had by then passed from French into American hands by the Louisiana Purchase.

Advocates like William Jones, Llangadfan (Monts.), encouraged emigration as the answer to landlord oppression about which one hears more and more after 1790. Though William Jones still cherished the ideal of a ' separate settlement ', his vision was entirely secular and he looked towards New York State rather than Pennsylvania. He was very active in the Bala area from which many emigrants left between 1791 and 1793. Morgan John Rhys was probably the greatest enthusiast for emigration because independent America came closest to his ideal of a free society untrammelled by tyranny of any kind. His intention to emigrate in 1785 was not accomplished till 1794 but be spent the meantime urging others to do so. It was his journeys in Caernarfonshire which sparked off the emigration movement in that county which had hardly been touched by it before. So high did the emigration ' mania ' run especially amongst his fellow Baptists that Christmas Evans made common cause with the Methodist, Robert Jones, Rhos-lan, and the Anglicans in denouncing it, the association between America and French revolutionary principles making it easier to discredit it. The following table indicating numbers of emigrants illustrates the strength of the movement in Caernarfonshire between 1794 and 1801 :

	Wales (incl. Mon.)	*Caerns.*		*Wales (incl. Mon.)*	*Caerns.*
1794	89	61	1798	5	0
1795	107	57	1799	4	0
1796	65	9	1800	227	72
1797	53	39	1801	799	348

The areas which supplied emigrants can be seen from the following table represented as percentages in declining order:

Caerns.	(1)	43·5%		Glam.	(7)	2·1%
Pembs.	(2)	11·3		Brecs.	(8)	1·8
Monts.	(3)	6·9		Denbs.	(9)	1·4
Cards.	(4)	5·4		Mon.	(10)	·8
Carms.	(4)	5·4		Rads.	(11)	·7
Mer.	(6)	3·3		Angl.	(12)	·4

Flints (13) ·2%

(This leaves 16·8% whose place of origin is indeterminate.)

The statistics indicate that the background of the emigrants was still predominantly rural since counties like Glamorgan, Monmouth, Flint and Denbigh were already beginning to experience economic stirrings which were creating better work prospects. Morgan John Rhys left for America in 1794 in the company of some Wrexham Baptists seeking a 'good spot' where the Welsh could settle together. He obtained land in west Pennsylvania which came to be known as Cambria county and he formed a Cambria Company of Philadelphia which sold off lots of 640 acres and assisted the immigrants to settle in their new home. The settlement succeeded but the administrative centre which Rhys had planned for it at Beulah wilted and was overshadowed by its twin town of Ebensburg into which there was a sizeable German migration. His undenominational church overcame religious prejudices for a time but sectarian differences finally re-asserted themselves especially after Rhys's death. His missionary zeal also provided the negroes with a church. His plans included provisions for education, a plot of land being set aside in the centre of Beulah for a school and a library. He was a pioneer of journalism on the American frontier with his *Western Sky* in 1798 and in this and from the pulpit he thundered against injustice including the institution of slavery which he regarded as a negation of human principles and even of constitutional right. Cambria turned out to be a disappointment and although contingents like that from Llanbryn-mair which crossed the Atlantic in 1796 settled there for a few years there was an exodus of Welsh settlers for other parts which were in the process of being opened up. One of the most important moves was that led by the Llanbryn-mair pioneers Ezekiel Hughes and Edward Bebb who explored the Ohio area and founded a settlement on the Whitewater which came to be known as Paddy's Run where a flourishing Welsh community blossomed. Henceforth, Cambria was more of a place to break the journey on the way to the interior and the concentration of Welsh settlers there made possible the peopling of many of the Ohio settlements.

Difficulties in finding transport in wartime conditions did not prevent the continuation of emigration especially after the treason trials of 1794. It abated somewhat after 1797 but was renewed on an unparalleled scale with the prospect of peace in 1801. A party which had left Caernarfonshire in 1795 became the nucleus of a settlement at Steuben in Utica. There was a mass emigration from that county in that year augmented by a few from Anglesey and Denbighshire which coincided with the departure of a large contingent from Llanbryn-mair, an old area of emigration. By this time slate ships were plying increasingly out of the small ports of Caernarfonshire and Merionethshire to the U.S.A. and the West Indies and so it was possible for individuals and families to make their own passage. The interest of industrial workers was also aroused and rumours circulated that Richard Crawshay had plans for opening iron furnaces in Pennsylvania and intended taking Welsh workers there. So many migrants were arriving in Pennsylvania from Wales, many of them destitute before their journey's end, that the Pennsylvania Welsh founded in 1798 a ' Society for the Relief of such Emigrants as may arrive in this country from Wales '. This was a successor to the earlier St. David's Society which had lapsed during the War of Independence. Between 1797 and 1801 a number of South Wales families settled in Oneida county and Carmarthenshire families, after a brief sojourn at Cambria, bought some 2,000 acres in the Welsh hills of Licking county in 1802. Radnor emigrants in 1803 still made for Radnor county, Delaware.

By 1815, Pennsylvania had absorbed more Welsh settlers than any state with New York State running second. Pennsylvania, originally looked to as the home of religious freedom, continued to attract on account of its great diversity and the opportunities which it offered. But the early exclusiveness of the Welsh had been broken down and even where Welsh communities existed there was a dispersal from them elsewhere. Although they continued to foster cultural and national ties with each other and with their homeland, Welsh settlers were becoming more individualistic and bent on private enterprise.

The main casualty was the language which lost ground in the second and third generation of settlers, lasting somewhat longer in the more isolated original communities.

The West Indies

The port records of Bristol and Liverpool disclose a considerable volume of Welsh emigrants to the West Indies especially in the early part of our period. The figures for Bristol are shown in this table :

1654-63	:	2,075
1663-79	:	1,700
1680-85	:	180

These emigrants originated mainly from Glamorganshire, Monmouthshire, Carmarthenshire, Pembrokeshire and Cardiganshire. Many went as indentured labourers to the plantations, Barbados being the most favoured destination. From the Liverpool records we gather that the age range of the indentured labourers who left for the plantations was from 11 to 30 years. The S.P.G. was just as assiduous in sending missionaries to the West Indies as to the mainland, the Rev. Griffith Hughes, F.R.S., of Tywyn (Mer.) among them, who, during his stay there, compiled the *Natural History of Barbados* published in 1750. Fortunes made in the West Indies fortified the situation of several Welsh families including the Maurices of Piercefield (Mon.) and the Pennants of Penrhyn (Caerns.).

India

India was not a place that Welshmen made for with a view to settlement as much as for making a fortune usually in the service of the East India Company. Elihu Yale, who had family connections with Denbighshire, was probably the most conspicuous success and he became Governor of Fort St. George, Madras. John Evans, who was the last Welsh-speaking Bishop of Bangor in our period, started his career as the first chaplain of the East India Co. but was kicked out of India for illicit trading which enabled him to bring home a sizeable fortune. There was a significant number of Welsh ' nabobs ' who used their fortunes to establish themselves as country gentry and sometimes to intervene in county politics as Sir William Paxton did in Carmarthenshire's ' Great Election ' in 1802.

India was already becoming a dumping ground for scapegrace sons by the end of our period. It had also attracted the interest of missionaries as early as the first decade of the eighteenth century and it was to join a Danish Mission on the Coromandel Coast that Griffith Jones expressed an intent. From John Evans and George Lewis, two Welsh clergymen, the Mission received much practical support.

SUGGESTED READING

C. H. Browning, *The Welsh settlement of Pennsylvania*, Philadelphia, 1912.

A. H. Dodd, *The character of early Welsh emigration to the United States*, Cardiff, 1957.

T. A. Glenn, *Welsh founders of Pennsylvania*, Oxford, 1913.

D. Williams, *Cymru ac America, Wales and America*, bilingual, Cardiff, 1946.

——, *John Evans and the legend of Madog*, Cardiff, 1963.

S. R. Williams, *The saga of Paddy's Run*, Oxford Ohio, 1945.

Articles:

A. H. Dodd, 'The background of the Welsh Quaker migration to Pennsylvania', *J. Mer. H. and R.S.*, III, 2, 1958.

R. Owen, 'Yr ymfudo o Sir Gaernarfon i'r Unol Daleithiau', *Trans. Caerns. H.S.*, XIII, 1952.

J. A. Thomas, 'Welsh Churchmen in colonial Pennsylvania', *J.H.S. Ch. in W.*, IV, 1954, V, 1955.

D. Williams, 'Some figures relating to emigration from Wales', *B.B.C.S.*, VII, 1935, VIII, 1936.

G. A. Williams, 'Morgan John Rhees and his Beula', *W.H.R.*, III, 4. 1967.

M. I. Williams, 'A note on Welsh emigration to America, 1697–1707', *N.L.W.Jnl.*, XVII, 1971.

Conclusion

The period we have reviewed, one must conclude, was one of unprecedented change which was accompanied by a revival in national life.

Loyalty to the Crown was conspicuous at the beginning of our period but, after the Revolution of 1688, the Welsh were weaned from this and, as the political balance shifted, contention between the leading county families for seats in Parliament became the nature of politics. By the end of the eighteenth century, the traditional leadership of the gentry in politics was being questioned as a growing estrangement between them and *y werin* appeared which caused the latter to turn towards new political leaders emerging from their own ranks. Most of them were prominent Nonconformists and with the development of the press as well, the political education of the nation was begun. But the mainstream of national life is not to be seen in politics since popular expression found a more congenial medium in religion and education.

Though the Anglican Church still claimed to be a national Church there was a growing alienation between it and the majority of the nation. The evangelicalism of the Methodists which also infected the Old Dissenters caused more and more people to desert it. Nonconformity became an increasingly powerful and virile force which became the strongest formative influence in national life in the nineteenth century.

The movement towards organisation on a national scale is best seen in the educational activity which was sustained throughout the period. Although education was still the handmaiden of religion and, as yet, little appreciated for its own sake, it achieved a high degree of literacy and stimulated an interest in intellectual activity. The lack of higher education was still felt and the highest point of development in this direction was the academies. These activities were not without their influence upon cultural development. From a situation of decline in language and literature there arose a great literary revival but economic poverty frustrated cultural developments in other directions. The most notable event was the revival of the *eisteddfod* with a decidedly more popular appeal than hitherto. In no sphere was the growing alienation of the gentry from national life more conspicuous than in that of culture.

National revival derived some stimulus from growing economic prosperity. Under the sponsorship of enterprising landlords agriculture became more productive but the economic dependence of the small farmer increased as a landlord-tenant relationship became more general with the continued growth of large estates. Farming activities were changing the landscape with fields and hedgerows becoming an ever more conspicuous feature in the process of enclosure. Even more indicative of the future was the steady concentration of heavy industry in certain areas of the coalfields of the south and north-east and the scale of this capitalist enterprise was unparalleled anywhere in the United Kingdom. The increase in trade which had prompted this development was also made possible by improvements in transport and communications hitherto so lacking.

Social change is implicit in economic advancement and the simple relationship of *bonedd a gwreng*[1] became increasingly complicated. A more numerous middle-class developed but even more significant was the emergence of a proletariat class completely divorced from the soil. Instead of small country towns dependent on the economy of the surrounding countryside we see the beginnings of a different type of town with an economy of its own usually connected with heavy industry.

Despite these changes which were hardly dreamt of at the beginning of our period, Welsh cultural traditions remained rooted in the soil. Whether they went to America or to a South Wales town this was the culture which migrants sought to transplant ; with what success is still a matter of historical controversy.

[1] gentry and commonalty.

Index

Aberystwyth, 203, 225
Acts, Corporation, 9, 32 ; Uniformity, 32, 36, 44 ; Conventicle, 32 ; Five Mile, 33, 44 ; Test, 34
Agricultural Societies, 134, 167, 246 ; Brecknockshire, 82, 134, 167 ; Glamorgan, 134, 167
Arnold, John, 18, 19
Assheton-Smith, Thomas, 159, 160, 170
Association Movement, 212-14

Bacon, Anthony, 150, 151, 155, 170, 209
Banking, 125, 147, 176, 178, 187, 204
Bayly, Sir Nicholas, 143 ; Paget (family), Earls Uxbridge, 6, 143, 144
Bevan, Madam Bridget, 103, 106, 107, 108
Beveridge, Bishop William, 27, 31
Bray, Dr. Thomas, 49, 56
Bulkeley (family), Baron Hill, 3, 6, 62 ; 4th Visct., 57, 59, 64 ; 7th, 209
Bulkeley, William, 58, 185, 199, 238, 244
Bull, Bishop George, 27, 28, 31, 98
Bute, Marquess of, 7, 10, 139, 183

Cambria, 259, 260
Cambrian, The, 14, 220, 229, 234
Campbell, John, of Stackpole, 10, 13, 209, 225 ; Earl Cawdor, 139, 226
Canals, Glamorgan, 174-5; Ellesmere, Montgomery, 175, 178
Caradogion, 221, 247-8
Cardiff, 169, 170, 171, 173, 178, 187, 195, 202, 214, 223, 244
Cartref, Y, 93, 209, 233
Charles, Thomas, 91, 94, 96, 108 ff, 227-8
charters remodelled, 19, 21, 22, 23
Cilgwyn and Cefn Du Slate Co., Nantlle, 160 ff
Corbet, Edward, 131, 132, 227
Cort process, 154, 157
Council in the Marches, 20, 22, 186
—, Lord President of, 18
Court of Great Sessions, 20, 186, 198-9, 212, 232
—, Justices of, 28, 33

Crawshay (family), Cyfarthfa, 150, 151, 152, 153, 154-5, 175, 176 ;
—, Richard, 260
Cycle of the White Rose, 58, 59, 61
Cylchgrawn Cynmraeg, Y, 111, 218, 220, 221, 233
Cymmrodorion Society, 72, 106, 231, 232, 240-1, 247
Cymreigyddion, 221, 247-8

Darby, Abraham, 148, 149, 154
Davies, Rev. David, Barkham, 191, 224
Davies, Rev. Howell, 77, 79, 84
Davies, Rev. Walter (Gwallter Mechain), 127, 166, 191, 192, 193
Davis, David, Castellhywel, 120, 218, 222
Declaration of Indulgence, 21, 34-5, 36, 38, 43, 44
Dinorwic Slate Co., 159 ff
Dowlais Iron Co., 149, 150, 151, 153

Edwards, Thomas (Twm o'r Nant), 125, 184, 185, 201, 225, 243, 244
Eisteddfod, 108, 221, 247, 248-9, 264
ejected ministers, 30, 36, 44, 118
Ellis, Rowland, Brynmawr, 252, 254
Evans, Evan (Ieuan Fardd), 232, 236, 238, 239, 241, 242
Evans, Bishop John, 52, 71, 74, 75-6, 261-2
Evans, Rev. John, 104, 105, 106
Evans, John, Waunfawr, 248, 258
Evans, Theophilus, 76, 86, 203, 237, 238
Evans, Thomas (Tomos Glyn Cothi), 218, 219, 228

Fishguard, French landing at, 226

'gathered' churches, 37-8, 39, 84, 85
Gouge, Thomas, 29, 44 ff
Guest (family), 151 ; —, John, 153
Gwyneddigion Society, 218, 219, 221, 241, 247, 248, 249

Hall, Benjamin, 13-14